Disney | SQUARE ENIX

KINGDOM HEARTS

P9-CCR-544

Volume 1
Adapted by
Shiro Amano

TOKYOPOP®

HAMBURG // LONDON // LOS ANGELES // TOKYO

# Kingdom Hearts II Volume 1
## Adapted by Shiro Amano

Assistant Editors - Alethea & Athena Nibley
Associate Editor - Peter Ahlstrom
Retouch and Lettering - Star Print Brokers
Production Artist - Michael Paolilli
Graphic Designer - James Lee

Editor - Bryce P. Coleman
Digital Imaging Manager - Chris Buford
Pre-Production Supervisor - Erika Terriquez
Art Director - Anne Marie Horne
Production Manager - Elisabeth Brizzi
Managing Editor - Vy Nguyen
VP of Production - Ron Klamert
Editor-in-Chief - Rob Tokar
Publisher - Mike Kiley
President and C.O.O. - John Parker
C.E.O. and Chief Creative Officer - Stuart Levy

A  Manga

TOKYOPOP Inc.
5900 Wilshire Blvd. Suite 2000
Los Angeles, CA 90036

E-mail: info@TOKYOPOP.com
Come visit us online at www.TOKYOPOP.com

ISBN: 978-1-4278-0781-6

First TOKYOPOP printing: July 2007

10 9 8 7 6 5 4 3 2 1

Printed in the USA

# KINGDOM HEARTS II

A scattered dream that's like a far-off memory. A far-off memory that's like a scattered dream.
I want to line the pieces up, yours and mine.

Adapted by
**Shiro Amano**
Original Concept by
**Tetsuya Nomura**

DISNEY · SQUARE ENIX

KINGDOM HEARTS
キングダム ハーツ II

# CONTENTS

KINGDOM HEARTS II

Chapter 1: Twilight Town     5

Chapter 2: Intruders     31

Chapter 3: Sea Salt Ice Cream     63

Chapter 4: The Distant Sound of Waves     89

Chapter 5: No. XIII     121

Chapter 6: A Letter With No Addressee     149

Chapter 7: What I Want to Ask Is...     171

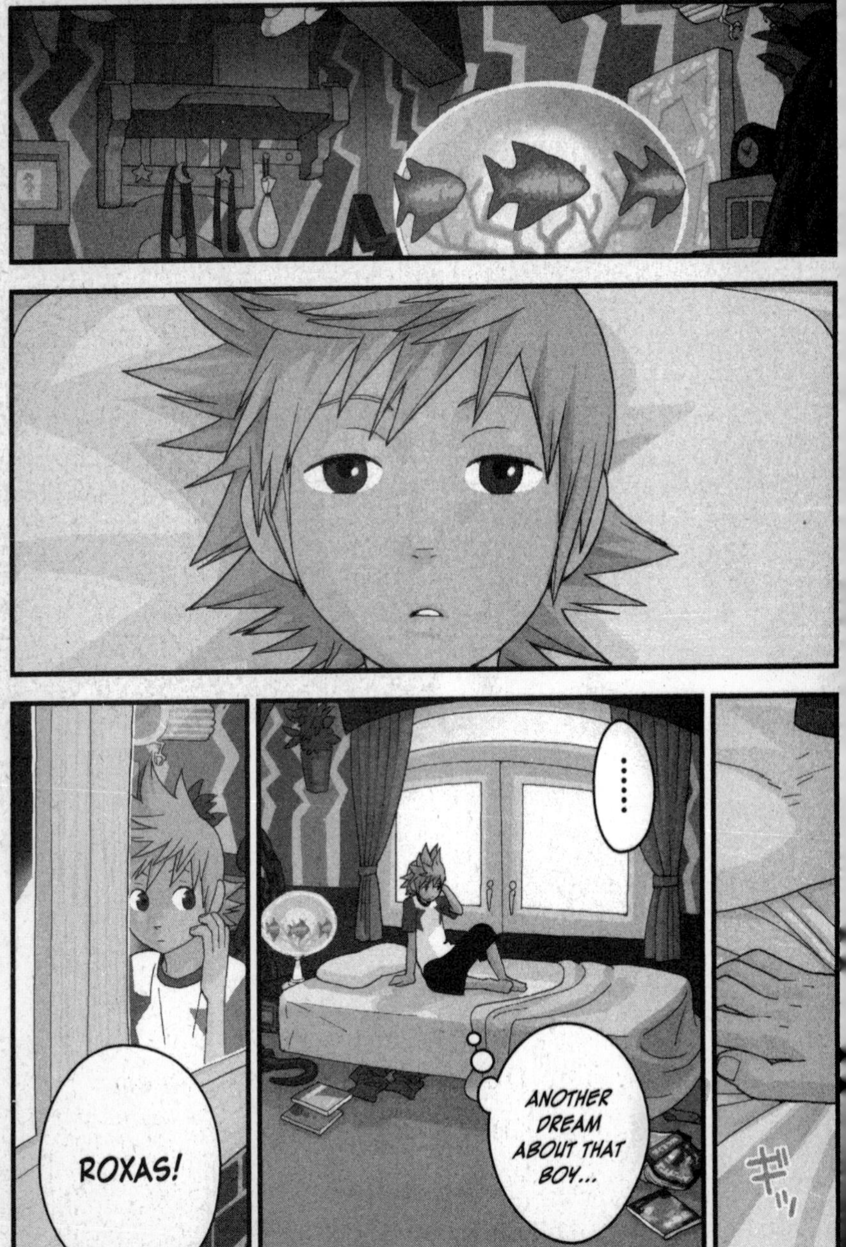
ギッ
......
ANOTHER DREAM ABOUT THAT BOY...
ROXAS!

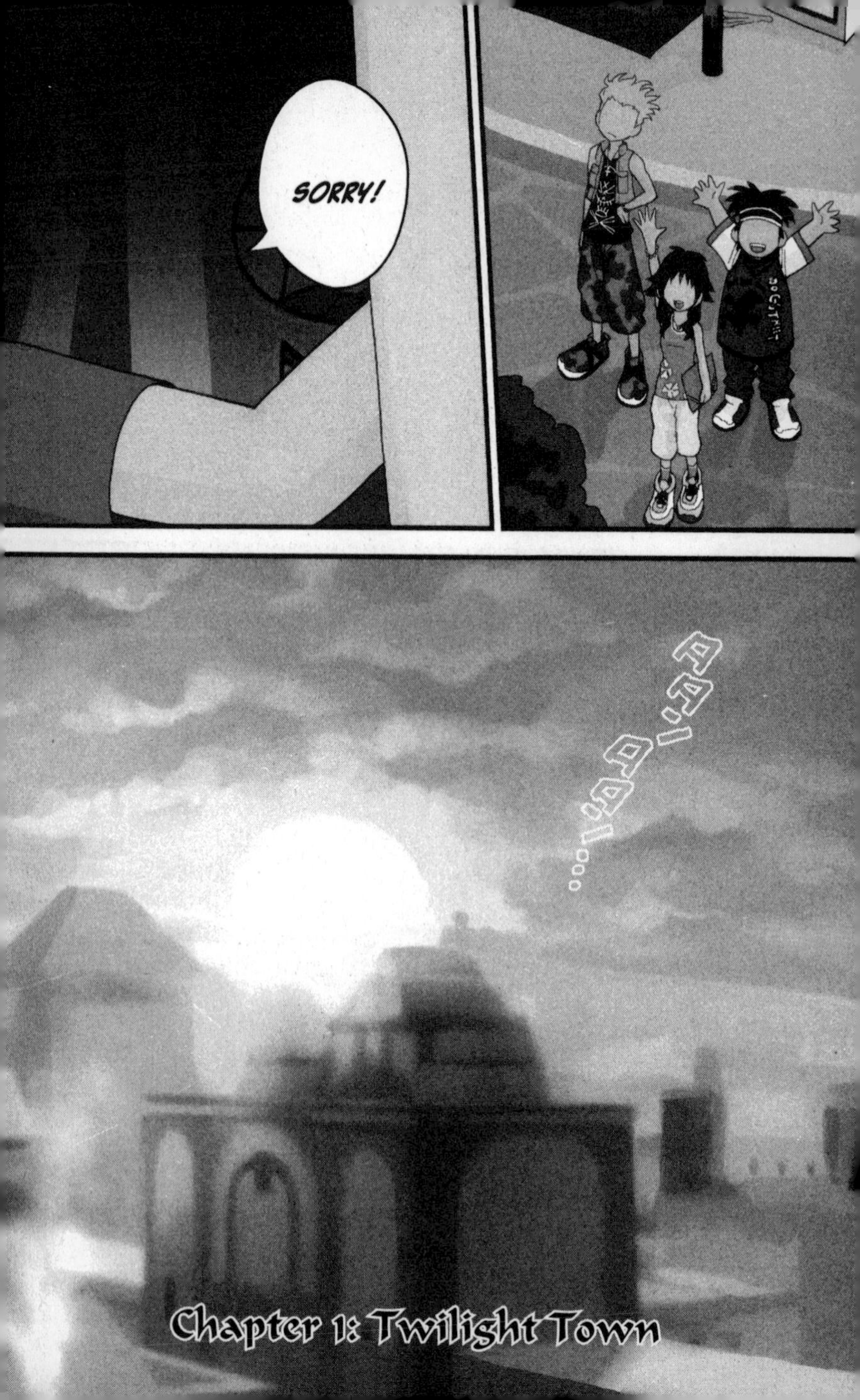
SORRY!
タ〜タ〜タ…
Chapter 1: Twilight Town

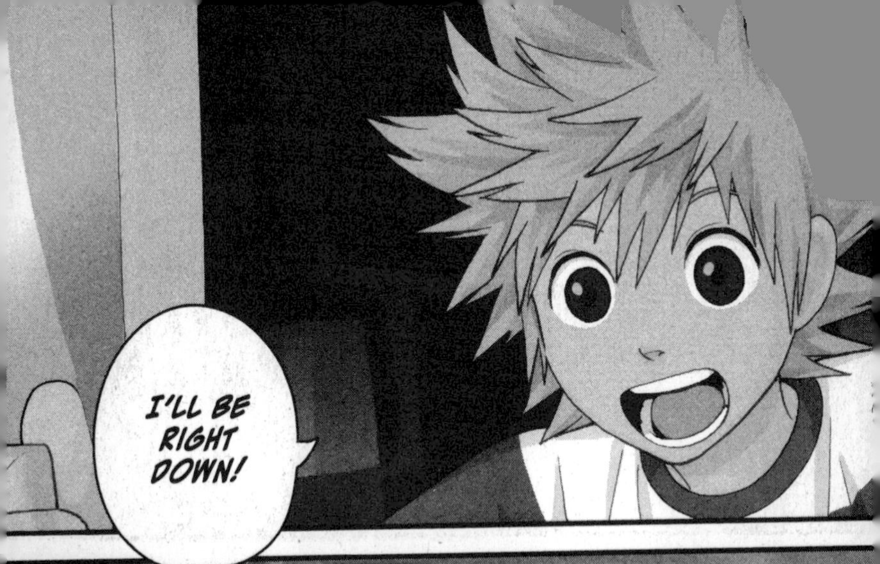
I'LL BE RIGHT DOWN!
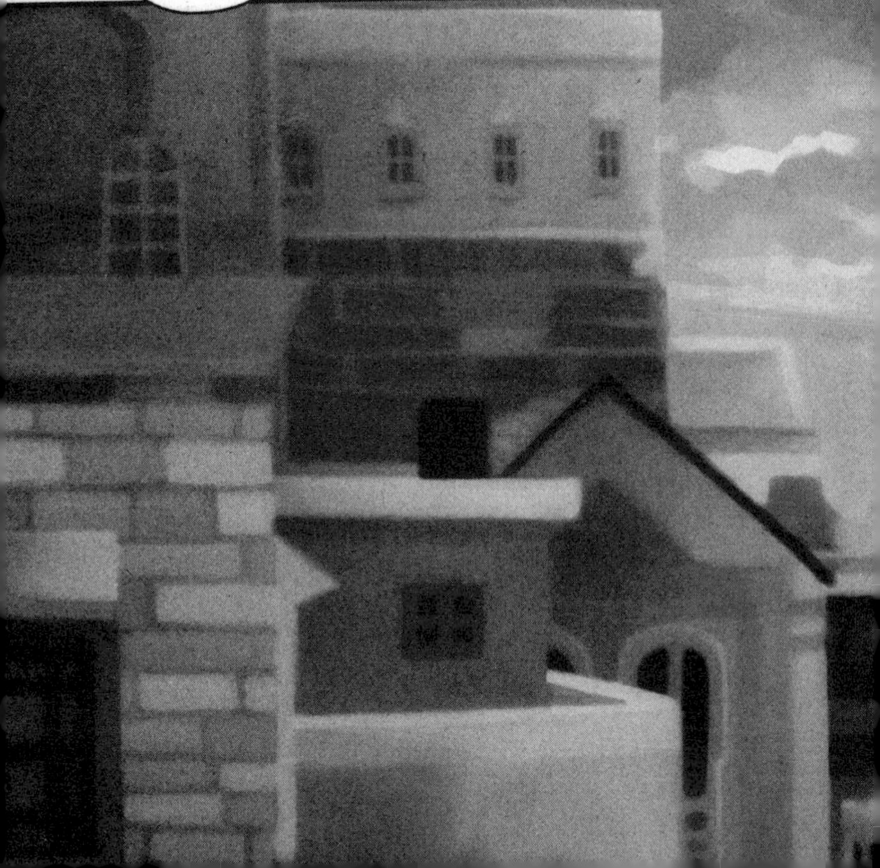

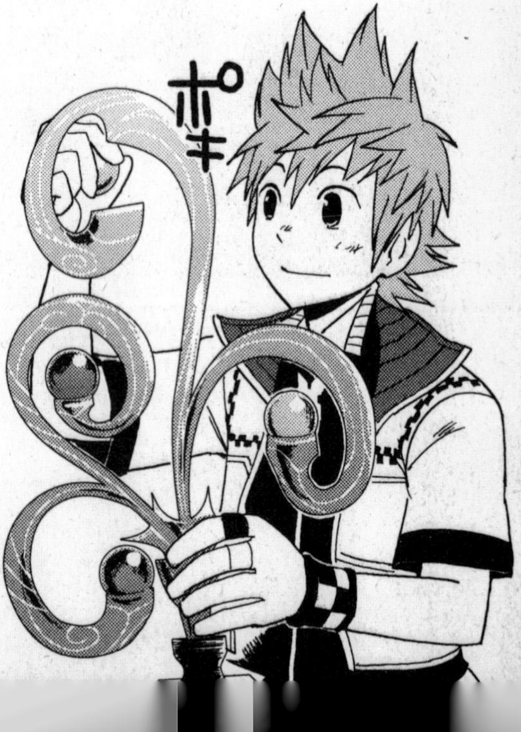
ポキ

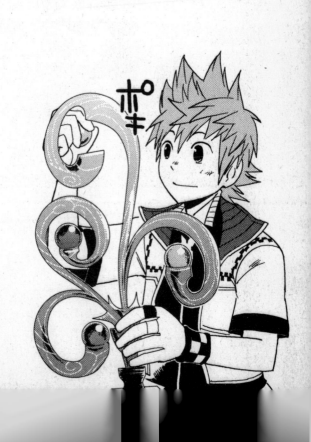

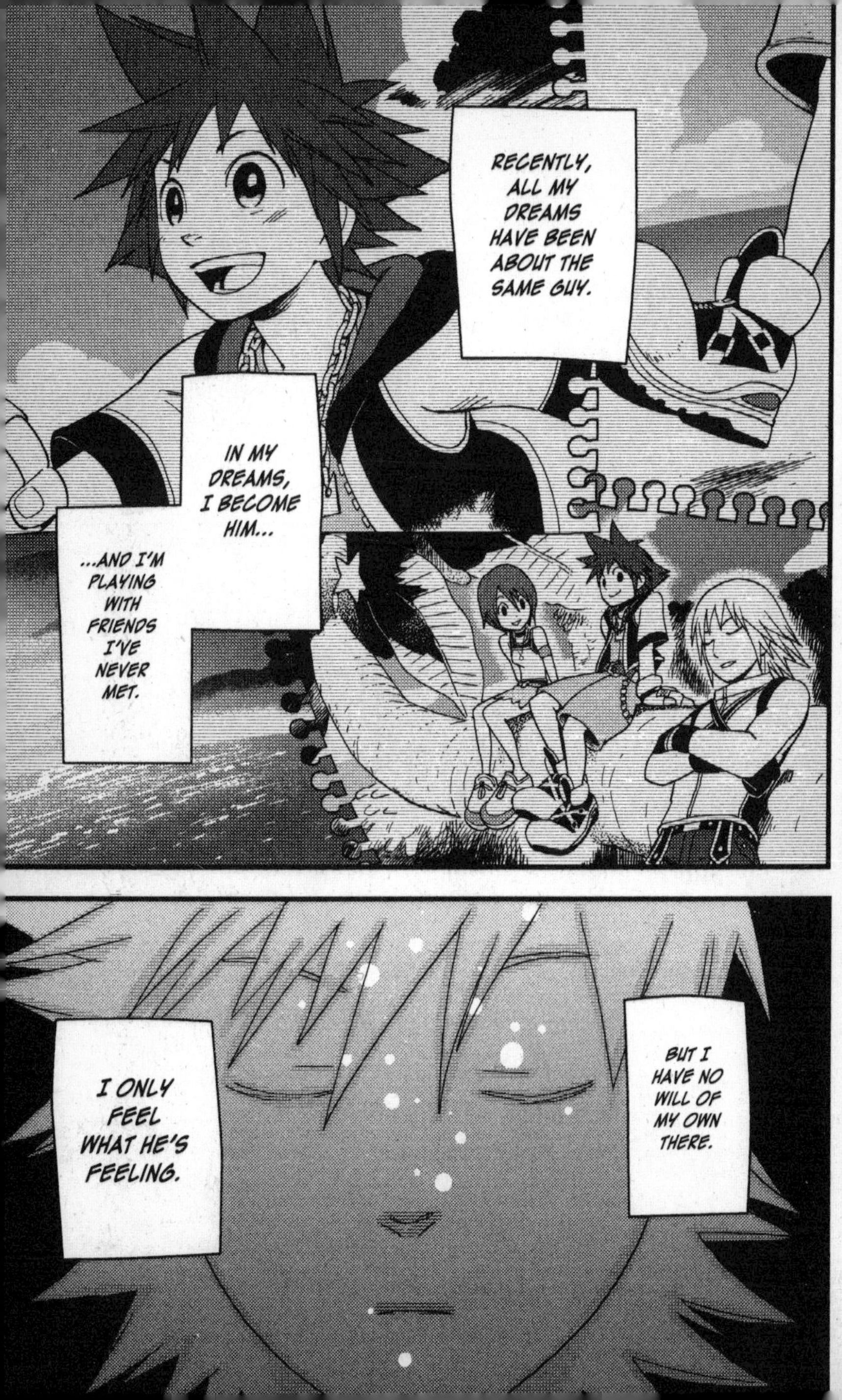
RECENTLY, ALL MY DREAMS HAVE BEEN ABOUT THE SAME GUY.
IN MY DREAMS, I BECOME HIM...
...AND I'M PLAYING WITH FRIENDS I'VE NEVER MET.
BUT I HAVE NO WILL OF MY OWN THERE.
I ONLY FEEL WHAT HE'S FEELING.

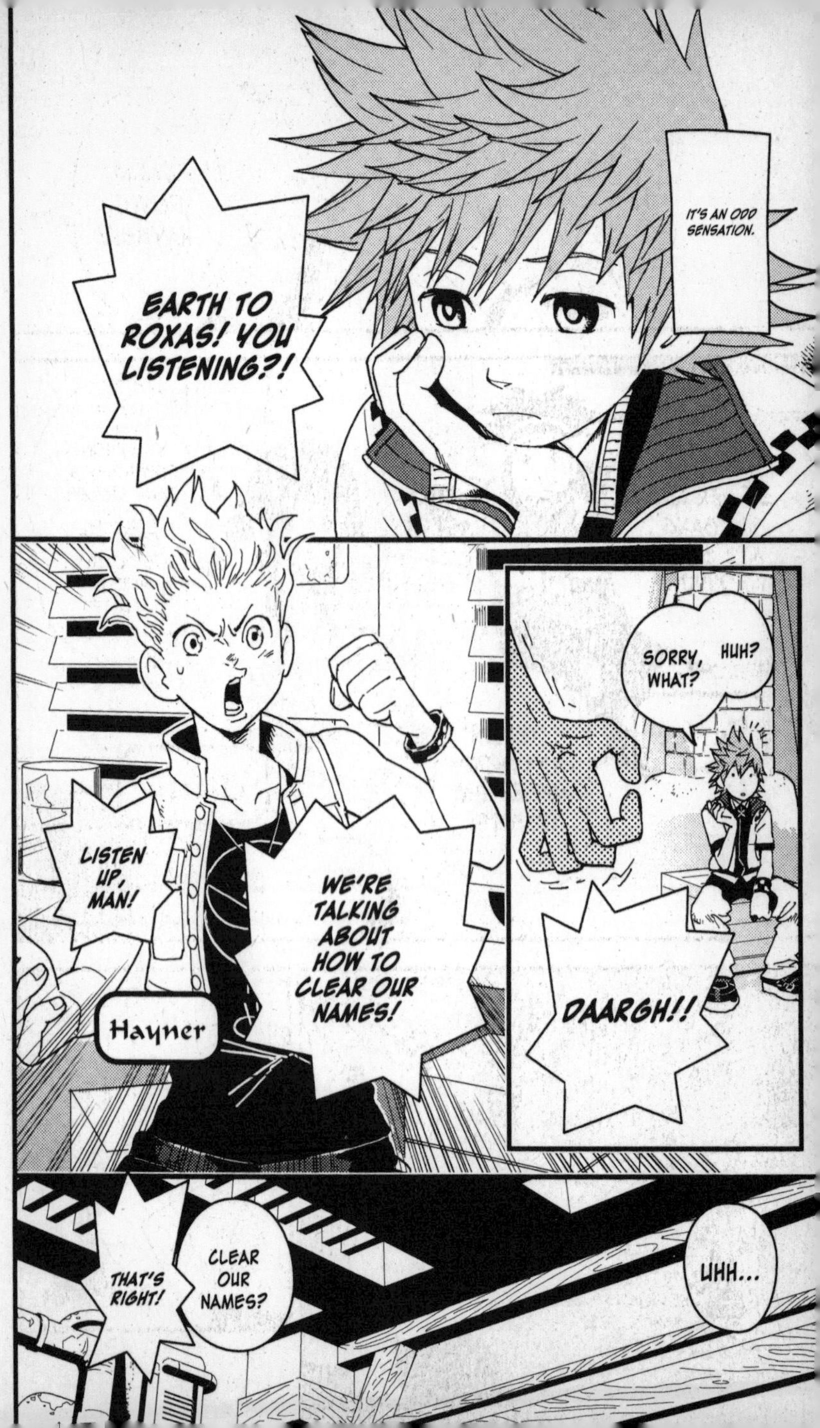
IT'S AN ODD SENSATION.
EARTH TO ROXAS! YOU LISTENING?!
HUH?
SORRY, WHAT?
DAARGH!!
LISTEN UP, MAN!
WE'RE TALKING ABOUT HOW TO CLEAR OUR NAMES!
Hayner
UHH...
CLEAR OUR NAMES?
THAT'S RIGHT!

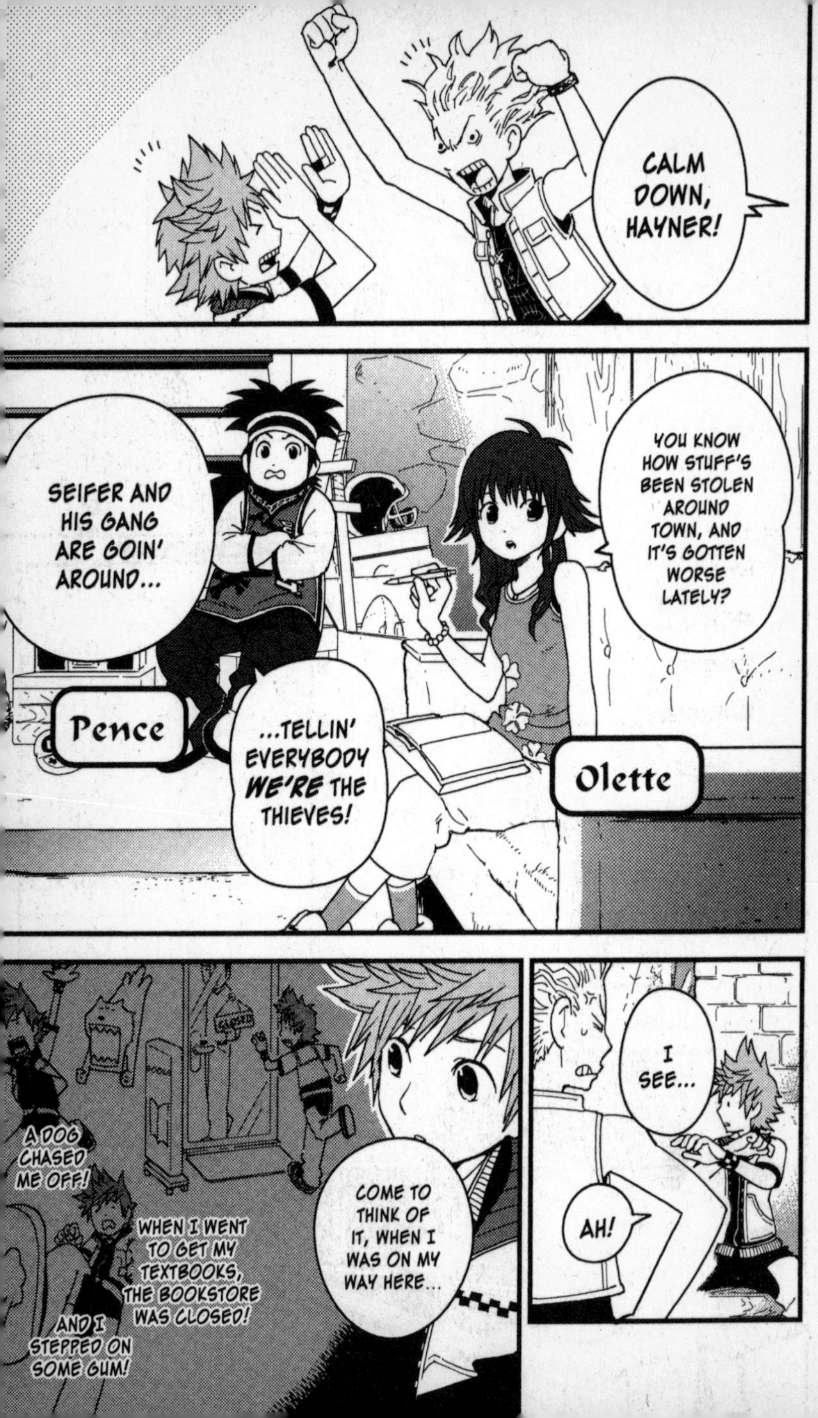
CALM DOWN, HAYNER!
YOU KNOW HOW STUFF'S BEEN STOLEN AROUND TOWN, AND IT'S GOTTEN WORSE LATELY?
Olette
SEIFER AND HIS GANG ARE GOIN' AROUND...
...TELLIN' EVERYBODY *WE'RE* THE THIEVES!
Pence
I SEE...
AH!
COME TO THINK OF IT, WHEN I WAS ON MY WAY HERE...
CLOSED
WHEN I WENT TO GET MY TEXTBOOKS, THE BOOKSTORE WAS CLOSED!
A DOG CHASED ME OFF!
AND I STEPPED ON SOME GUM!

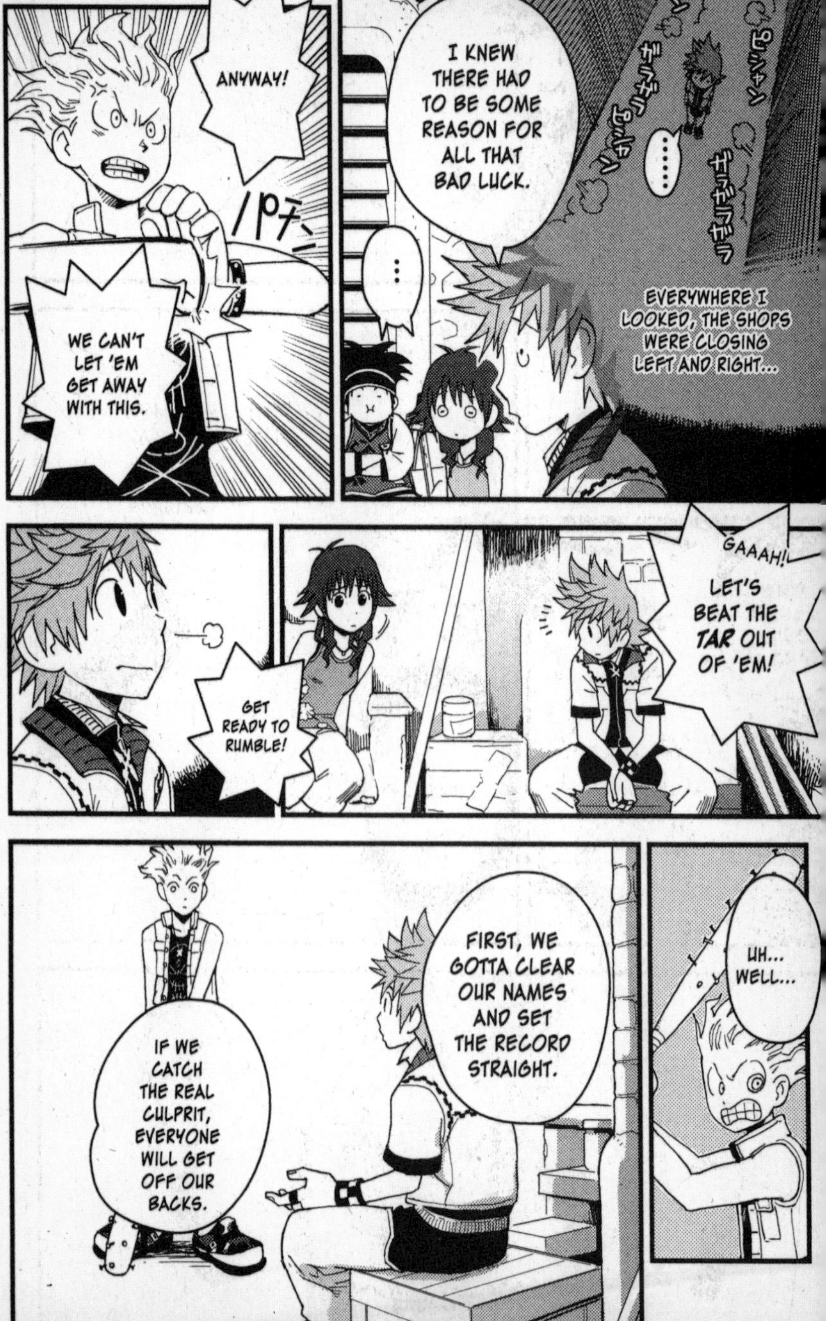

......
EVERYWHERE I LOOKED, THE SHOPS WERE CLOSING LEFT AND RIGHT...
I KNEW THERE HAD TO BE SOME REASON FOR ALL THAT BAD LUCK.
...
ANYWAY!
WE CAN'T LET 'EM GET AWAY WITH THIS.
GAAAH!
LET'S BEAT THE TAR OUT OF 'EM!
GET READY TO RUMBLE!
UH... WELL...
FIRST, WE GOTTA CLEAR OUR NAMES AND SET THE RECORD STRAIGHT.
IF WE CATCH THE REAL CULPRIT, EVERYONE WILL GET OFF OUR BACKS.

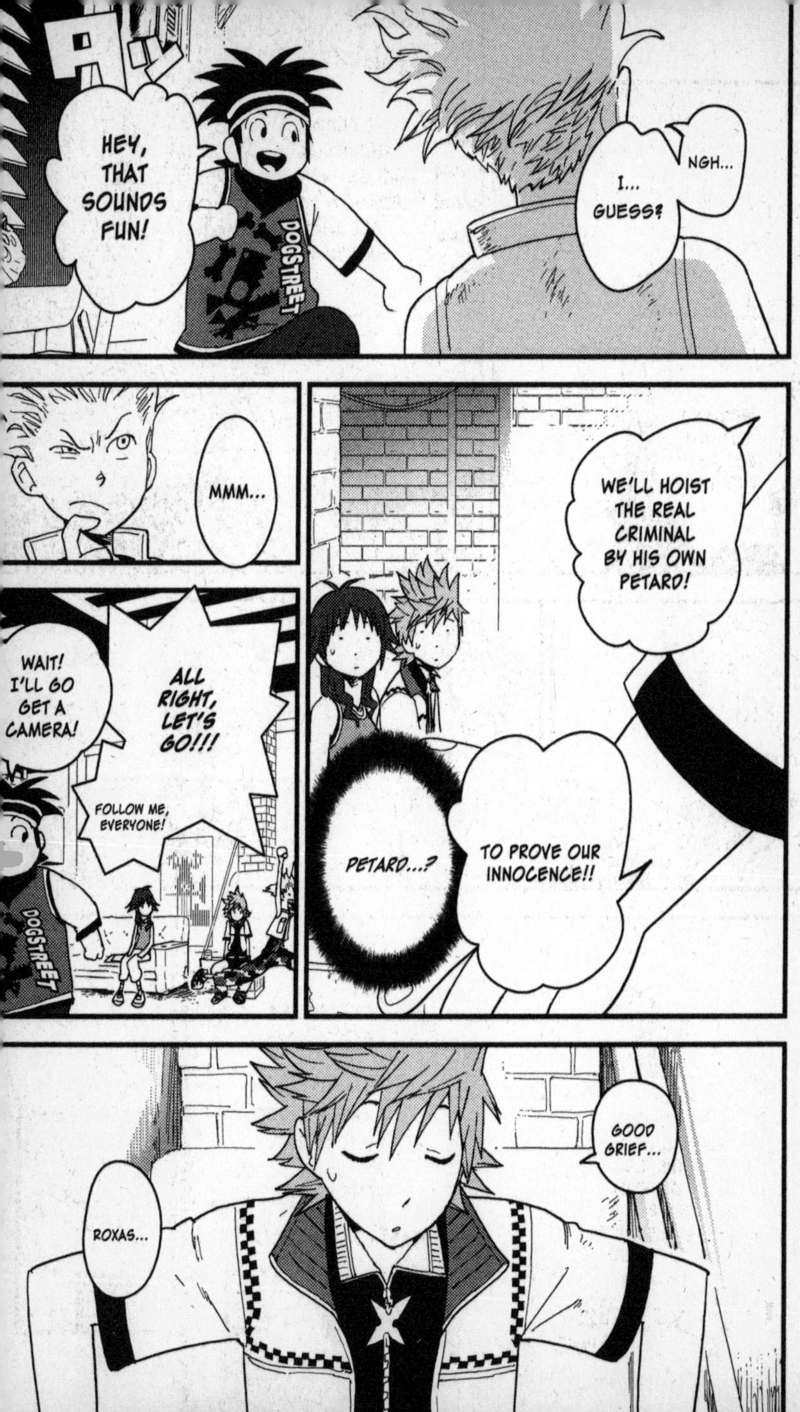
NGH... I... GUESS?
HEY, THAT SOUNDS FUN!
WE'LL HOIST THE REAL CRIMINAL BY HIS OWN PETARD!
TO PROVE OUR INNOCENCE!!
PETARD...?
MMM...
ALL RIGHT, LET'S GO!!!
FOLLOW ME, EVERYONE!
WAIT! I'LL GO GET A CAMERA!
GOOD GRIEF...
ROXAS...

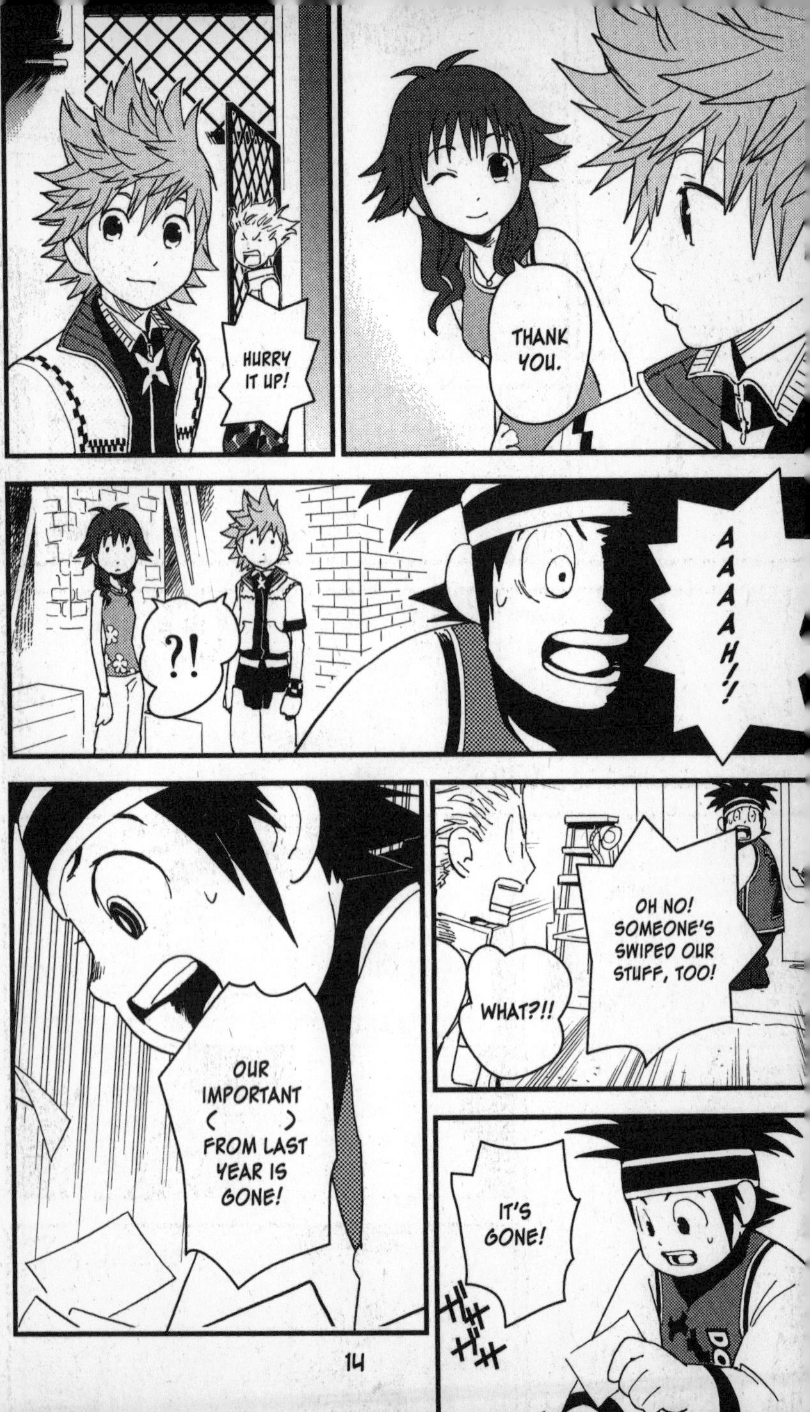
THANK YOU.
HURRY IT UP!
AAAAAH!!
?!
OH NO! SOMEONE'S SWIPED OUR STUFF, TOO!
WHAT?!!
IT'S GONE!
OUR IMPORTANT ( ) FROM LAST YEAR IS GONE!

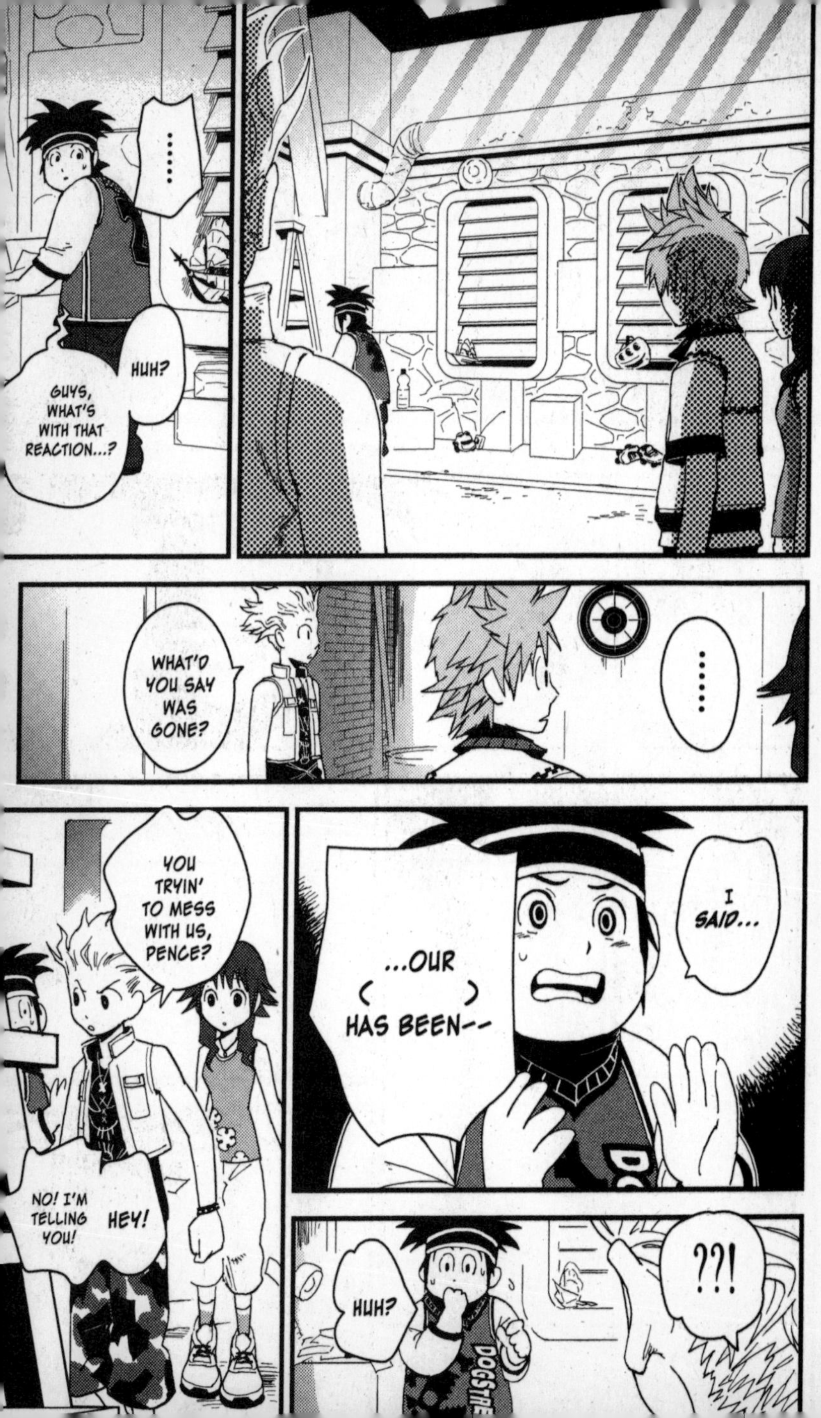
......
HUH?
GUYS, WHAT'S WITH THAT REACTION...?
......
WHAT'D YOU SAY WAS GONE?
I SAID...
...OUR ( ) HAS BEEN--
??!
HUH?
YOU TRYIN' TO MESS WITH US, PENCE?
HEY!
NO! I'M TELLING YOU!

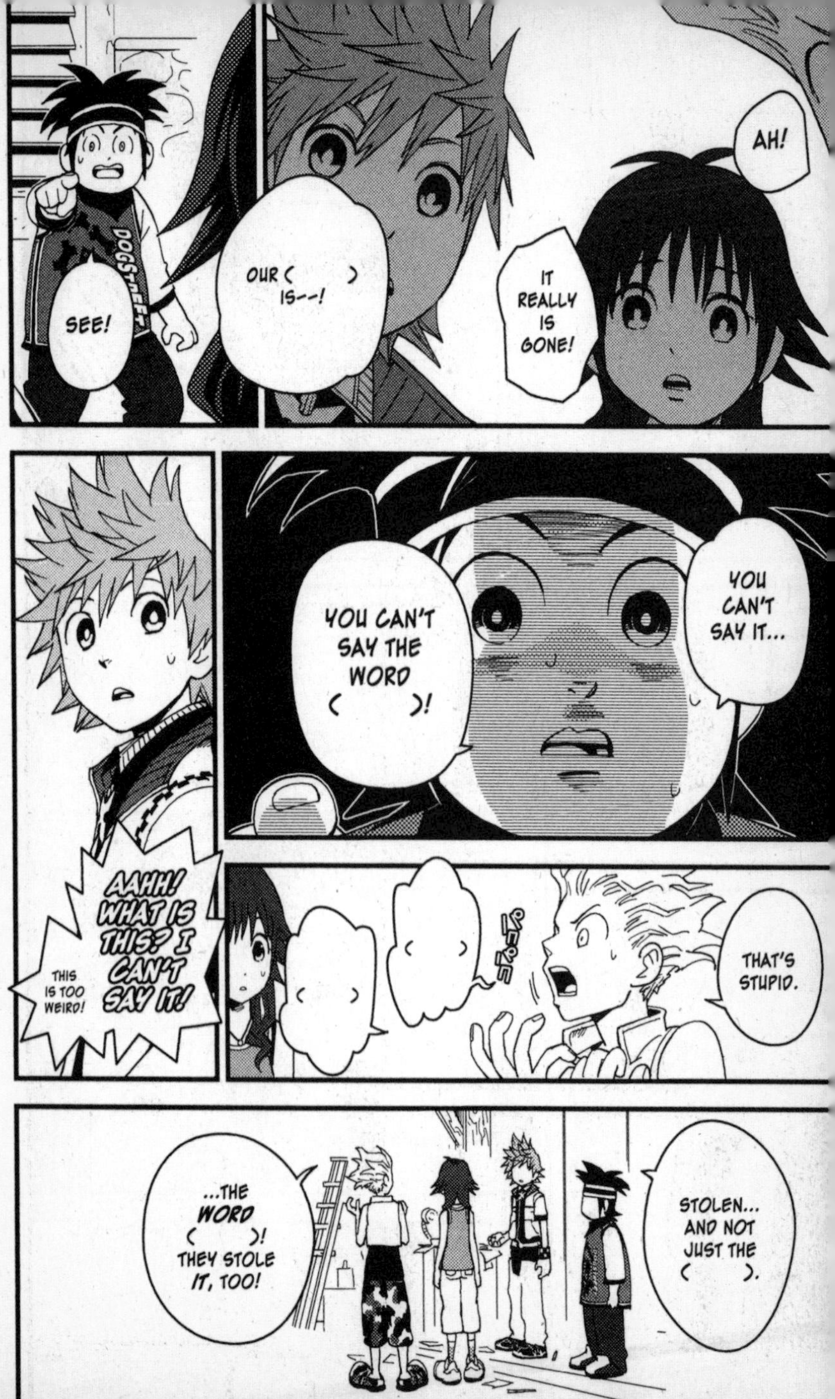
AH!
IT REALLY IS GONE!
OUR (      ) IS--!
SEE!
YOU CAN'T SAY IT...
YOU CAN'T SAY THE WORD (      )!
THAT'S STUPID.
(   )
(   )
AAHH! WHAT IS THIS? I CAN'T SAY IT!
THIS IS TOO WEIRD!
STOLEN... AND NOT JUST THE (      ).
...THE *WORD* (      )! THEY STOLE *IT*, TOO!

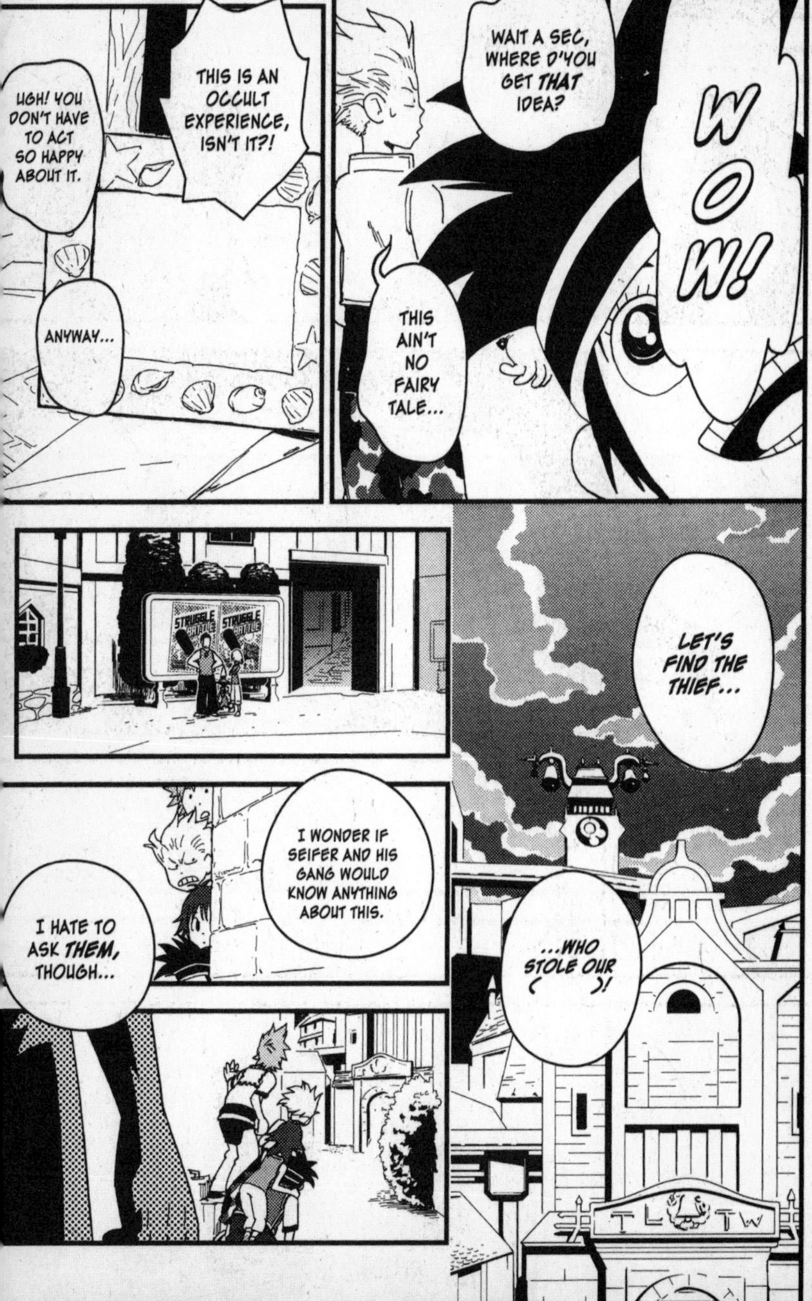
WOW!
WAIT A SEC, WHERE D'YOU GET *THAT* IDEA?
THIS AIN'T NO FAIRY TALE...
THIS IS AN OCCULT EXPERIENCE, ISN'T IT?!
UGH! YOU DON'T HAVE TO ACT SO HAPPY ABOUT IT.
ANYWAY...
*LET'S FIND THE THIEF...*
*...WHO STOLE OUR ( )!*
STRUGGLE BATTLE
STRUGGLE BATTLE
I WONDER IF SEIFER AND HIS GANG WOULD KNOW ANYTHING ABOUT THIS.
I HATE TO ASK *THEM*, THOUGH...
TL TW

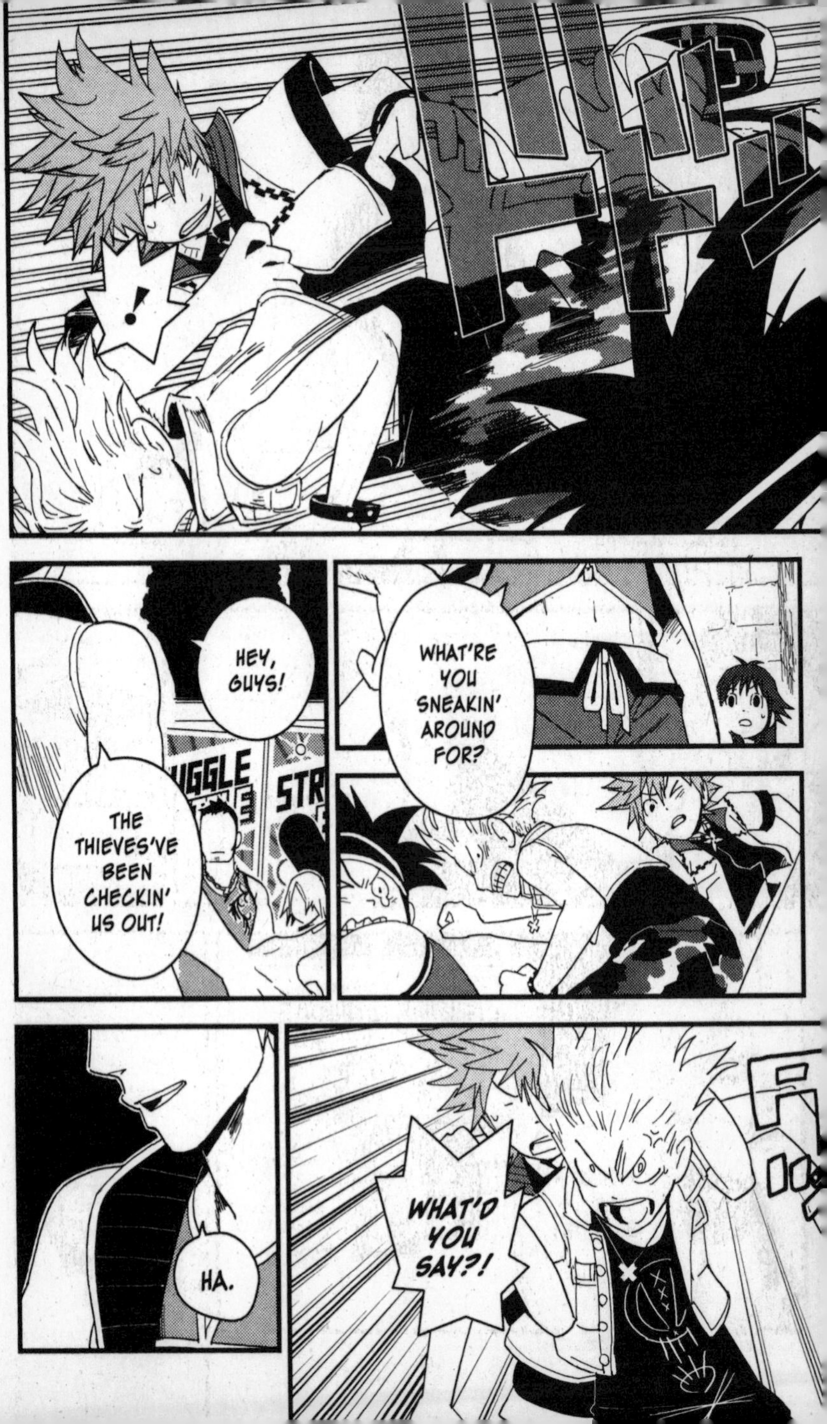
!
HEY, GUYS!
THE THIEVES'VE BEEN CHECKIN' US OUT!
WHAT'RE YOU SNEAKIN' AROUND FOR?
HA.
WHAT'D YOU SAY?!

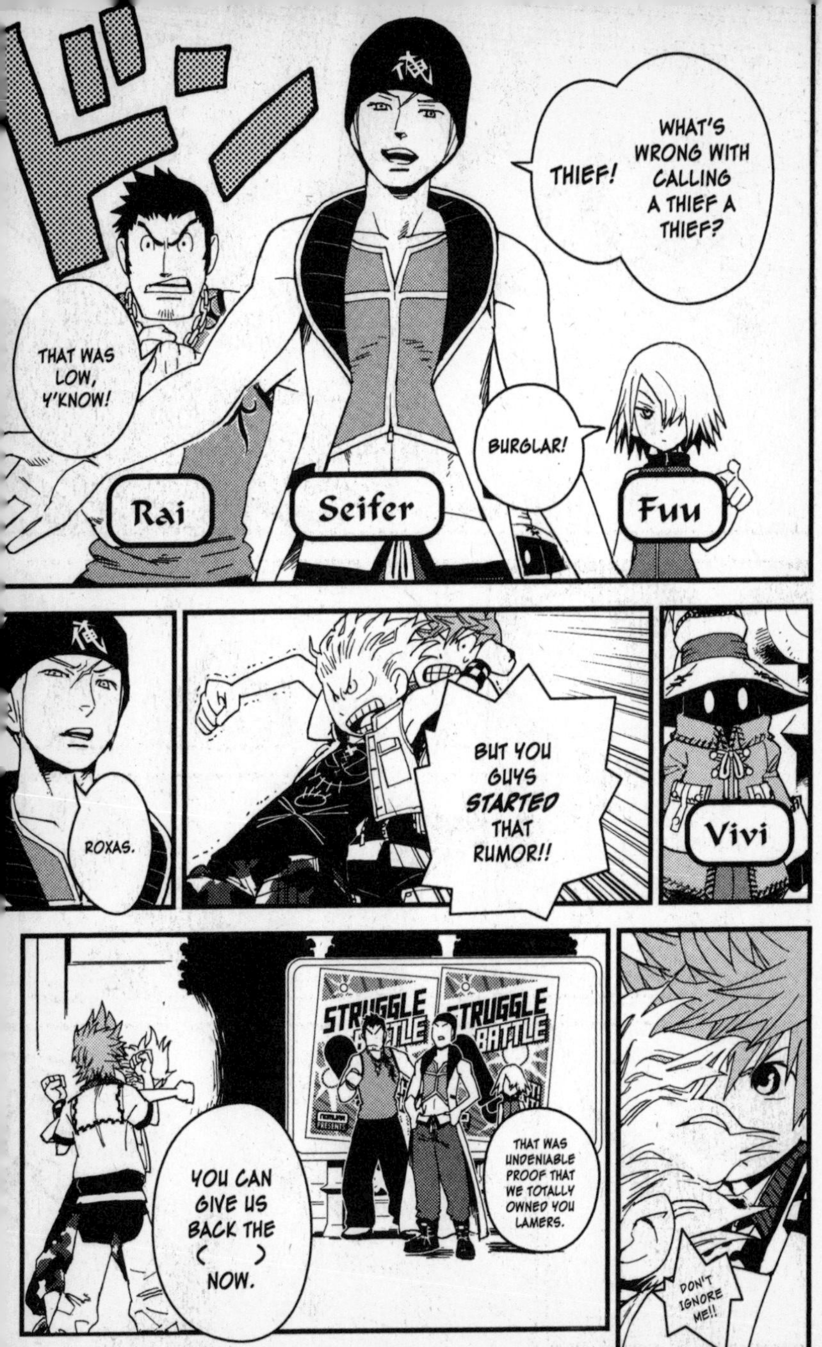
WHAT'S WRONG WITH CALLING A THIEF A THIEF?
THIEF!
BURGLAR!
THAT WAS LOW, Y'KNOW!
Fuu
Seifer
Rai
Vivi
BUT YOU GUYS STARTED THAT RUMOR!!
ROXAS.
DON'T IGNORE ME!!
THAT WAS UNDENIABLE PROOF THAT WE TOTALLY OWNED YOU LAMERS.
STRUGGLE BATTLE
STRUGGLE BATTLE
YOU CAN GIVE US BACK THE ( ) NOW.

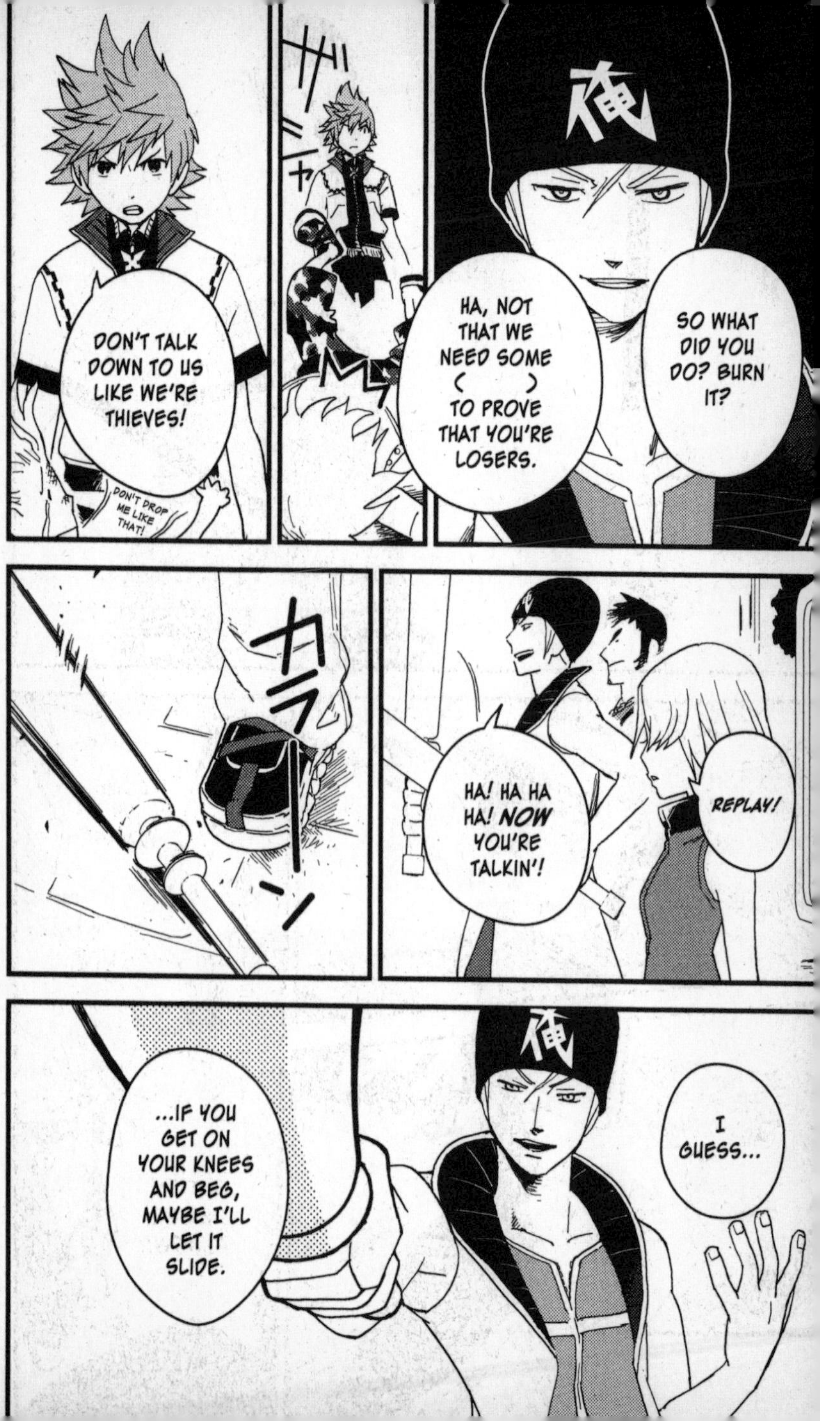
SO WHAT DID YOU DO? BURN IT?
HA, NOT THAT WE NEED SOME ( ) TO PROVE THAT YOU'RE LOSERS.
DON'T TALK DOWN TO US LIKE WE'RE THIEVES!
DON'T DROP ME LIKE THAT!
REPLAY!
HA! HA HA HA! NOW YOU'RE TALKIN'!
I GUESS...
...IF YOU GET ON YOUR KNEES AND BEG, MAYBE I'LL LET IT SLIDE.

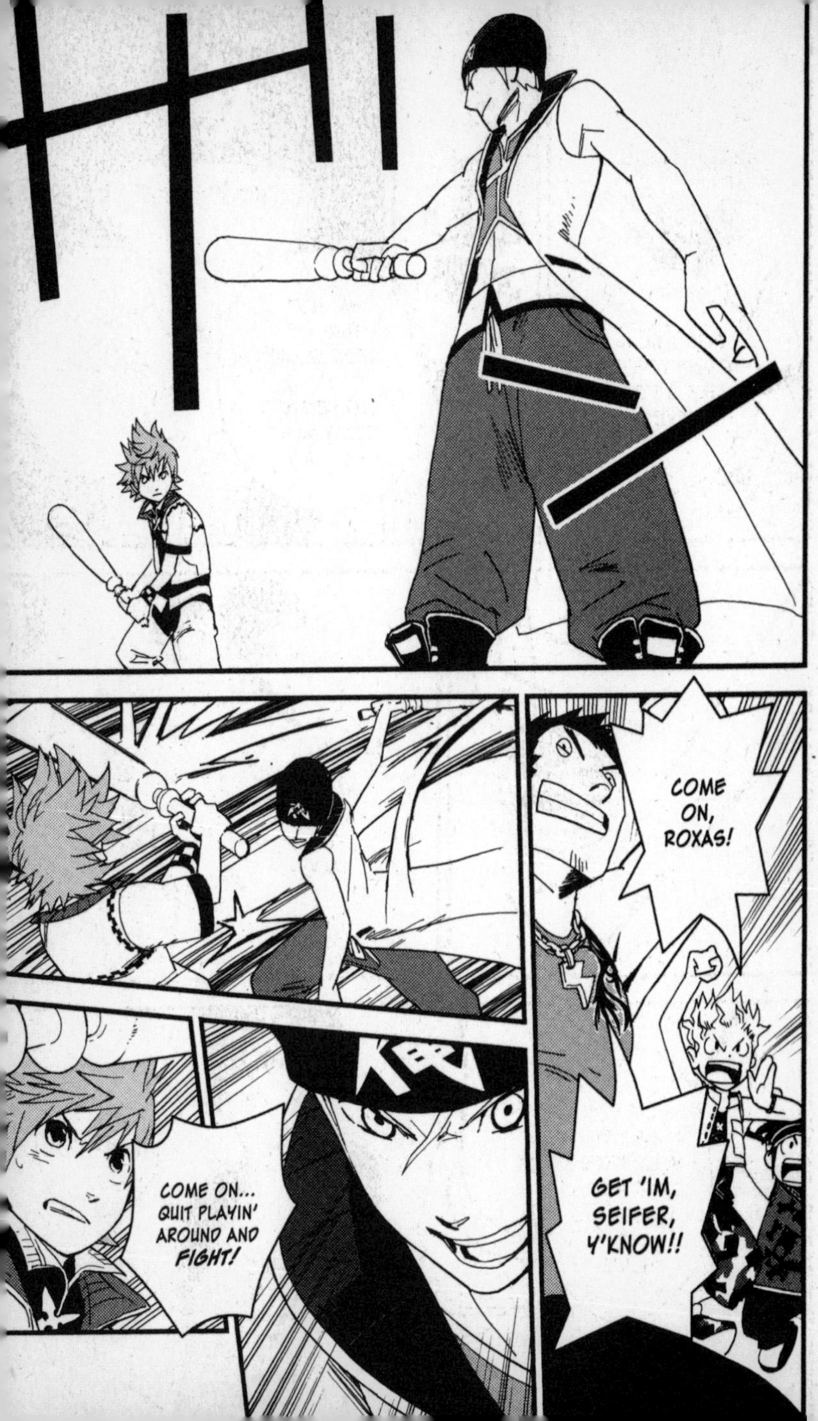
COME ON, ROXAS!
GET 'IM, SEIFER, Y'KNOW!!
COME ON... QUIT PLAYIN' AROUND AND *FIGHT!*

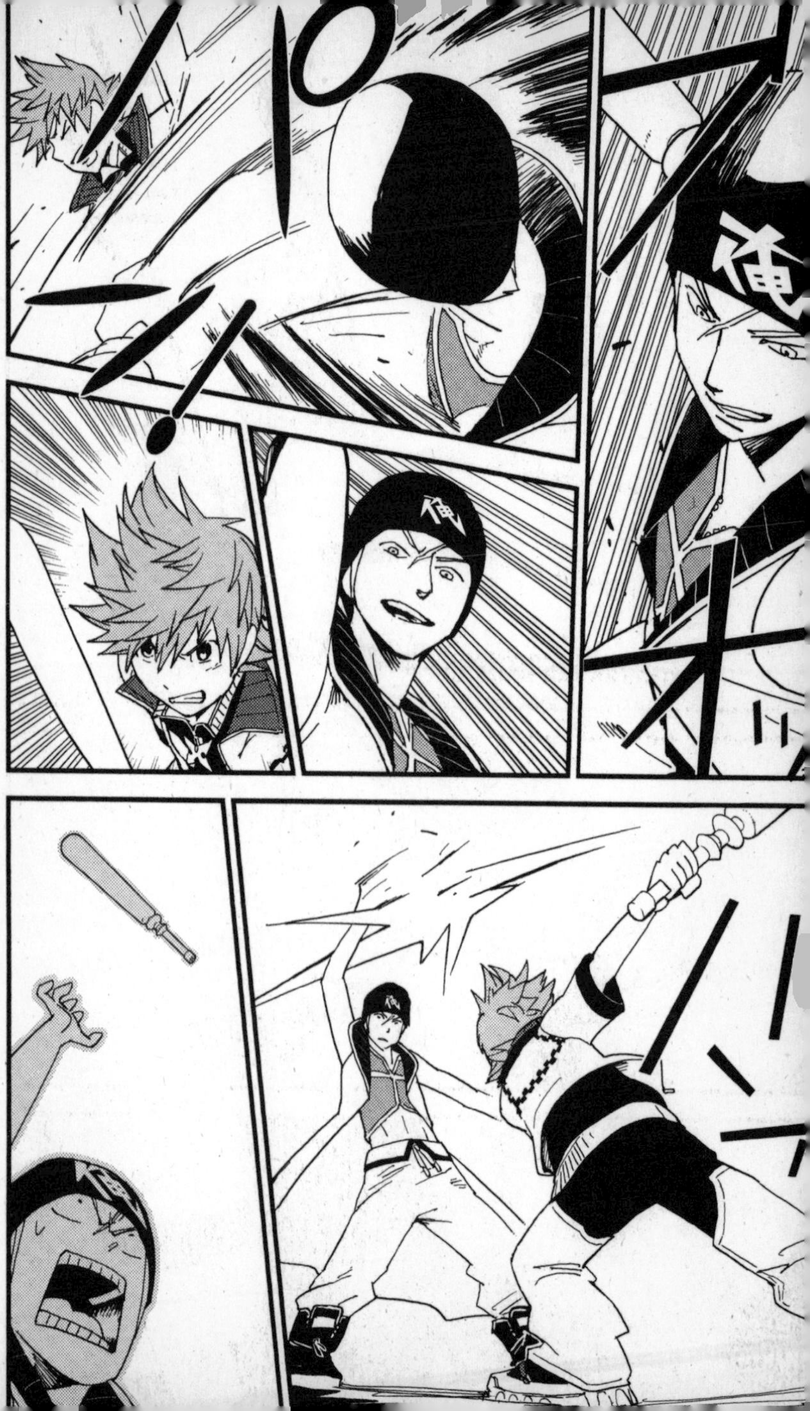
俺

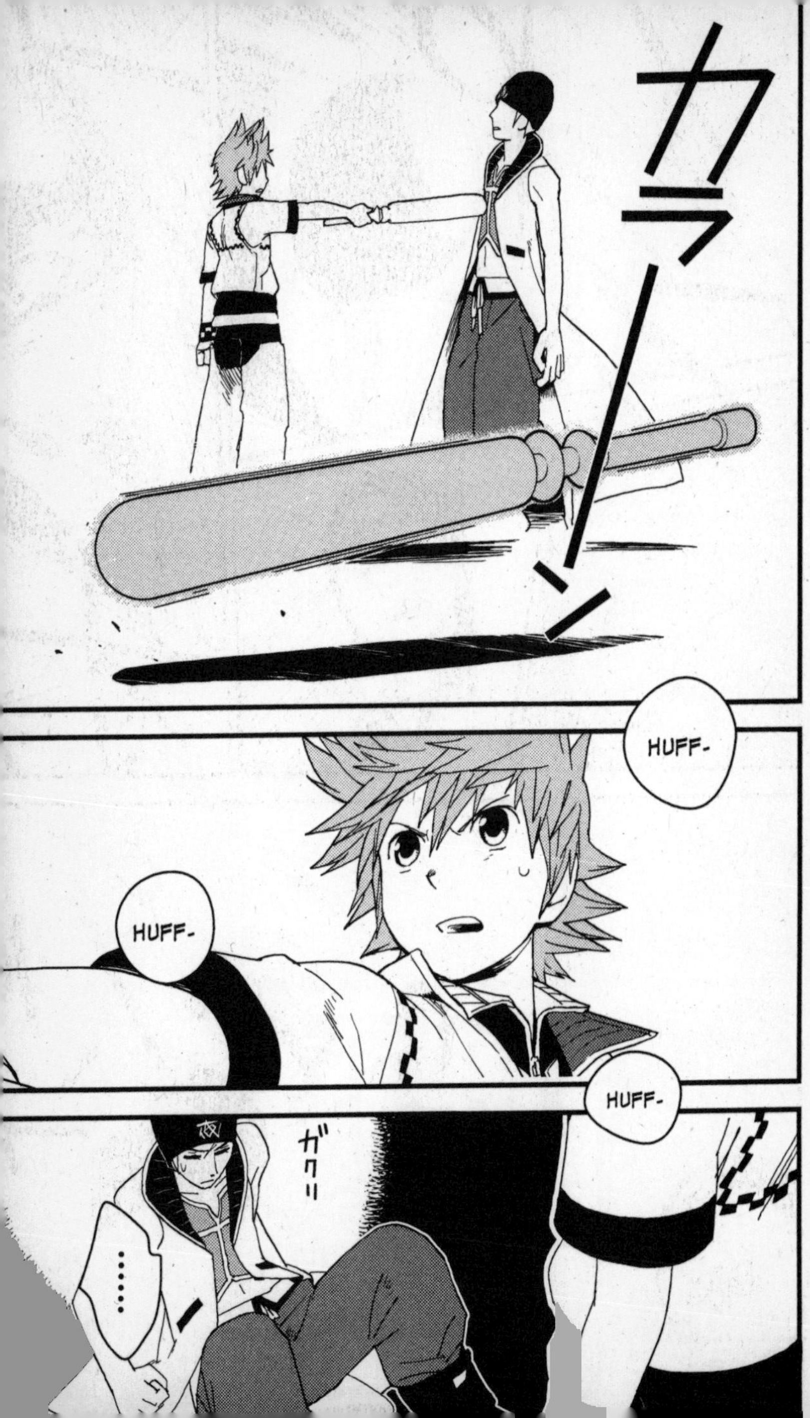
カラーン
HUFF-
HUFF-
HUFF-
ガクリ
......

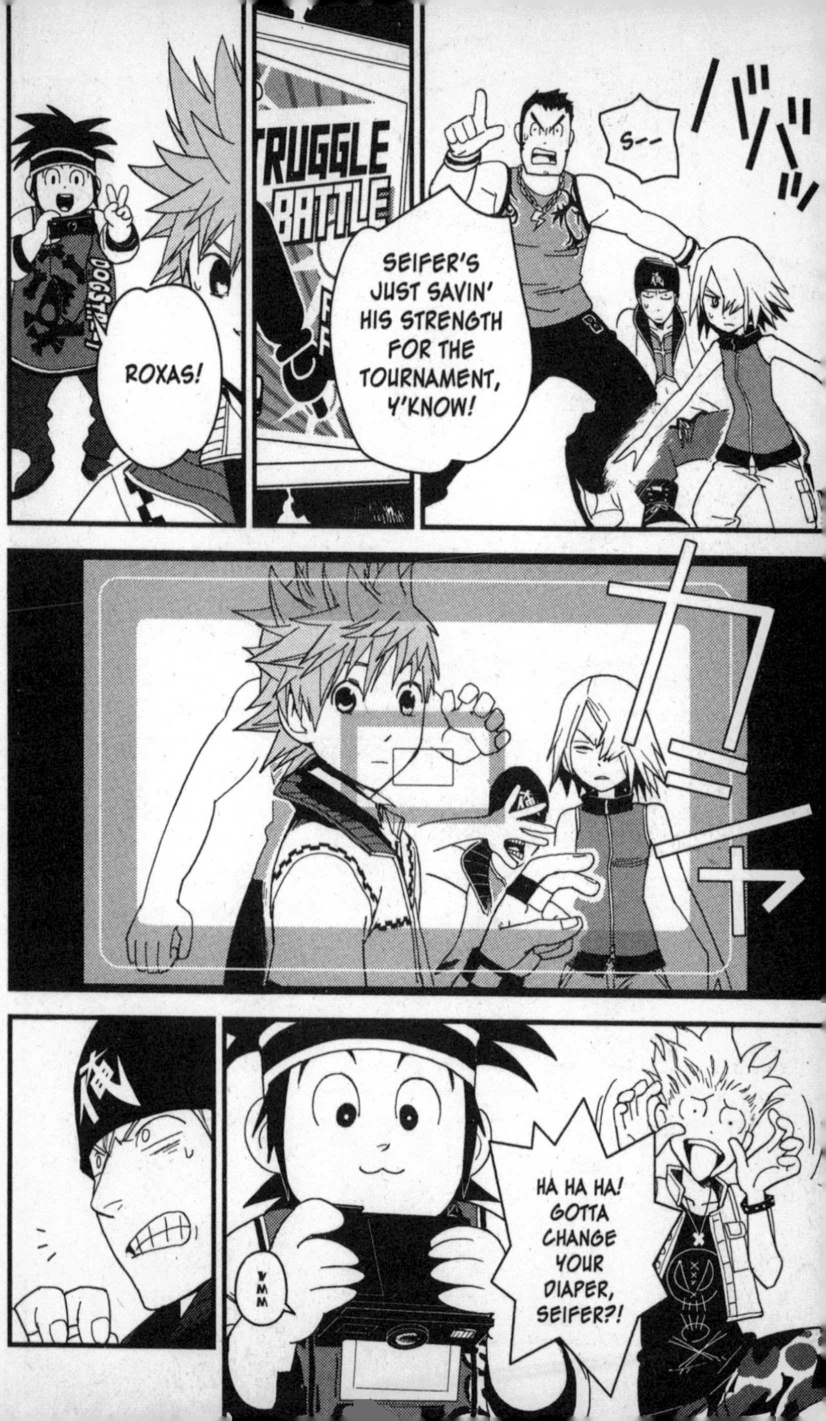
S--
バババッ
SEIFER'S JUST SAVIN' HIS STRENGTH FOR THE TOURNAMENT, Y'KNOW!
ROXAS!
カシャ
HA HA HA! GOTTA CHANGE YOUR DIAPER, SEIFER?!

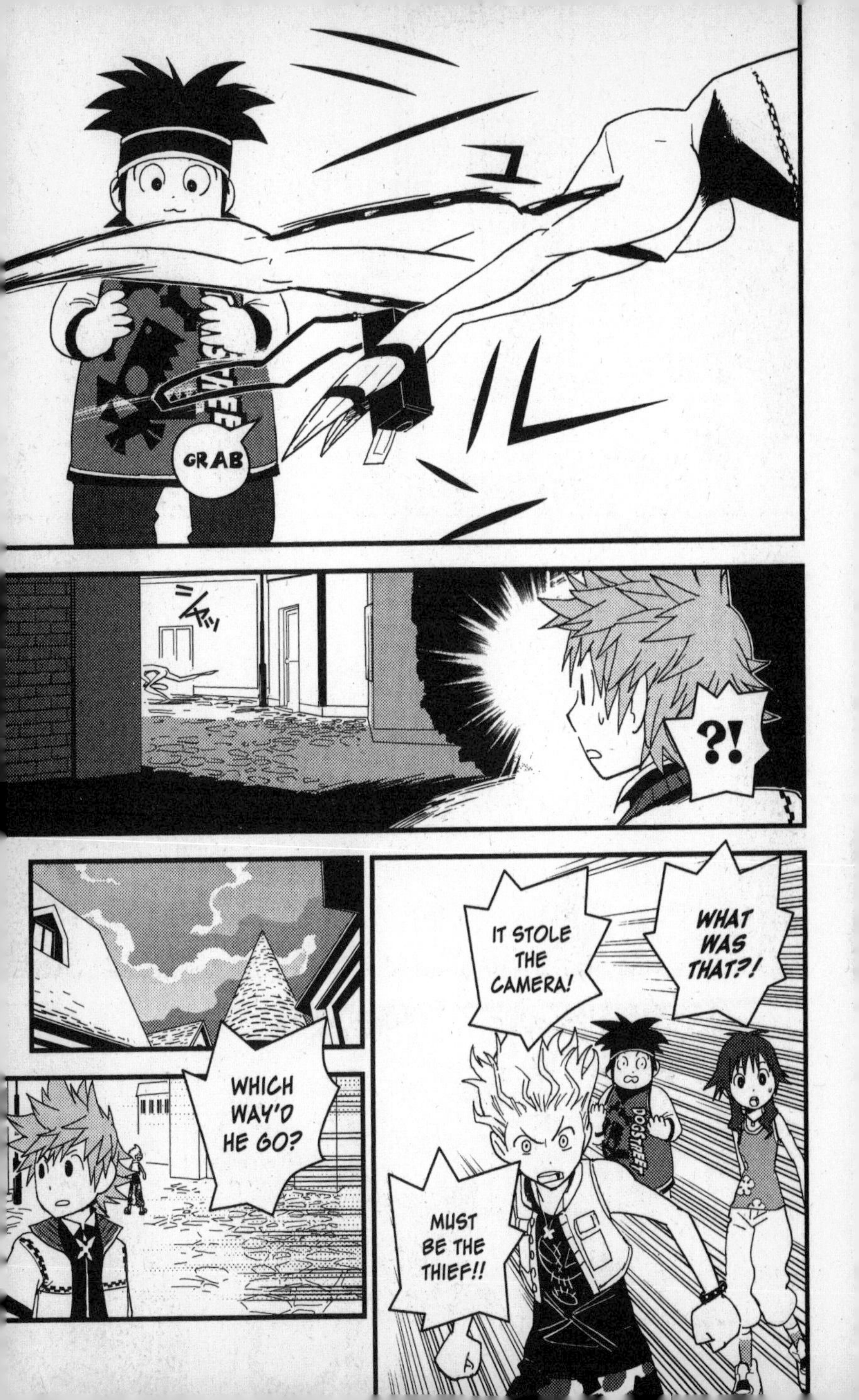
GRAB
?!
WHAT WAS THAT?!
IT STOLE THE CAMERA!
MUST BE THE THIEF!!
WHICH WAY'D HE GO?

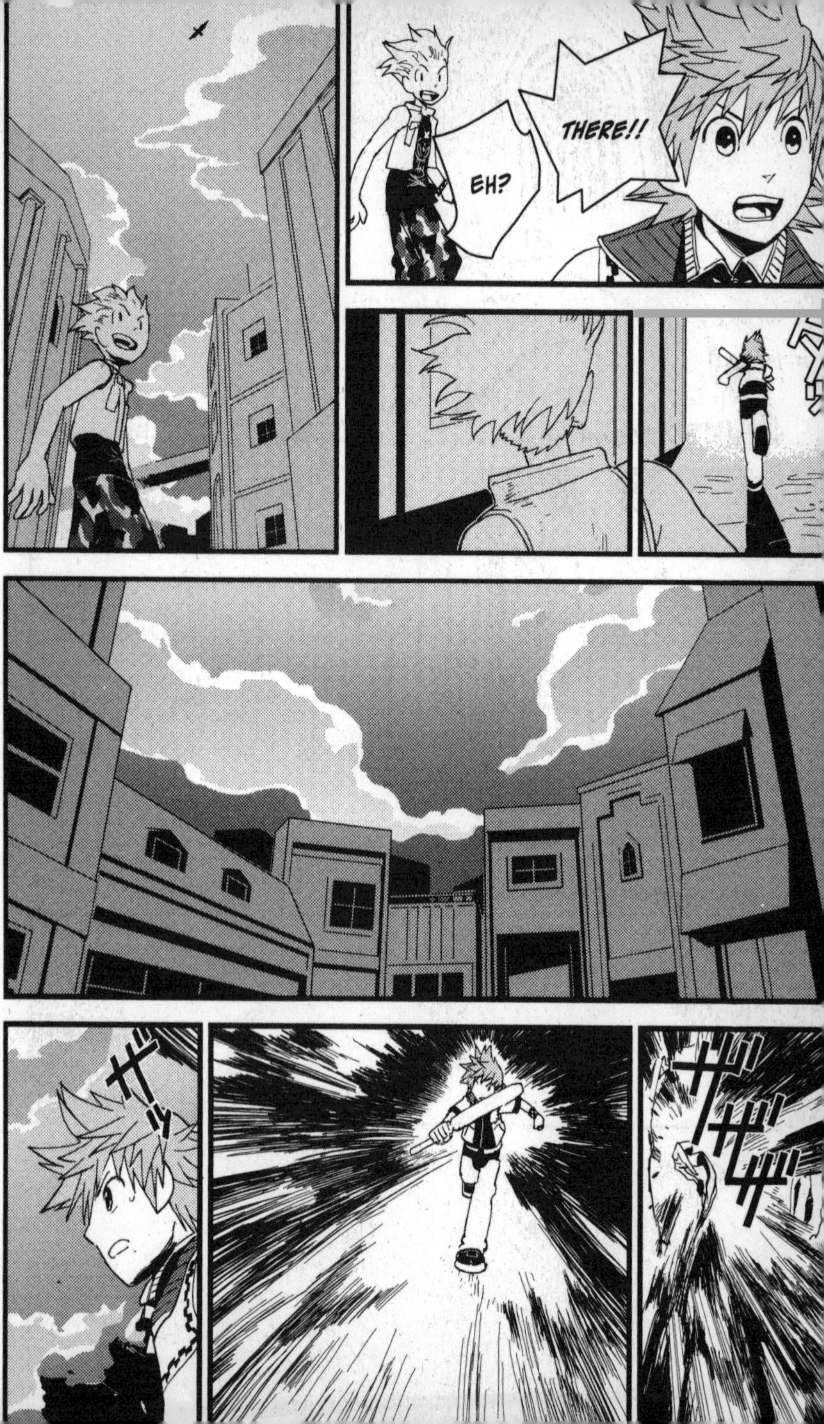
THERE!!
EH?

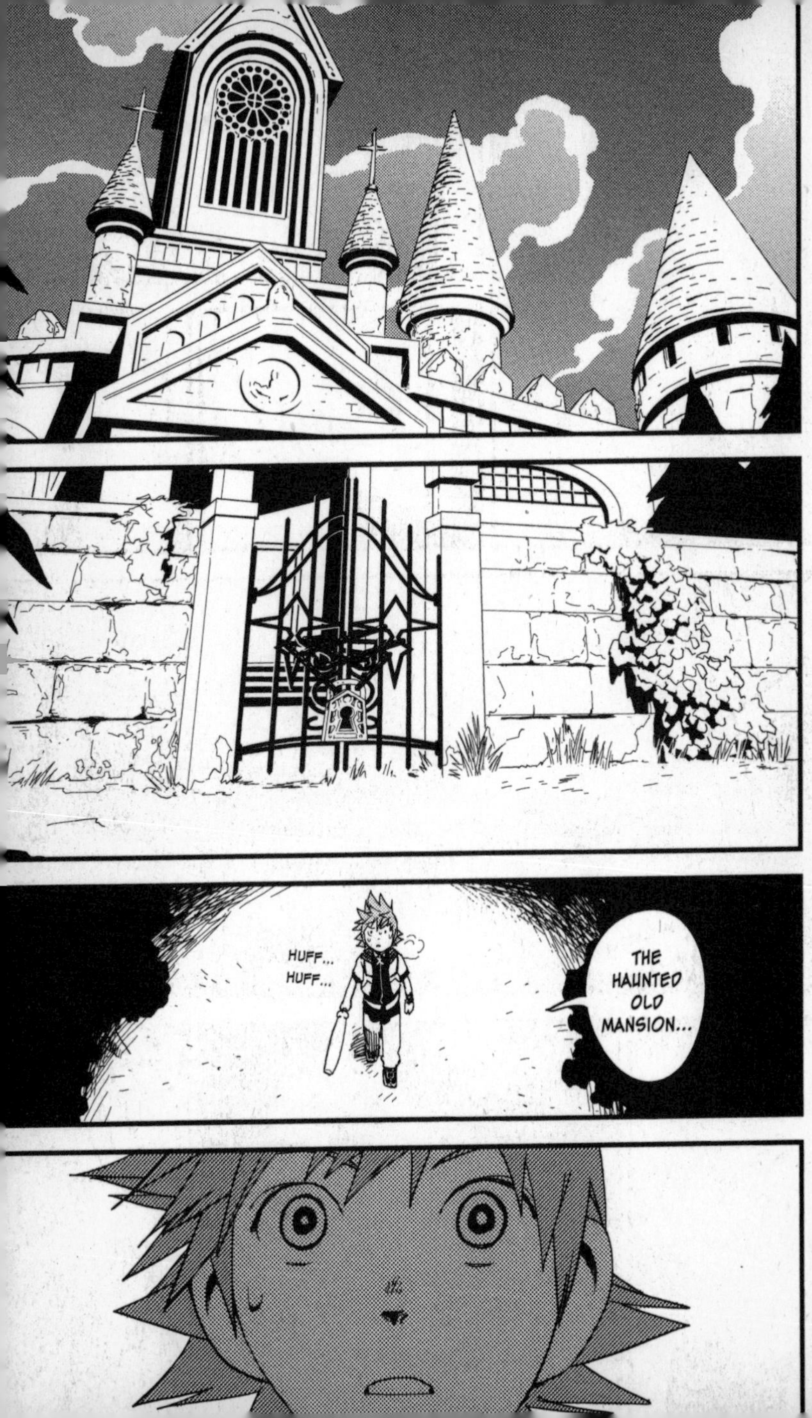
HUFF... HUFF...
THE HAUNTED OLD MANSION...

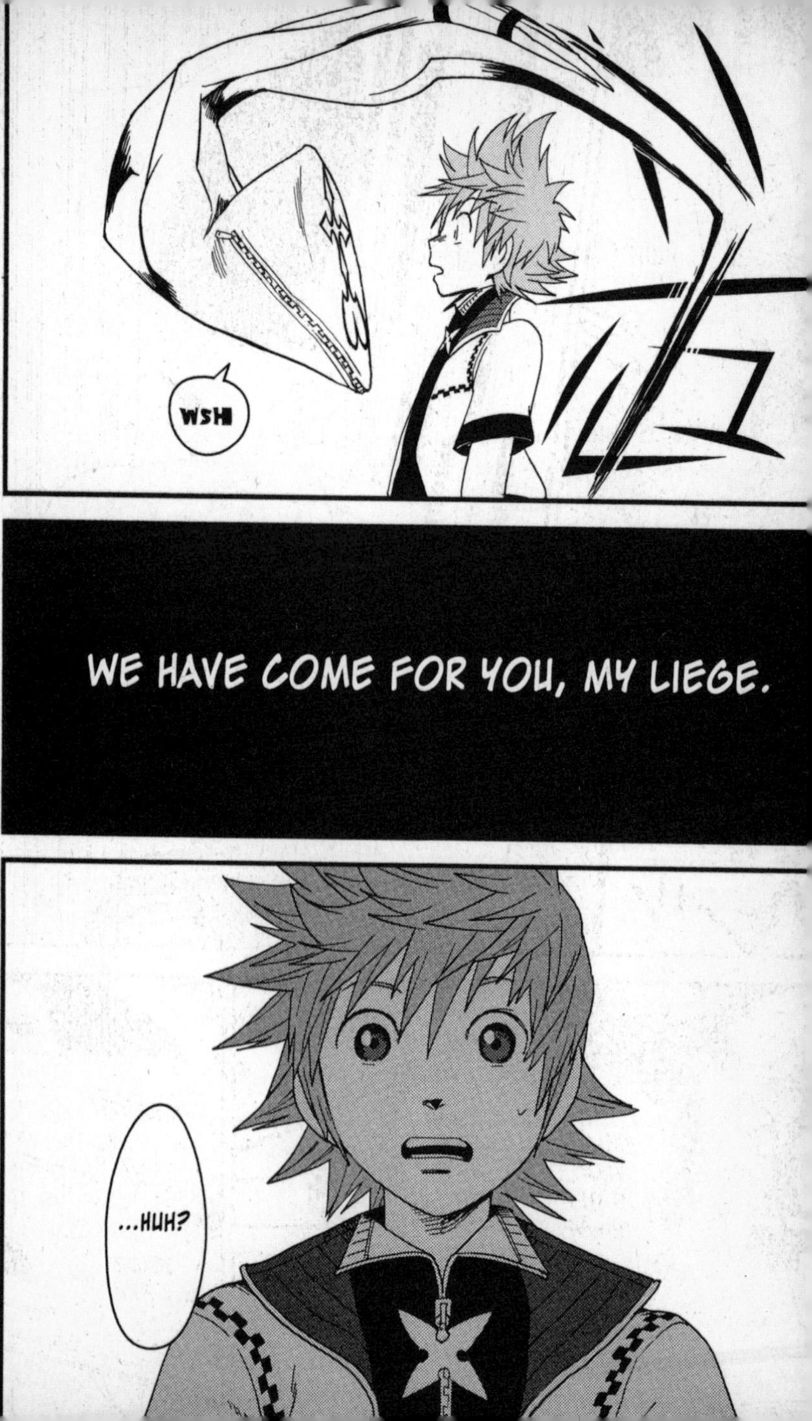
WSH
WE HAVE COME FOR YOU, MY LIEGE.
...HUH?

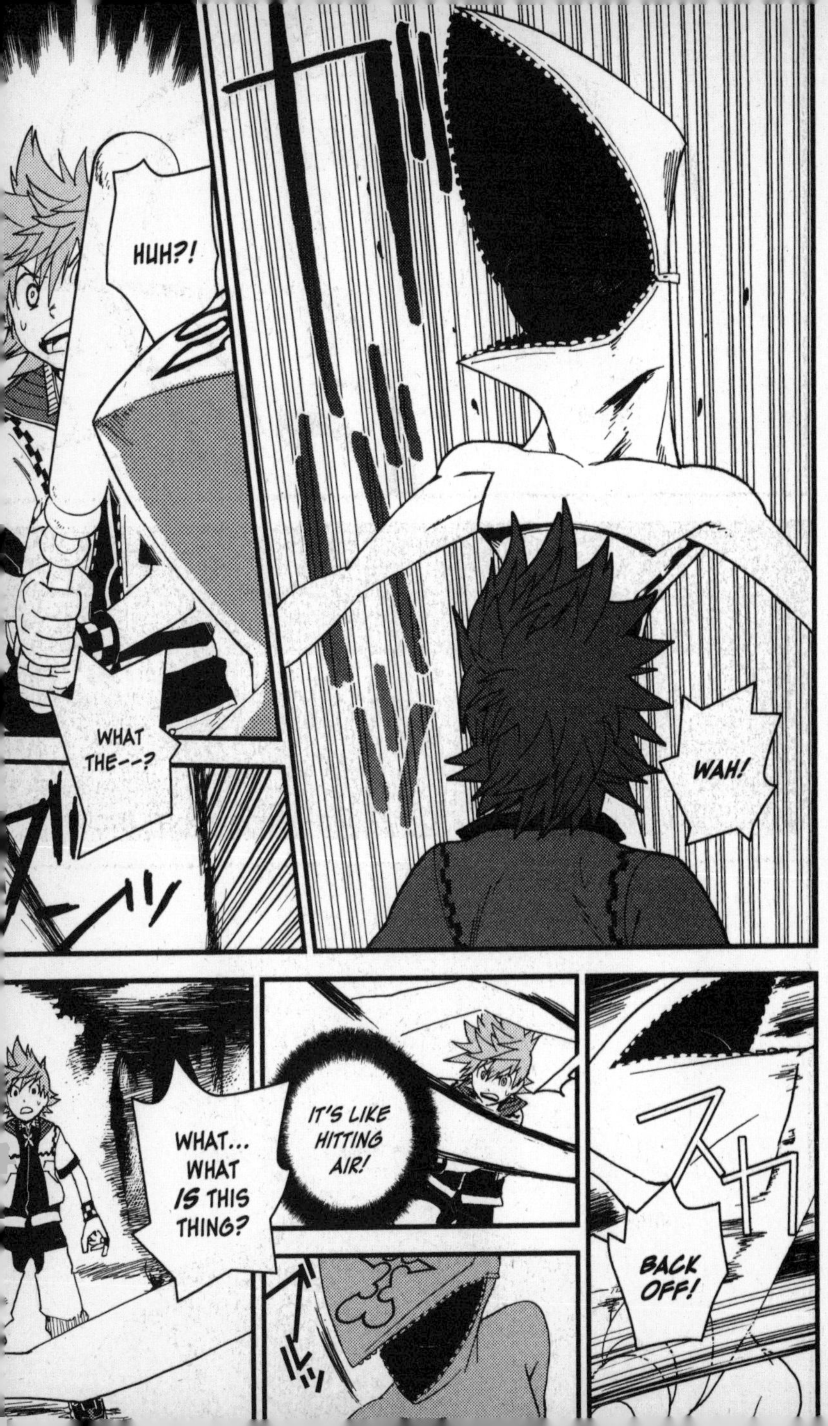
WAH!
HUH?!
WHAT THE--?
BACK OFF!
IT'S LIKE HITTING AIR!
WHAT... WHAT *IS* THIS THING?

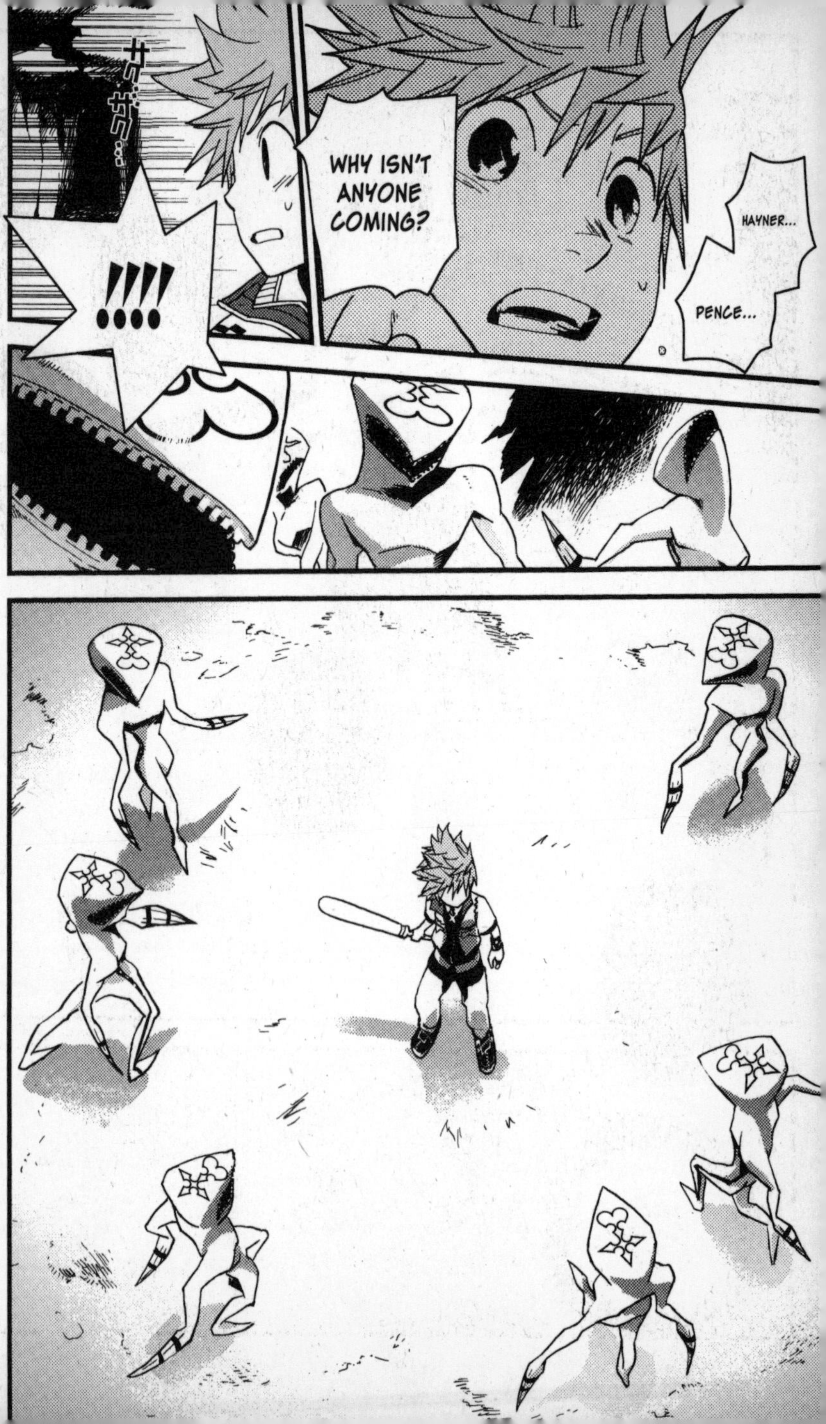
HAYNER...
PENCE...
WHY ISN'T ANYONE COMING?
ザク ザク…
!!!!

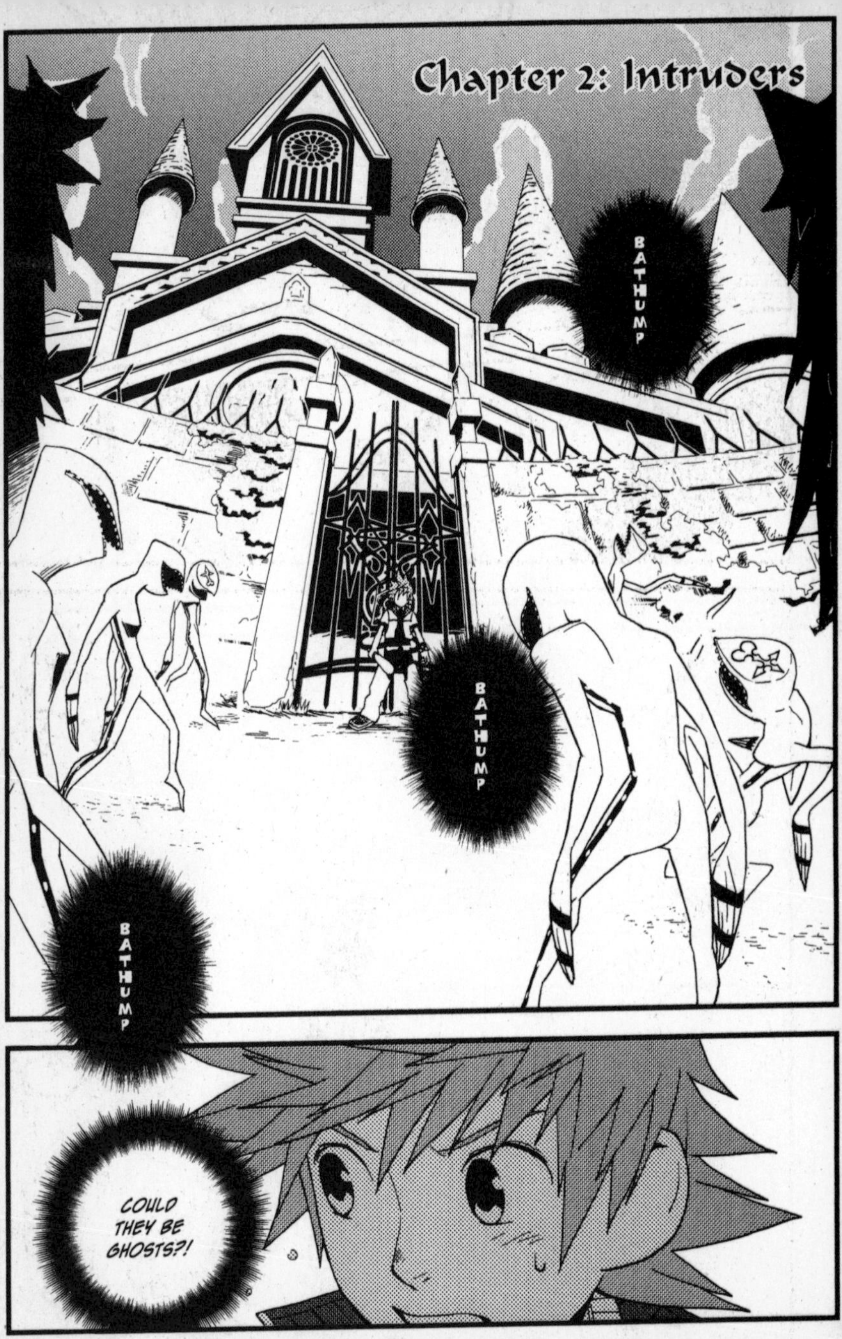
Chapter 2: Intruders
BATHUMP
BATHUMP
BATHUMP
COULD THEY BE GHOSTS?!

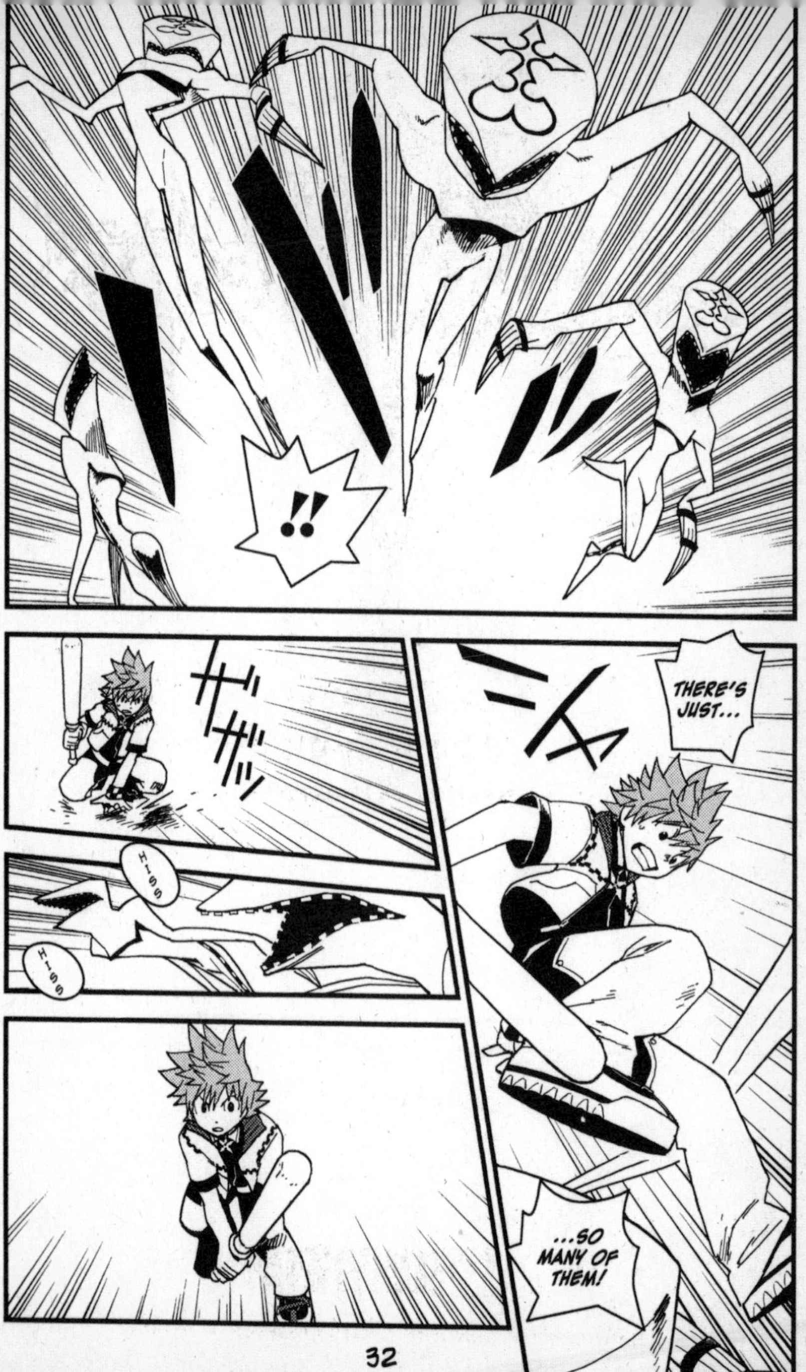
!!
THERE'S JUST...
...SO MANY OF THEM!
HISS
HISS

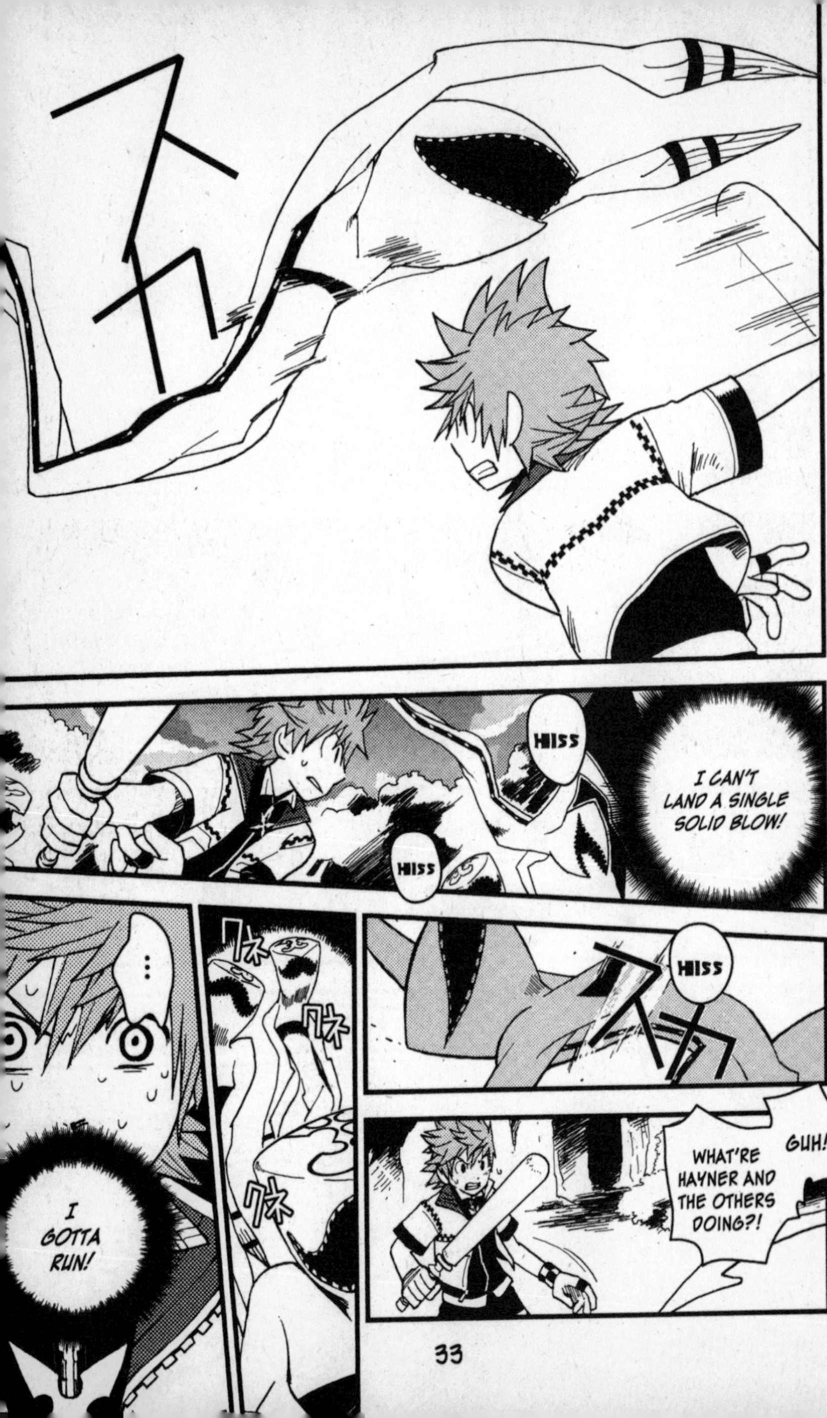
スカ
HISS
I CAN'T LAND A SINGLE SOLID BLOW!
HISS
HISS
スカ
GUH!
WHAT'RE HAYNER AND THE OTHERS DOING?!
クネ
クネ
クネ
...
I GOTTA RUN!

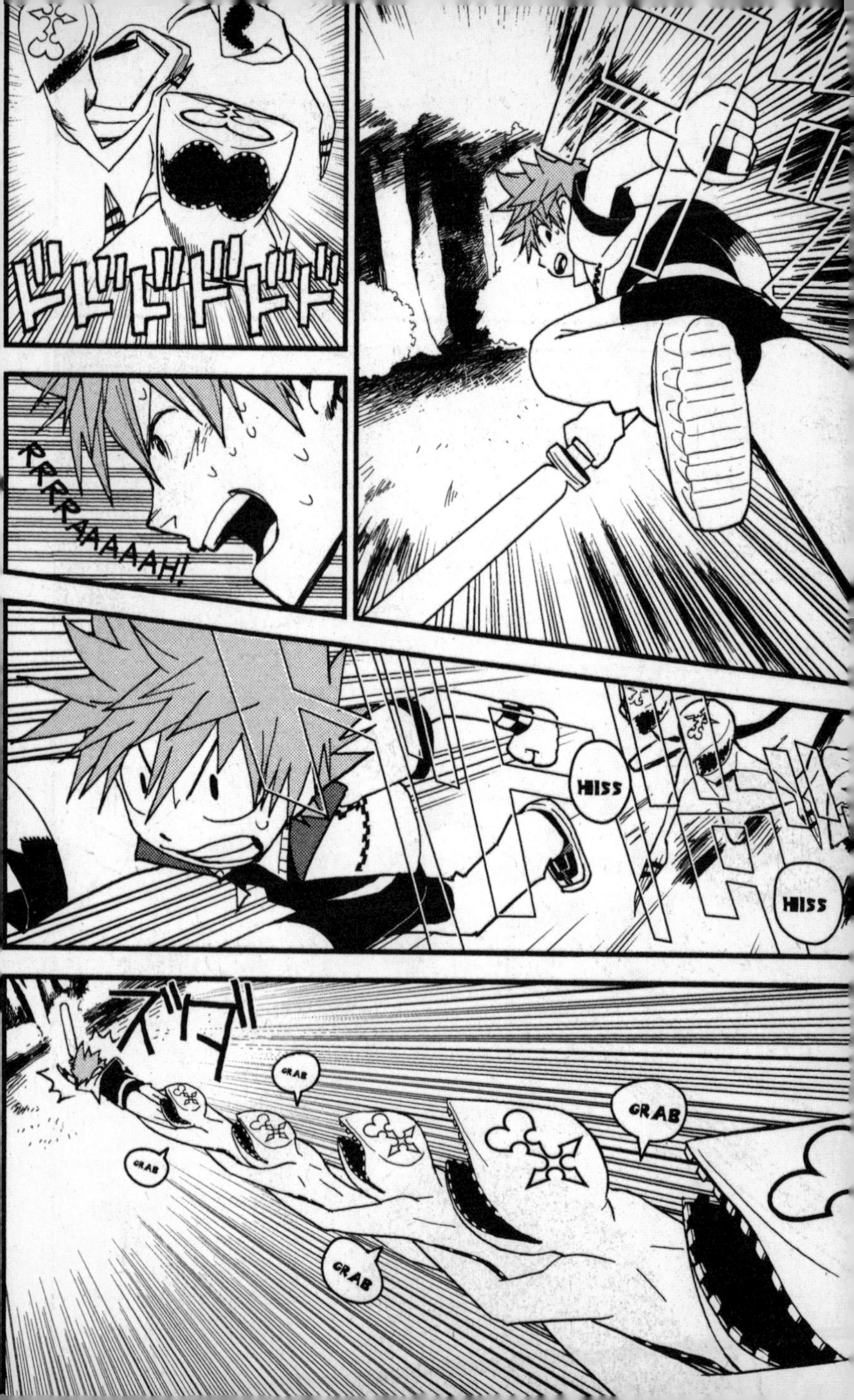
RRRRAAAAAAH!
HISS
HISS
GRAB
GRAB
GRAB
GRAB

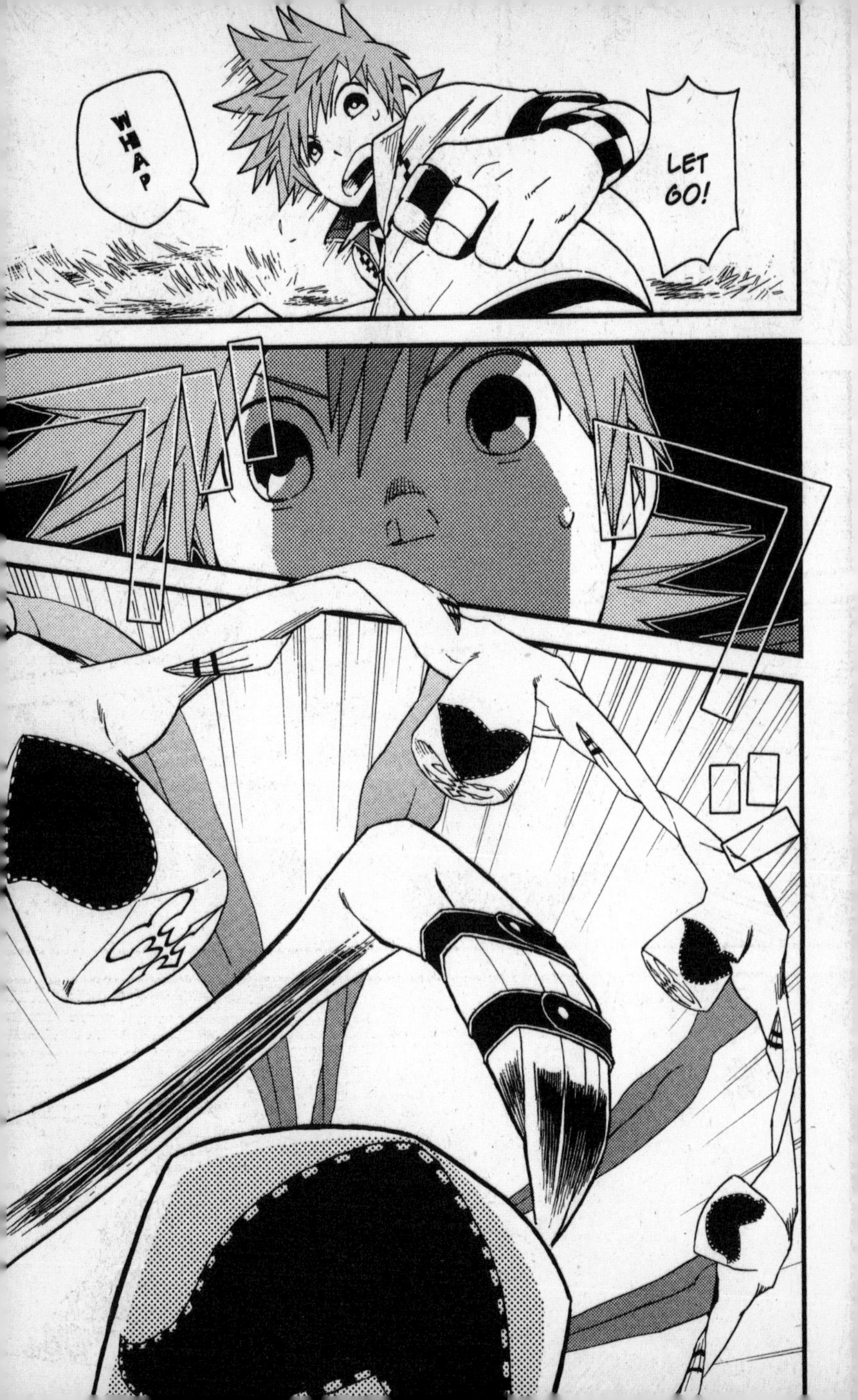
LET GO!
WHAP

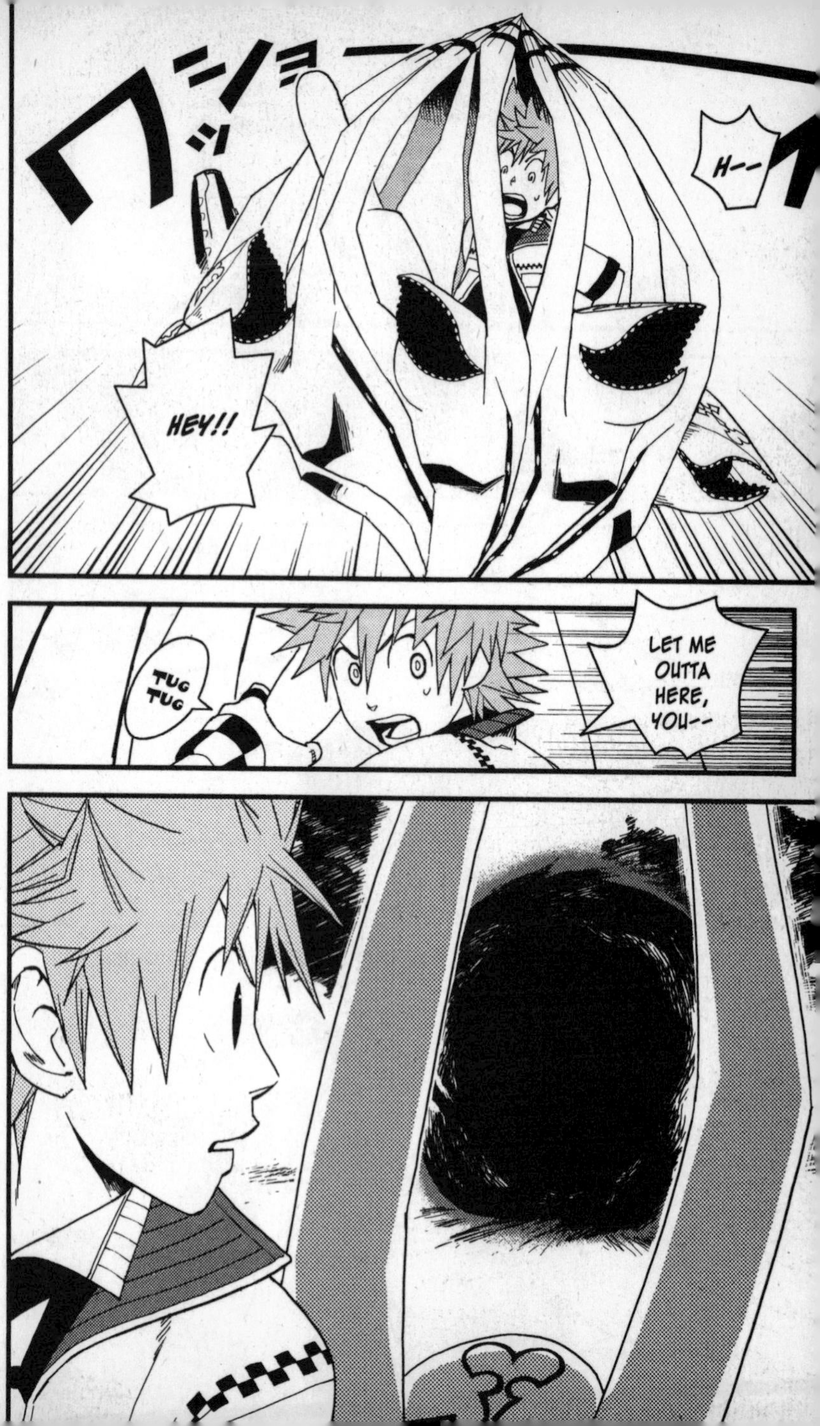
H--
HEY!!
LET ME OUTTA HERE, YOU--
TUG TUG

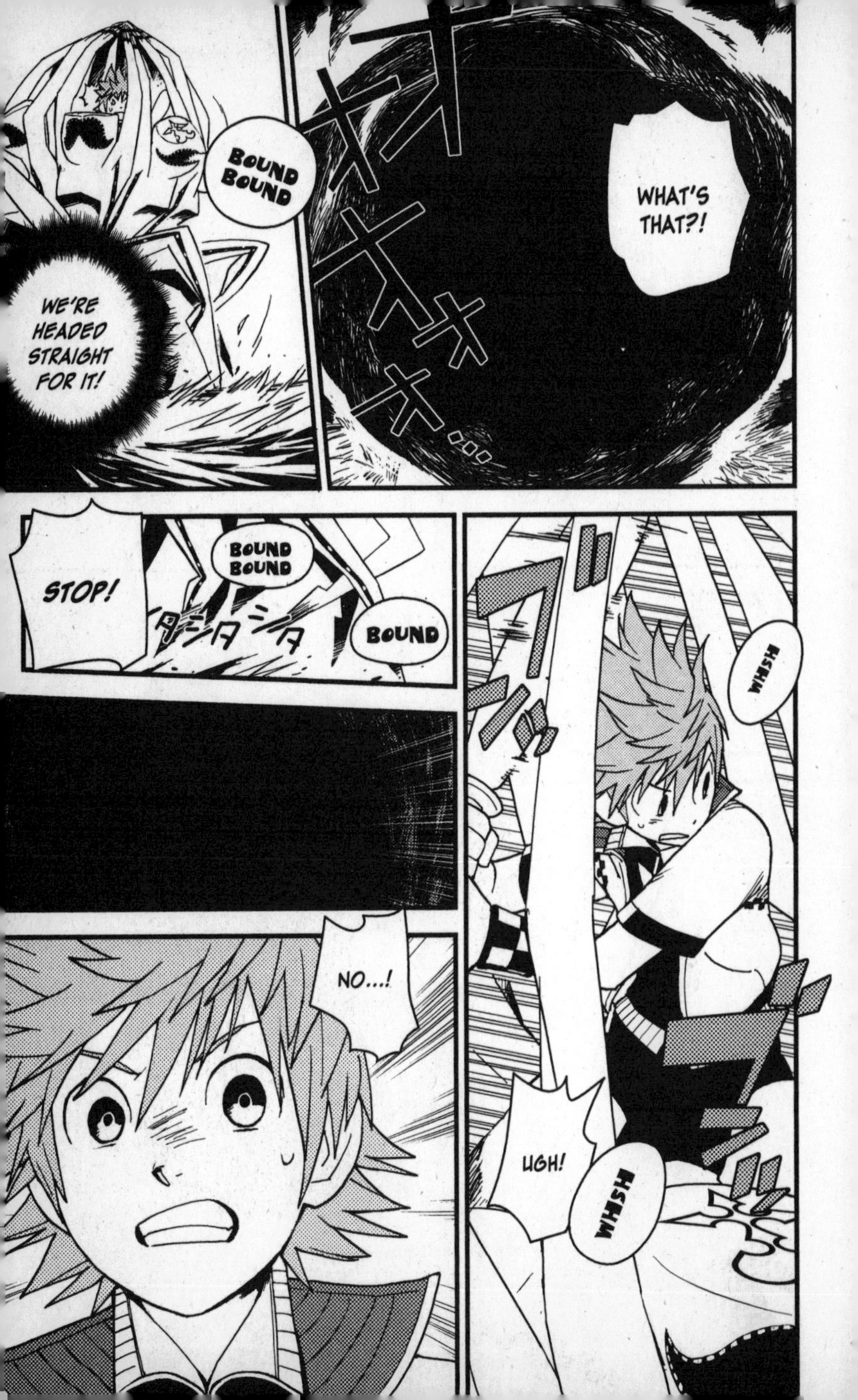
WHAT'S THAT?!
BOUND BOUND
WE'RE HEADED STRAIGHT FOR IT!
WHSH
UGH!
WHSH
STOP!
BOUND BOUND
BOUND
NO...!

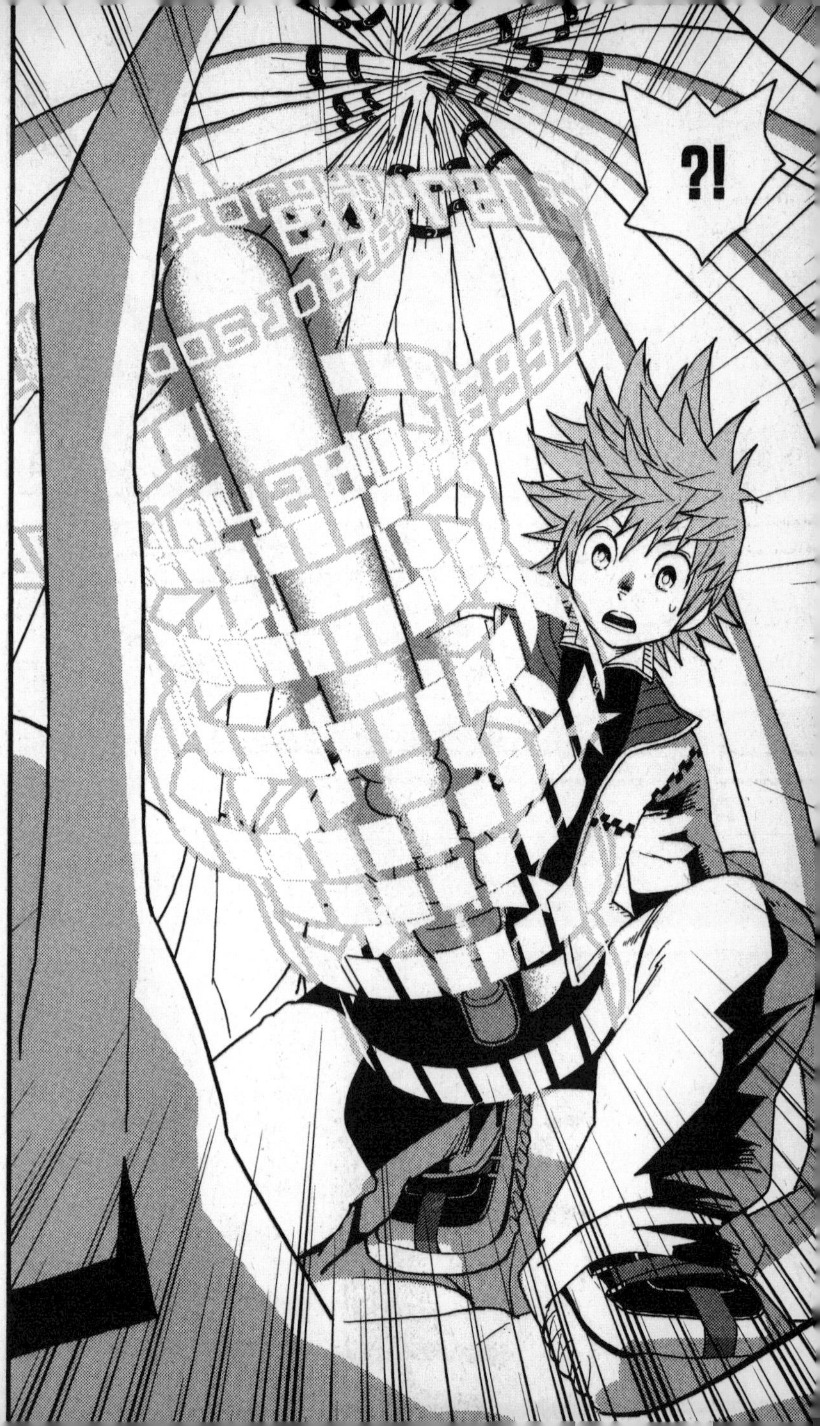
?!

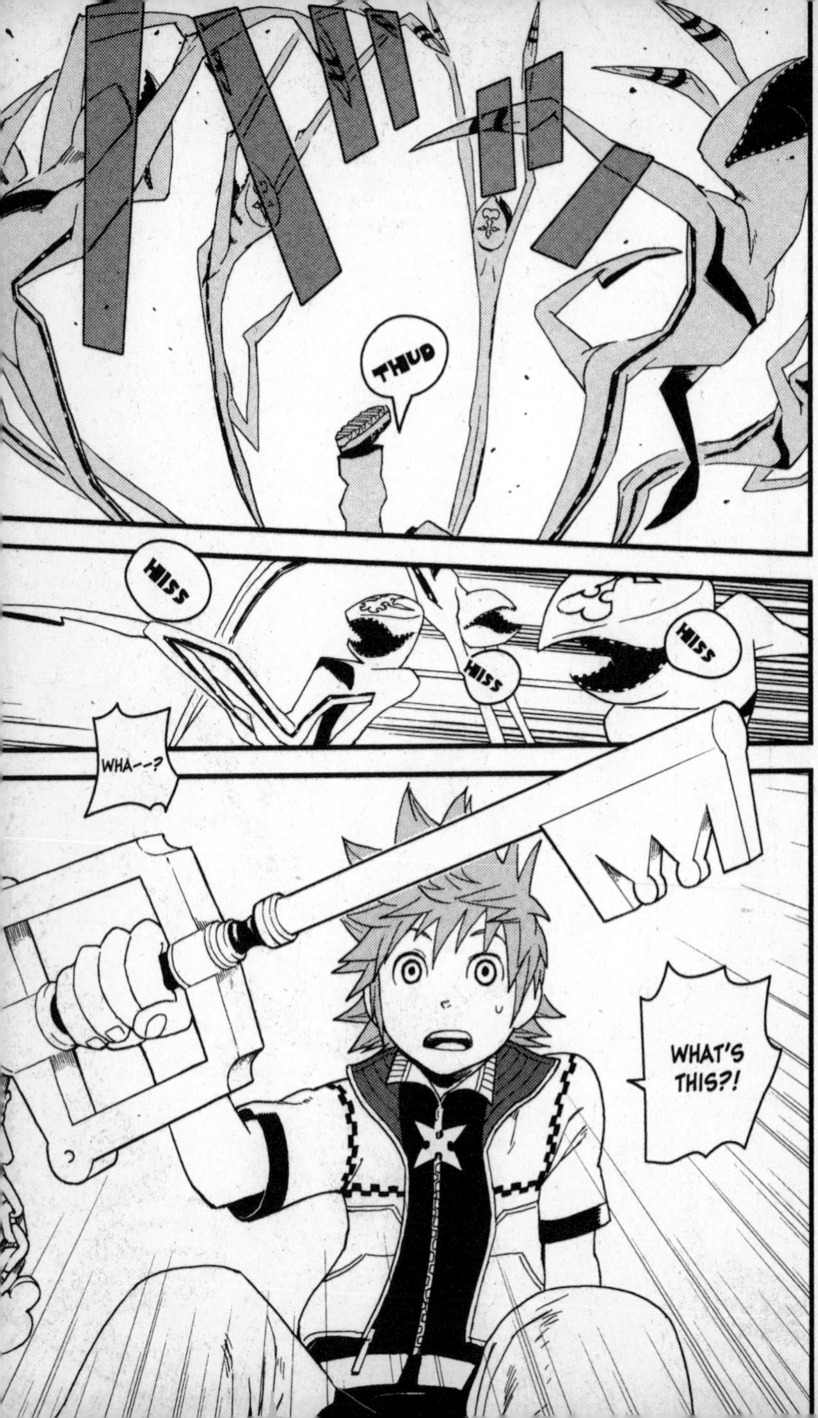
THUD
HISS
HISS
HISS
WHA--?
WHAT'S THIS?!

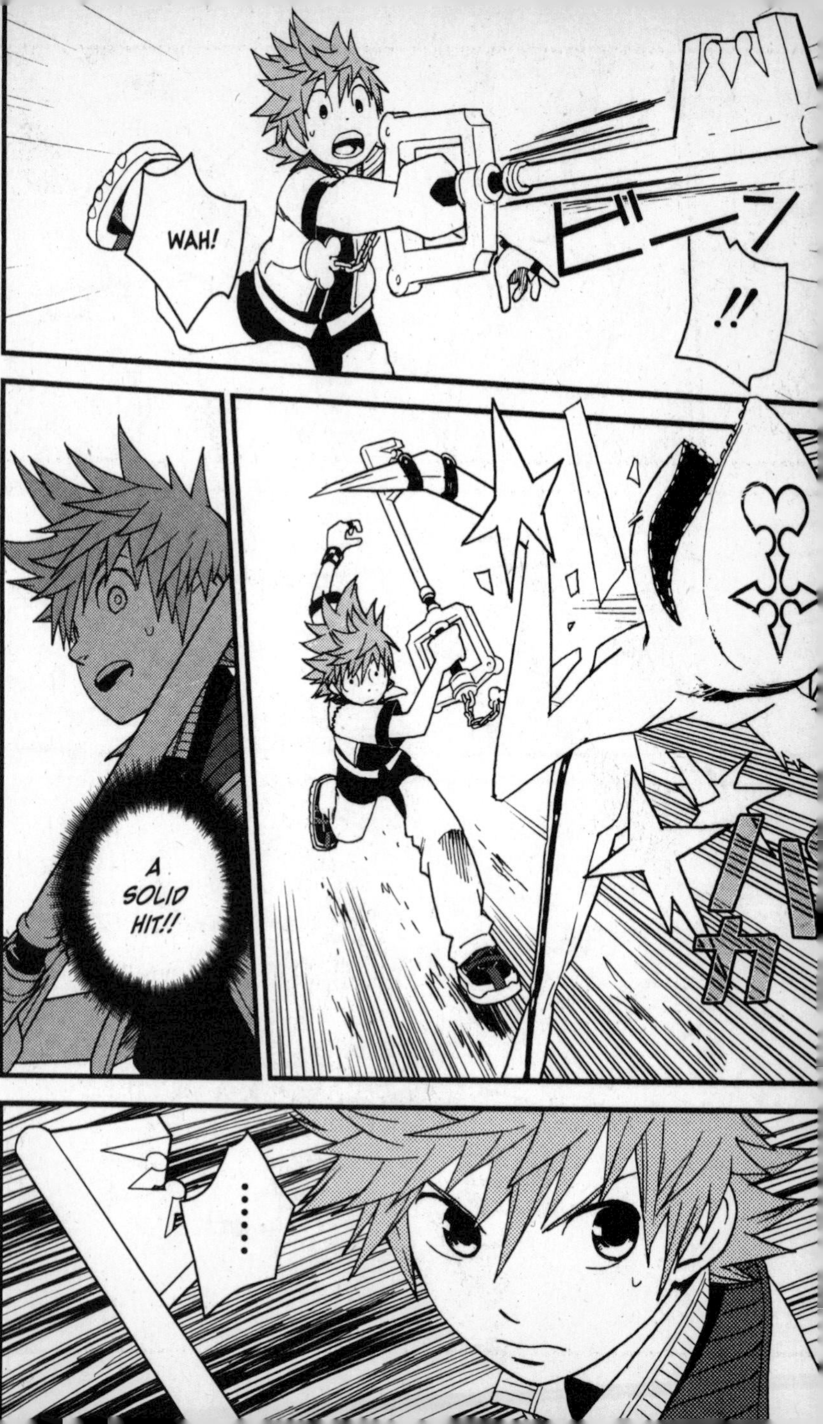
ビーン
!!
WAH!
A SOLID HIT!!
......

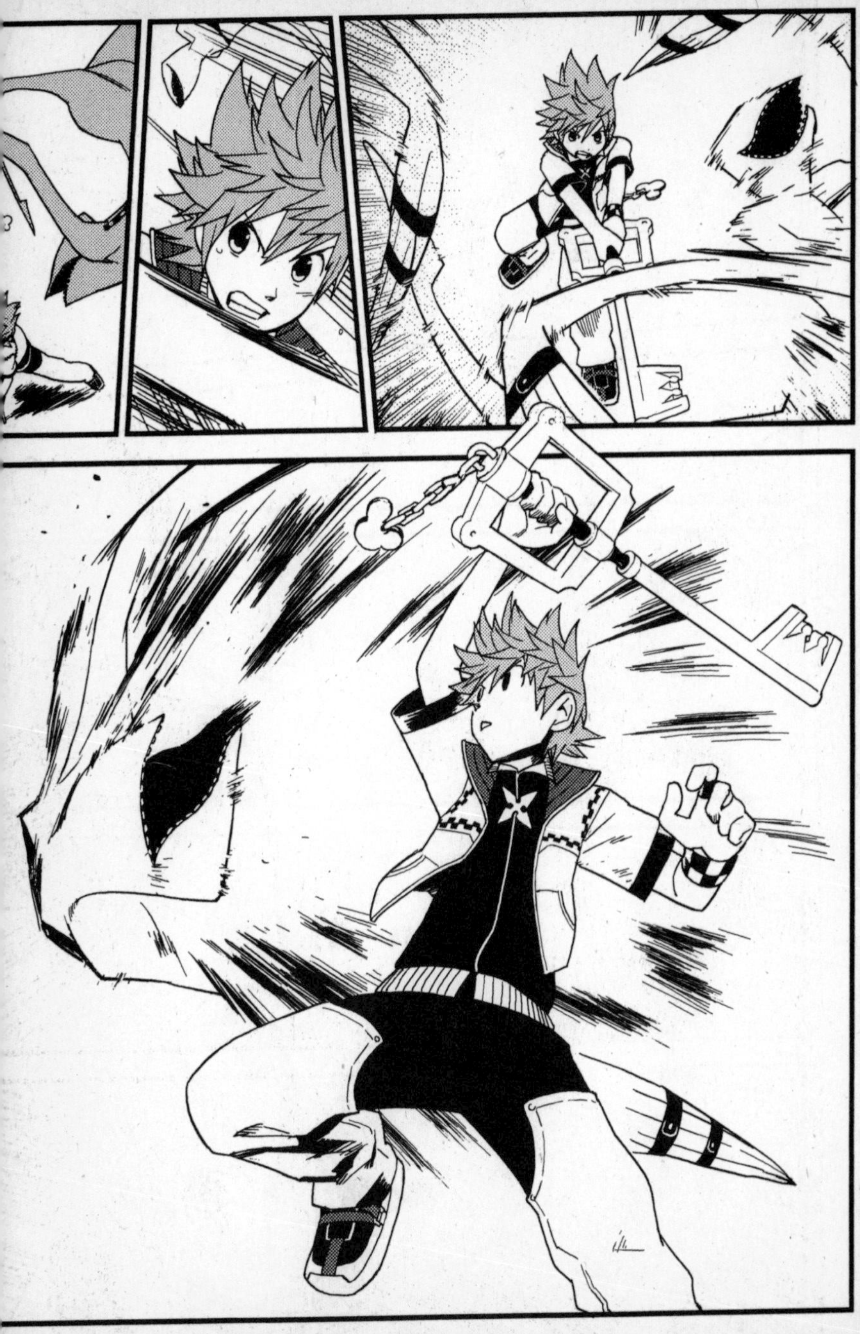

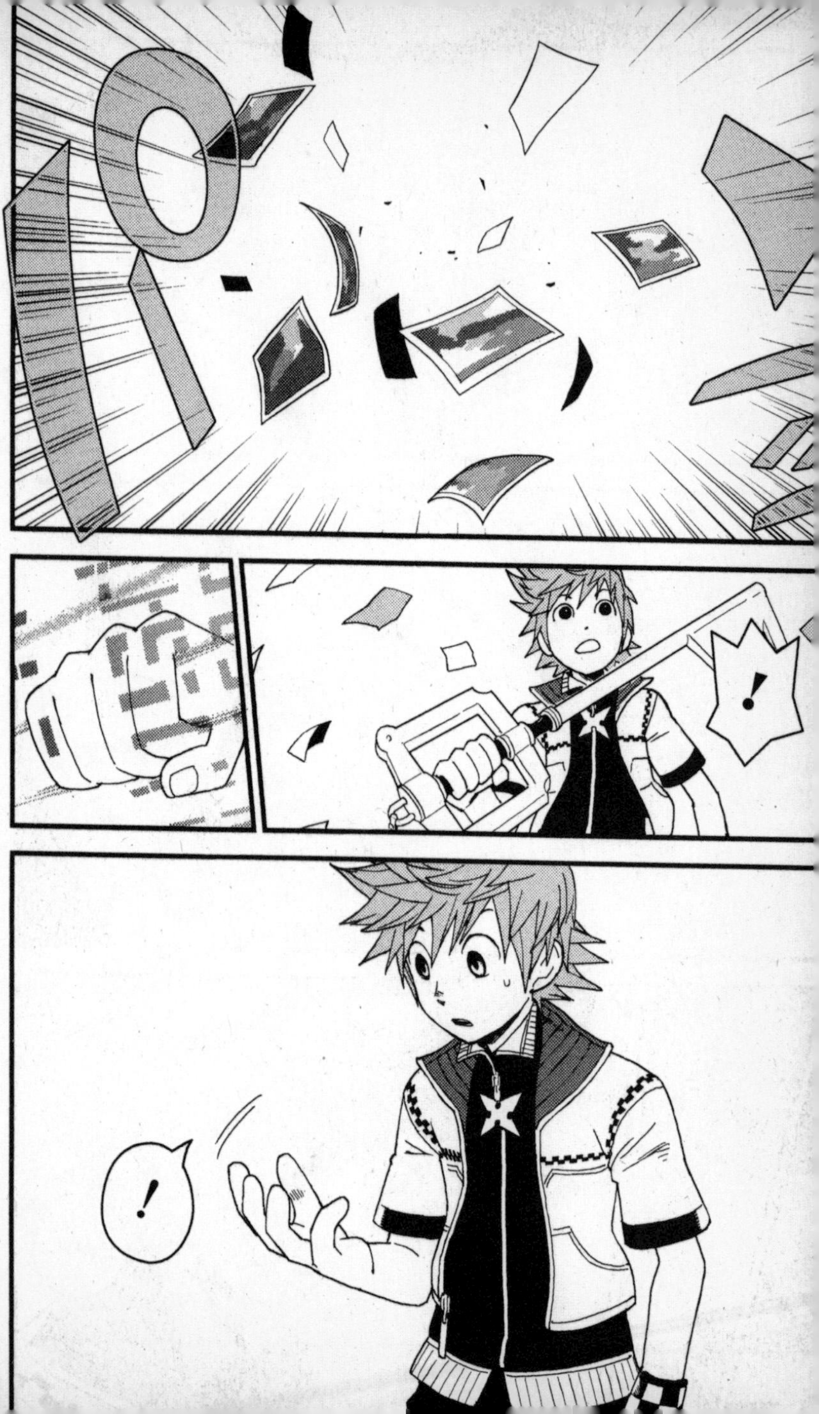
!
!

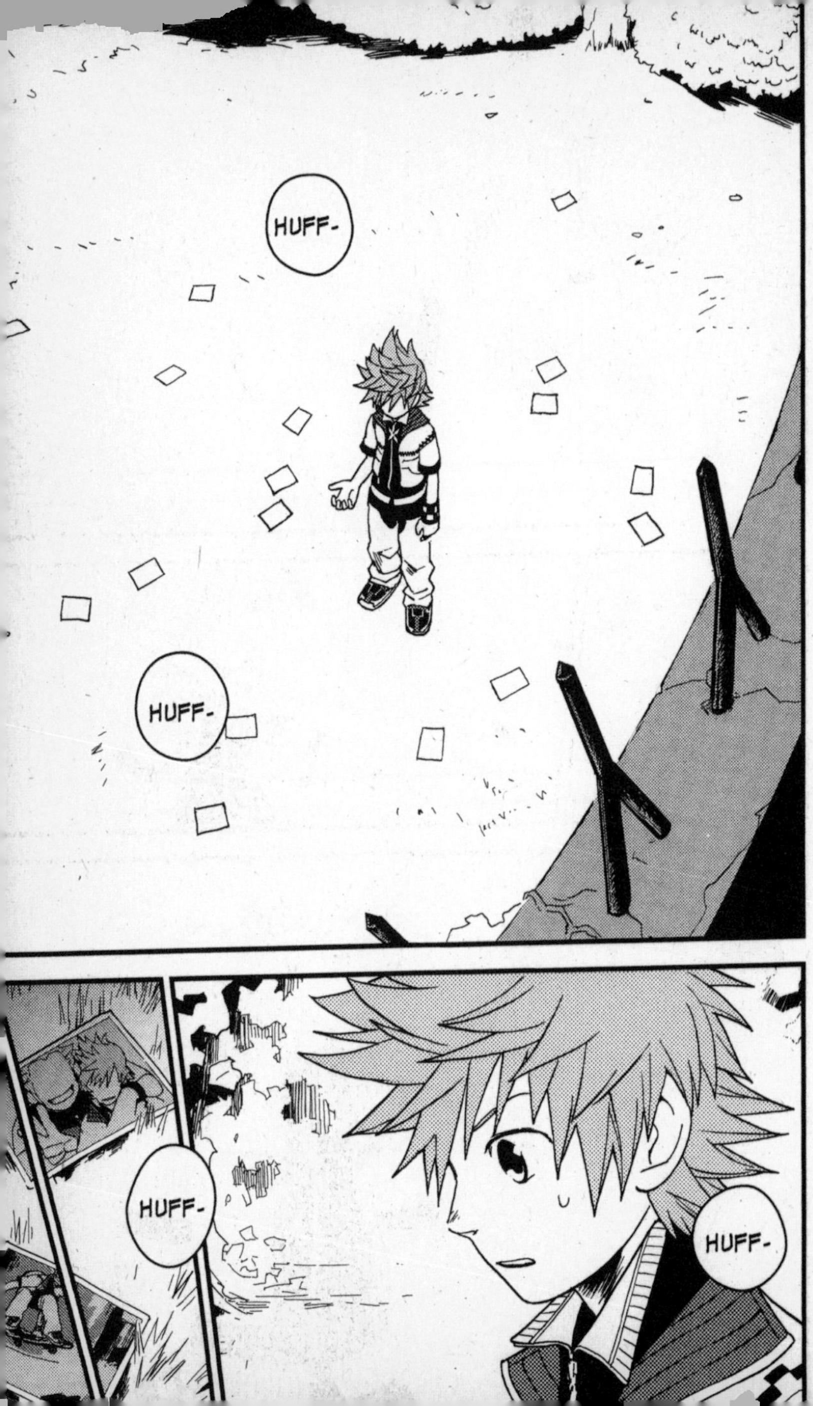
HUFF-
HUFF-
HUFF-
HUFF-

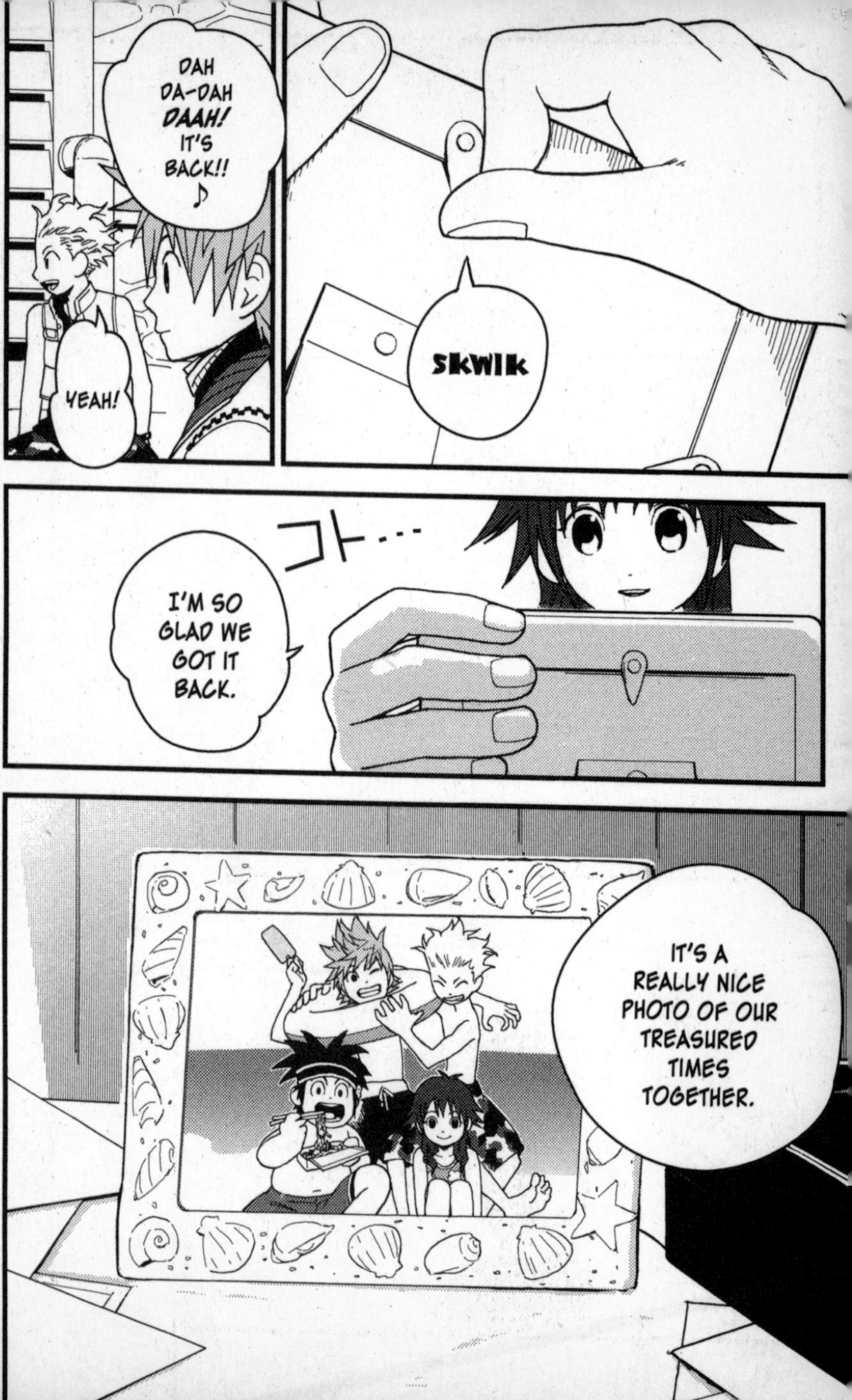
SKWIK
DAH DA-DAH DAAH! IT'S BACK!! ♪
YEAH!
コト...
I'M SO GLAD WE GOT IT BACK.
IT'S A REALLY NICE PHOTO OF OUR TREASURED TIMES TOGETHER.

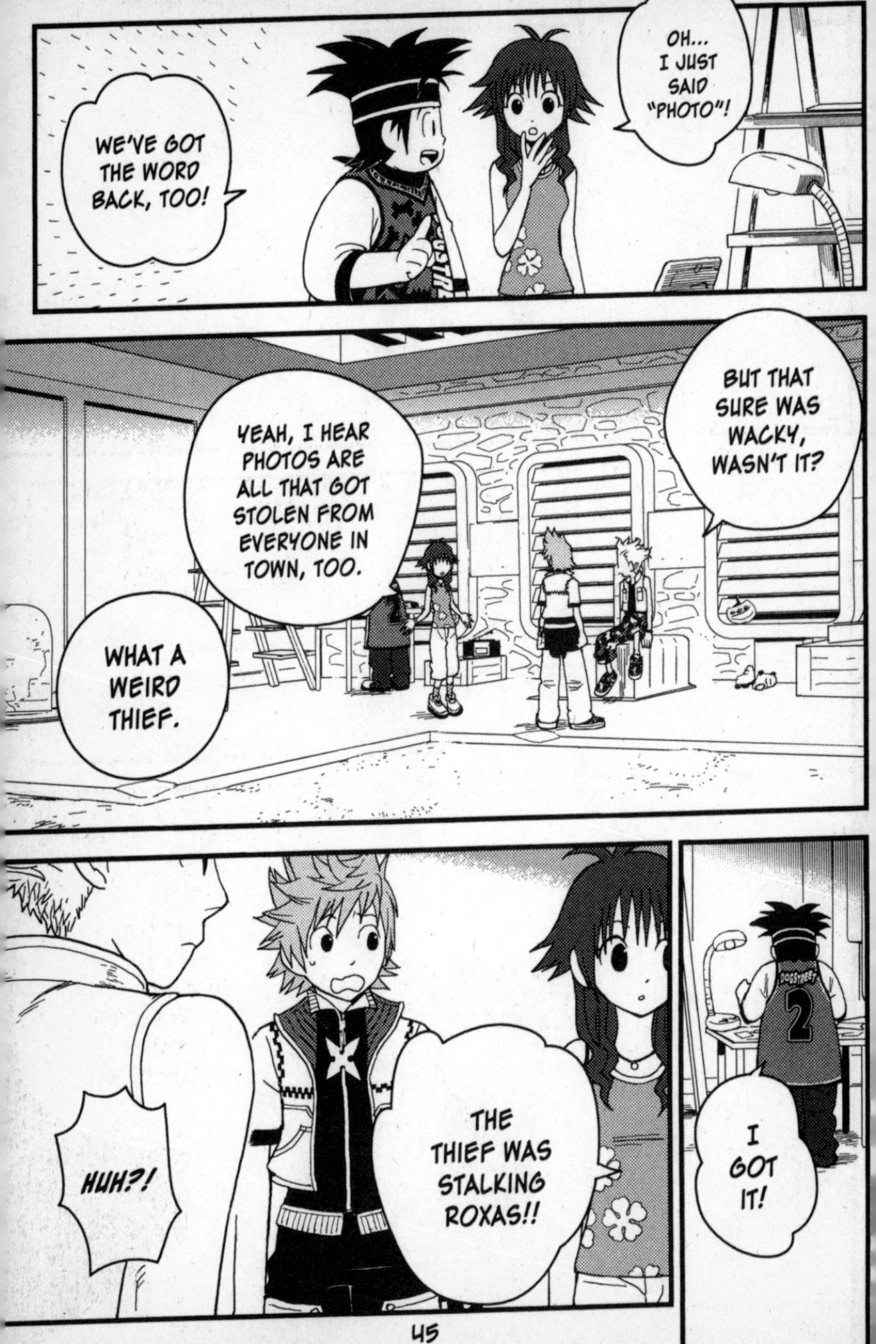
OH... I JUST SAID "PHOTO"!
WE'VE GOT THE WORD BACK, TOO!
BUT THAT SURE WAS WACKY, WASN'T IT?
YEAH, I HEAR PHOTOS ARE ALL THAT GOT STOLEN FROM EVERYONE IN TOWN, TOO.
WHAT A WEIRD THIEF.
I GOT IT!
THE THIEF WAS STALKING ROXAS!!
HUH?!

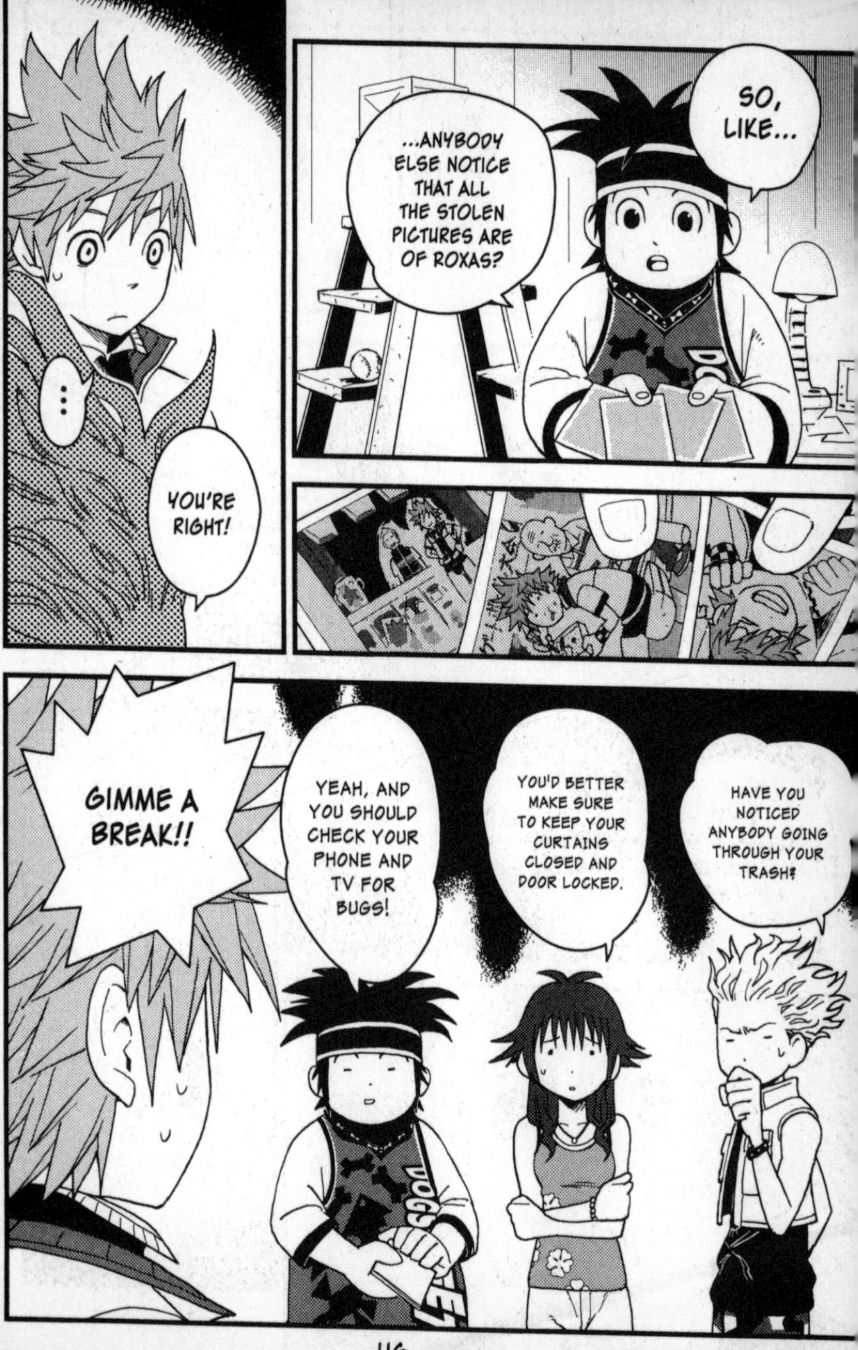
SO, LIKE...
...ANYBODY ELSE NOTICE THAT ALL THE STOLEN PICTURES ARE OF ROXAS?
...
YOU'RE RIGHT!
HAVE YOU NOTICED ANYBODY GOING THROUGH YOUR TRASH?
YOU'D BETTER MAKE SURE TO KEEP YOUR CURTAINS CLOSED AND DOOR LOCKED.
YEAH, AND YOU SHOULD CHECK YOUR PHONE AND TV FOR BUGS!
GIMME A BREAK!!

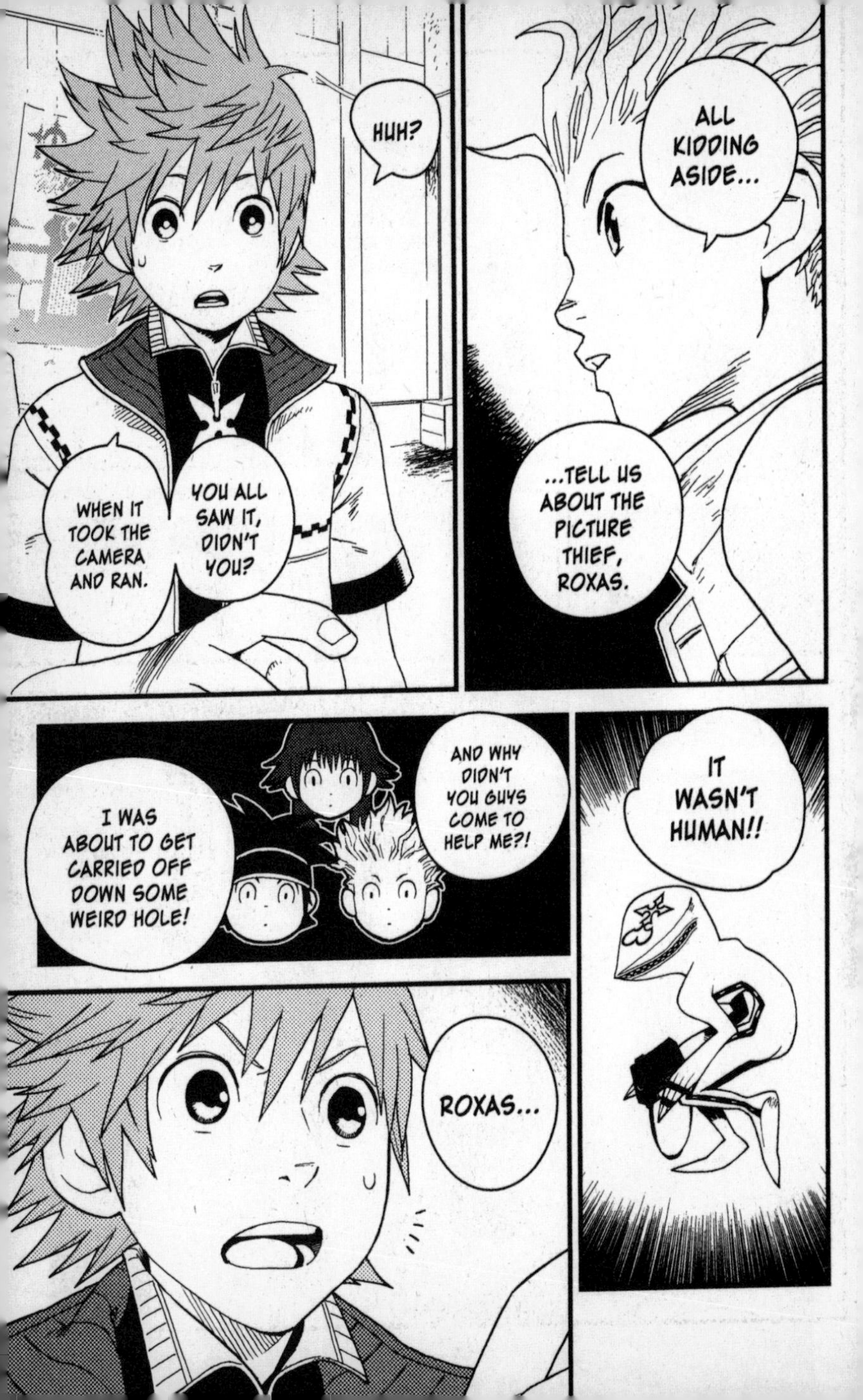
ALL KIDDING ASIDE...
...TELL US ABOUT THE PICTURE THIEF, ROXAS.
HUH?
YOU ALL SAW IT, DIDN'T YOU?
WHEN IT TOOK THE CAMERA AND RAN.
IT WASN'T HUMAN!!
AND WHY DIDN'T YOU GUYS COME TO HELP ME?!
I WAS ABOUT TO GET CARRIED OFF DOWN SOME WEIRD HOLE!
ROXAS...

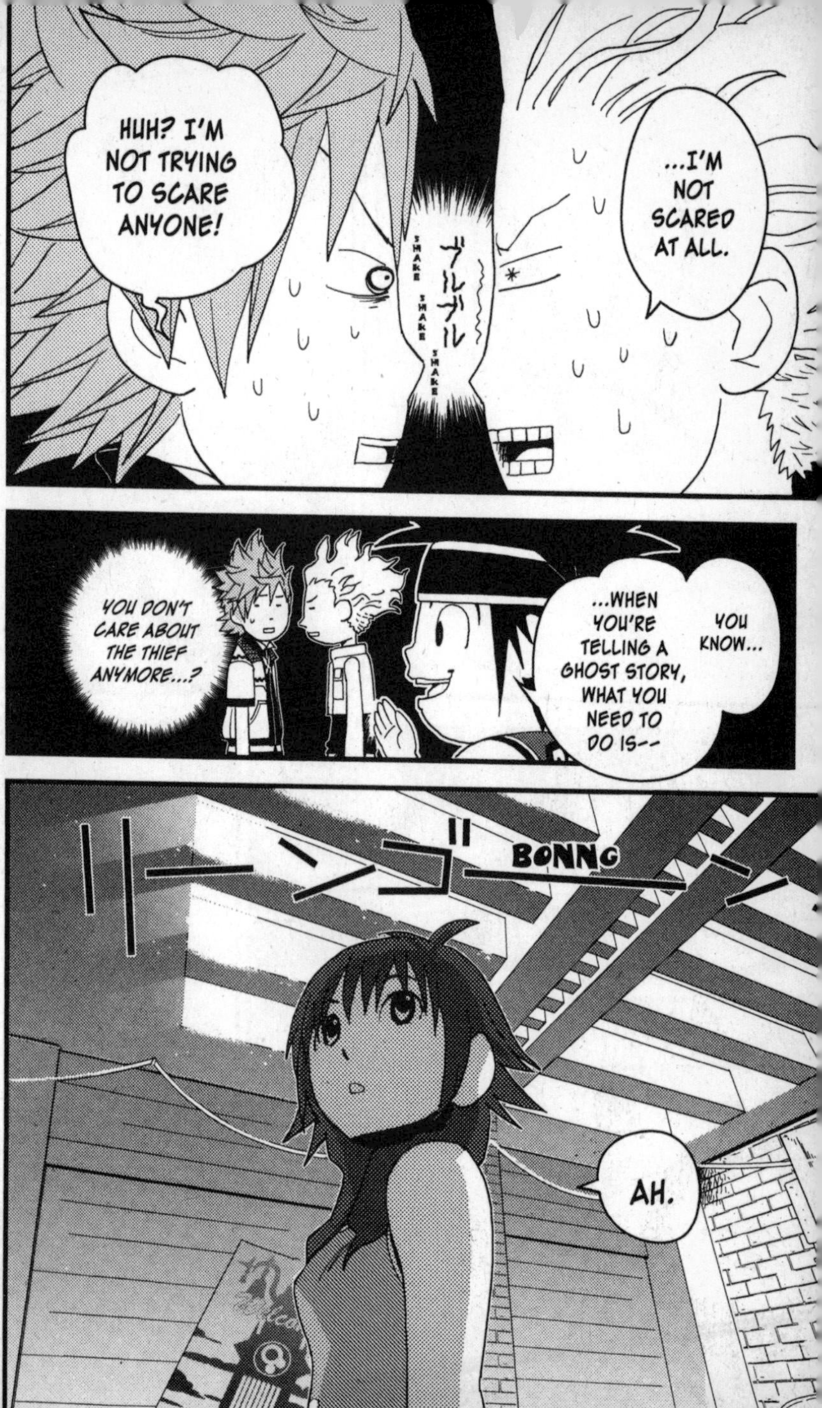
...I'M NOT SCARED AT ALL.
ブルブル
SHAKE SHAKE SHAKE
HUH? I'M NOT TRYING TO SCARE ANYONE!
YOU KNOW...
...WHEN YOU'RE TELLING A GHOST STORY, WHAT YOU NEED TO DO IS--
YOU DON'T CARE ABOUT THE THIEF ANYMORE...?
リーンゴーン
BONNG
AH.

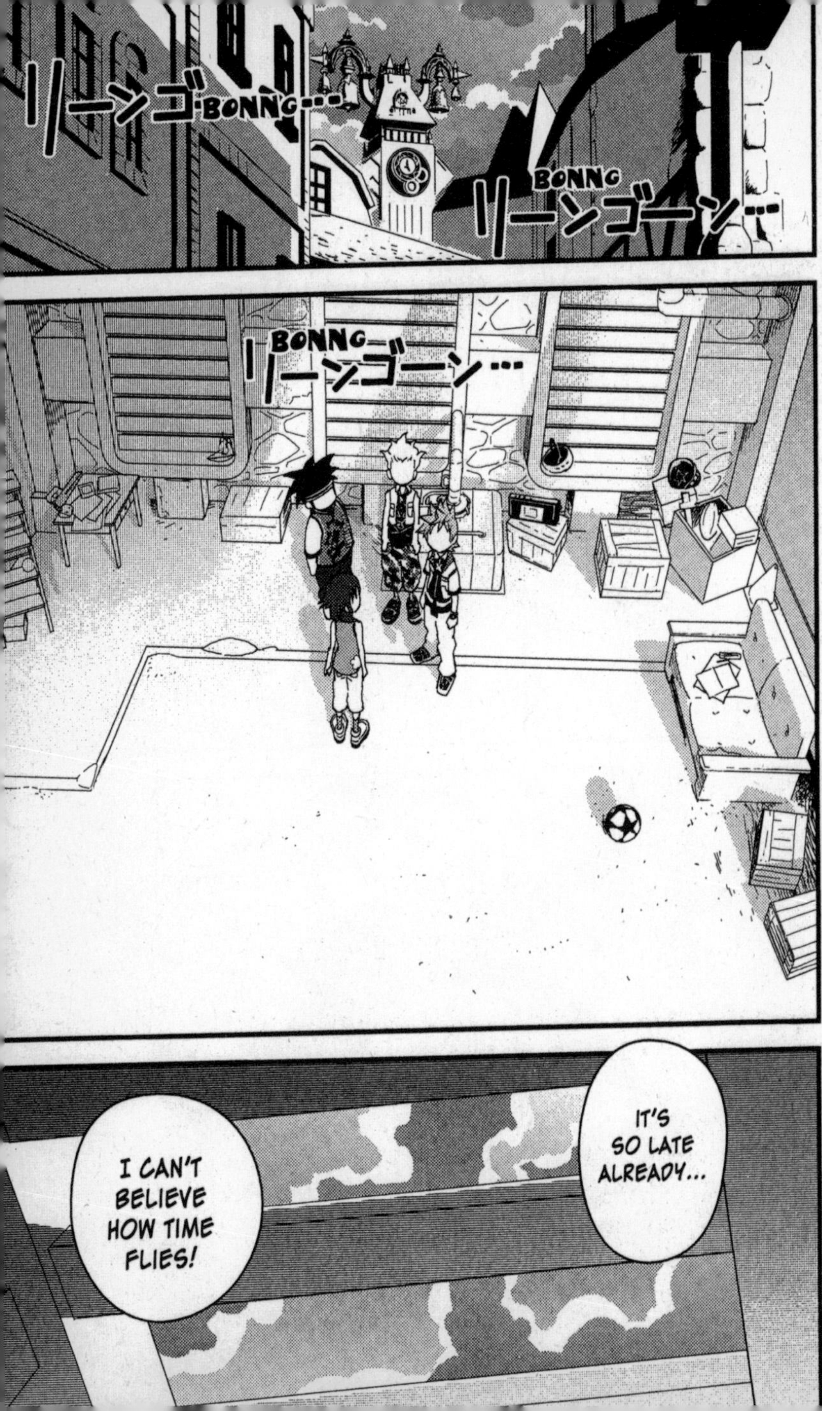

リーンゴ BONNG...
BONNG リーンゴーン...
BONNG リーンゴーン...
IT'S SO LATE ALREADY...
I CAN'T BELIEVE HOW TIME FLIES!

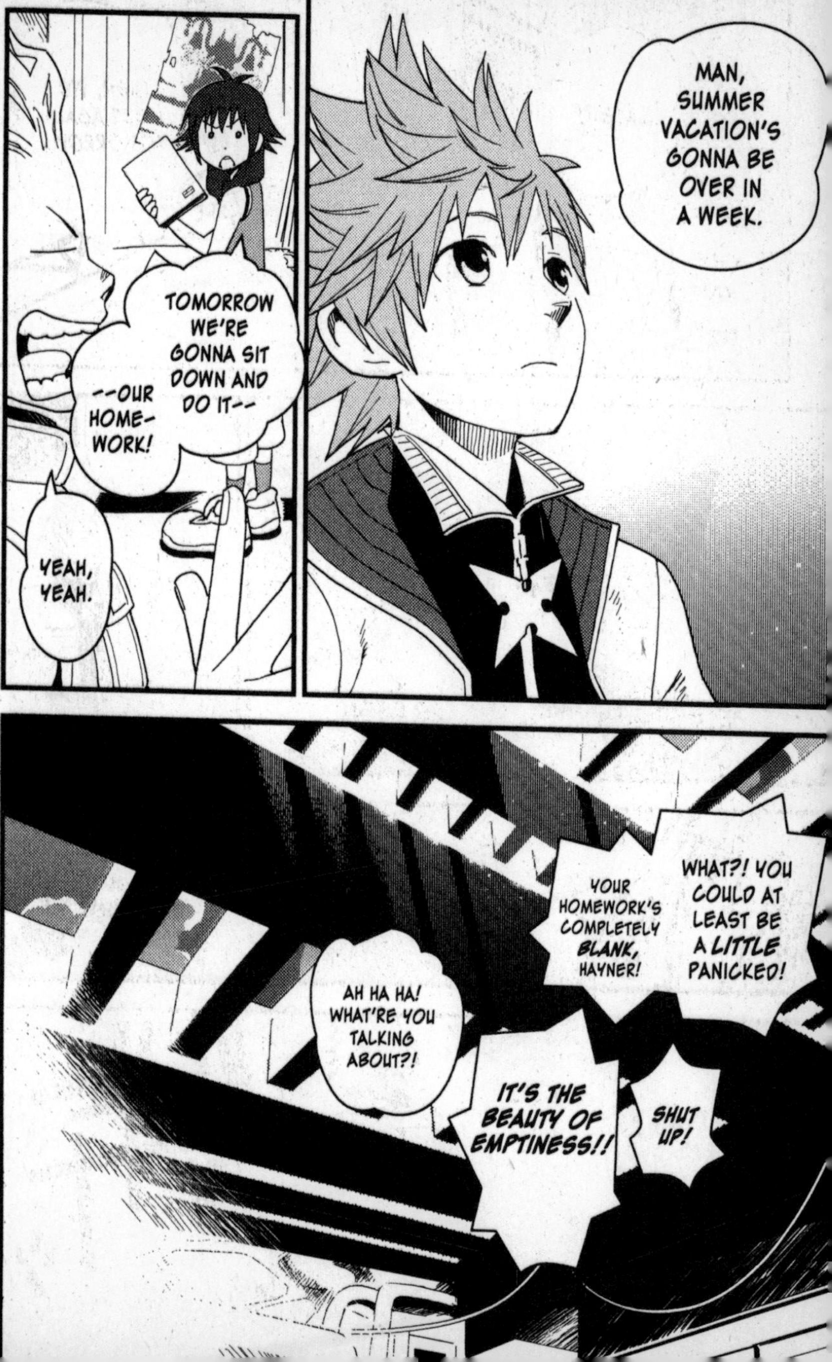
MAN, SUMMER VACATION'S GONNA BE OVER IN A WEEK.
TOMORROW WE'RE GONNA SIT DOWN AND DO IT--
--OUR HOMEWORK!
YEAH, YEAH.
WHAT?! YOU COULD AT LEAST BE A *LITTLE* PANICKED!
YOUR HOMEWORK'S COMPLETELY *BLANK*, HAYNER!
AH HA HA! WHAT'RE YOU TALKING ABOUT?!
SHUT UP!
IT'S THE BEAUTY OF EMPTINESS!!

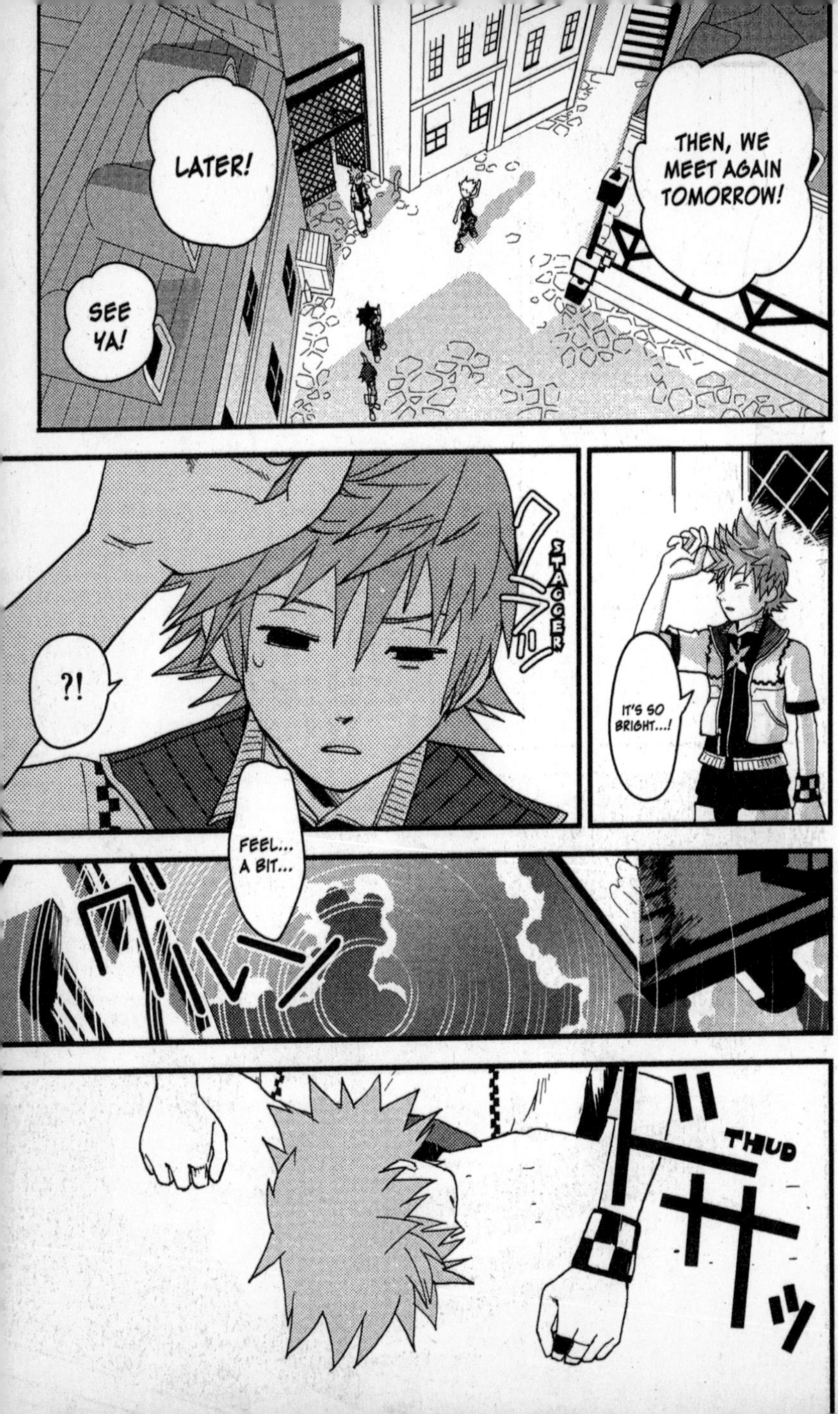
THEN, WE MEET AGAIN TOMORROW!
LATER!
SEE YA!
IT'S SO BRIGHT...!
STAGGER
?!
FEEL... A BIT...
THUD

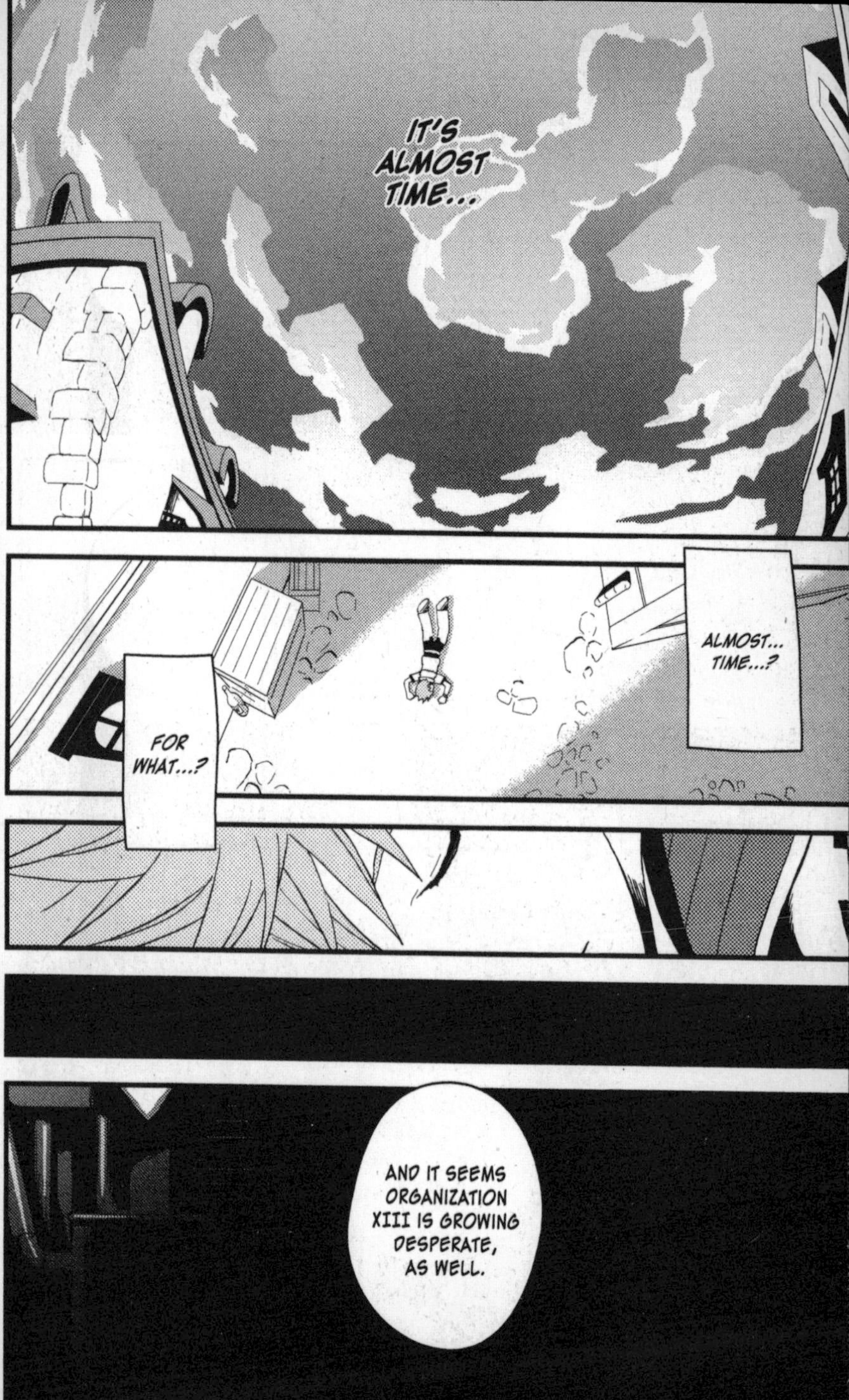
IT'S ALMOST TIME...
ALMOST... TIME...?
FOR WHAT...?
AND IT SEEMS ORGANIZATION XIII IS GROWING DESPERATE, AS WELL.

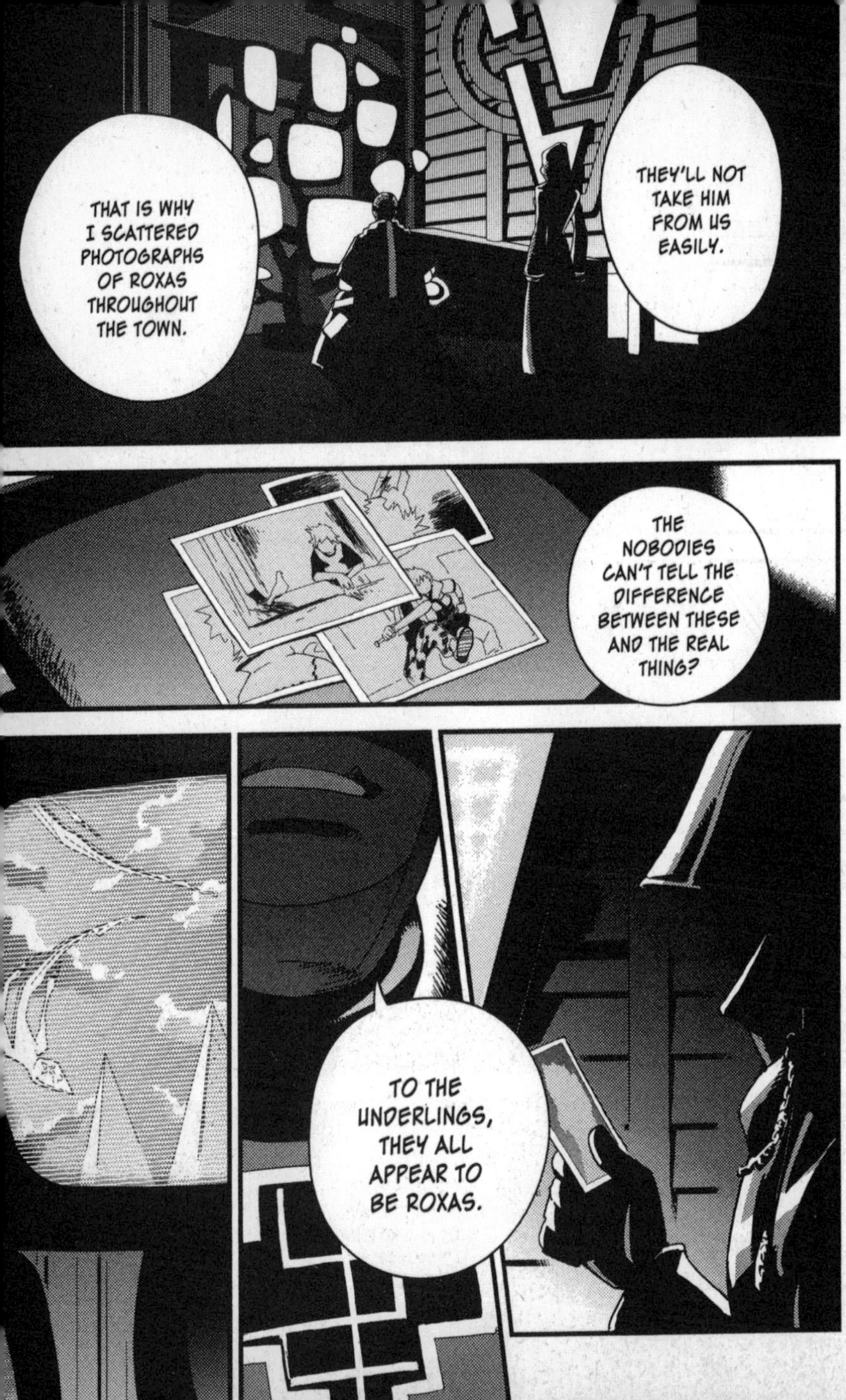
THEY'LL NOT TAKE HIM FROM US EASILY.
THAT IS WHY I SCATTERED PHOTOGRAPHS OF ROXAS THROUGHOUT THE TOWN.
THE NOBODIES CAN'T TELL THE DIFFERENCE BETWEEN THESE AND THE REAL THING?
TO THE UNDERLINGS, THEY ALL APPEAR TO BE ROXAS.

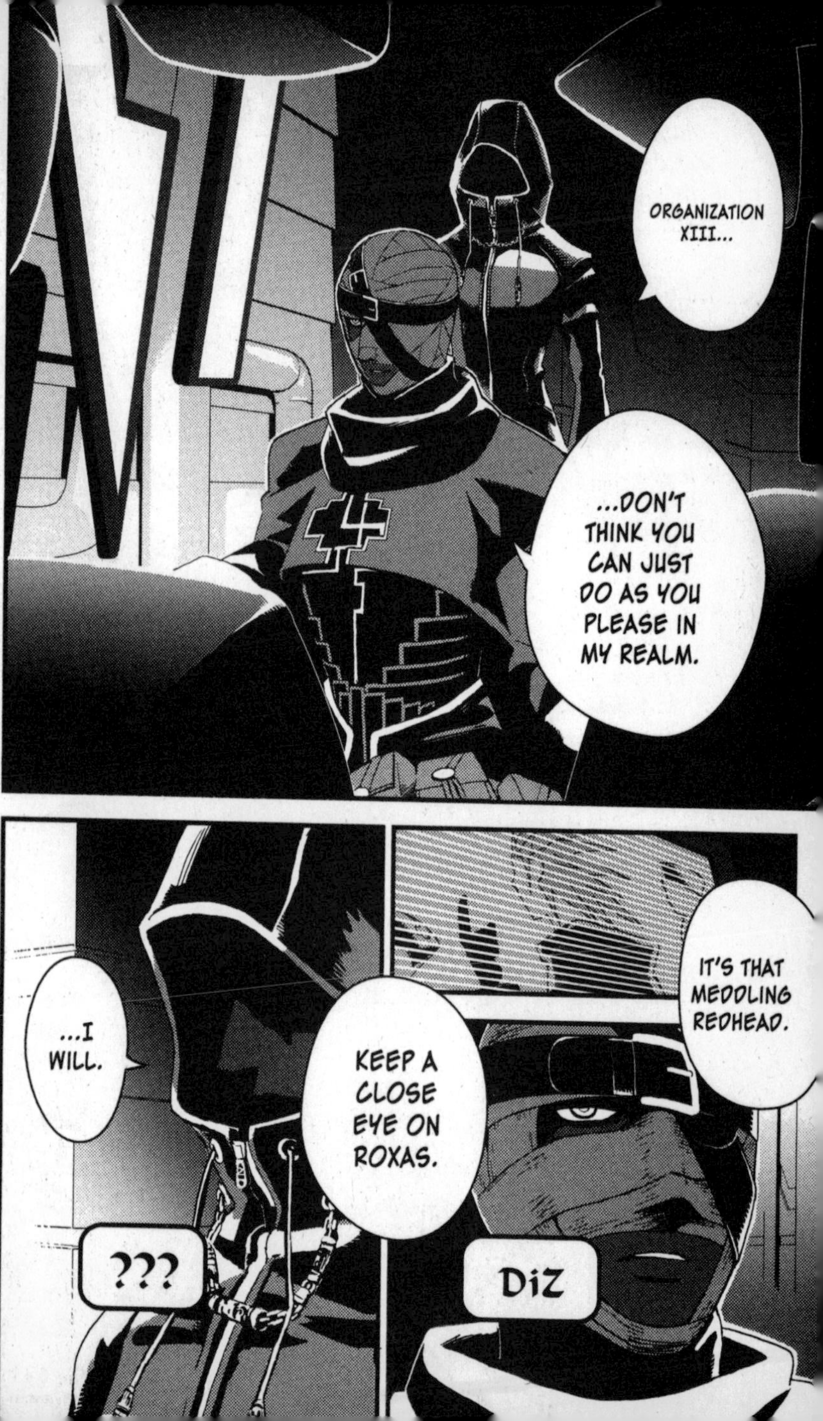
ORGANIZATION XIII...
...DON'T THINK YOU CAN JUST DO AS YOU PLEASE IN MY REALM.
IT'S THAT MEDDLING REDHEAD.
KEEP A CLOSE EYE ON ROXAS.
DiZ
...I WILL.
???

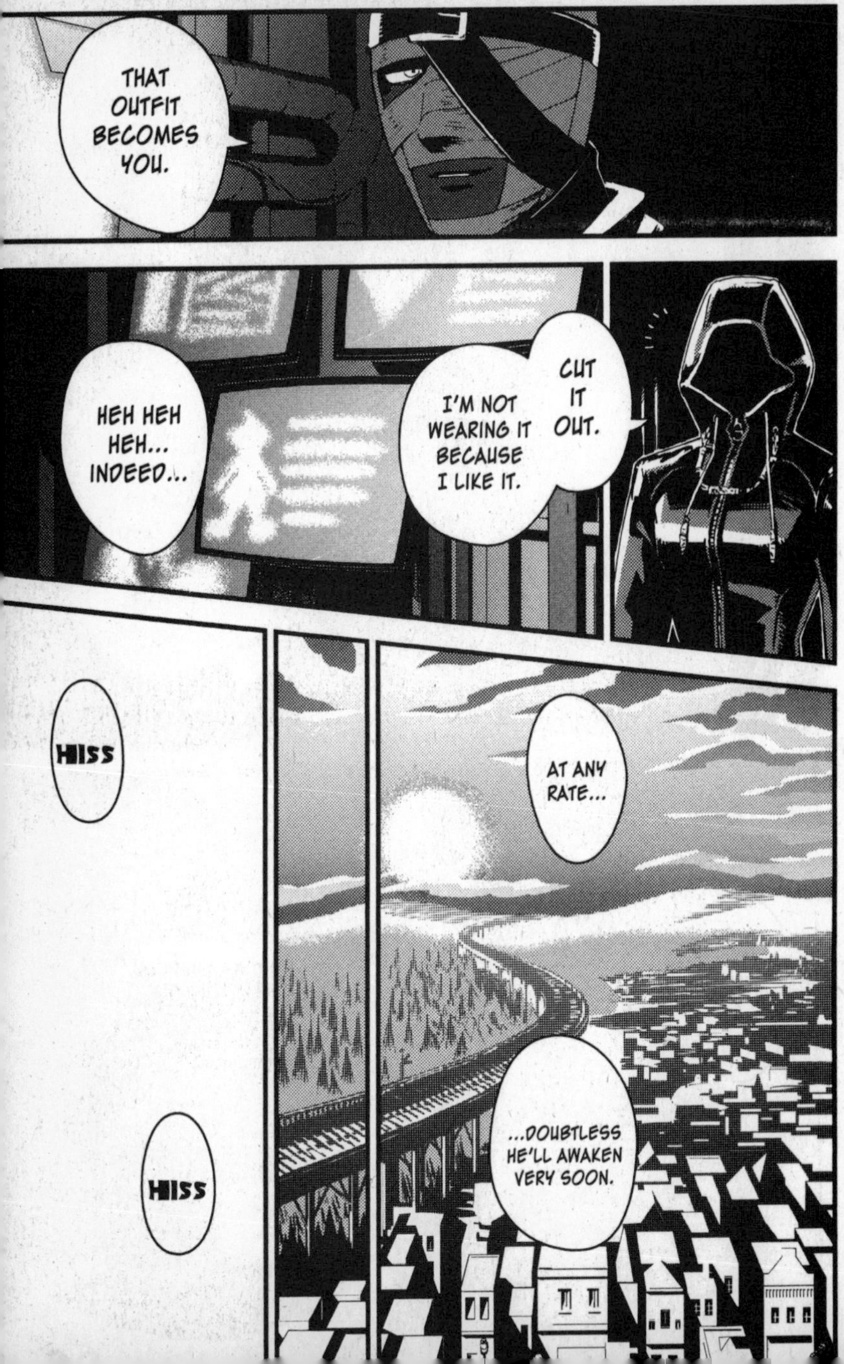
THAT OUTFIT BECOMES YOU.
CUT IT OUT.
I'M NOT WEARING IT BECAUSE I LIKE IT.
HEH HEH HEH... INDEED...
AT ANY RATE...
...DOUBTLESS HE'LL AWAKEN VERY SOON.
HISS
HISS

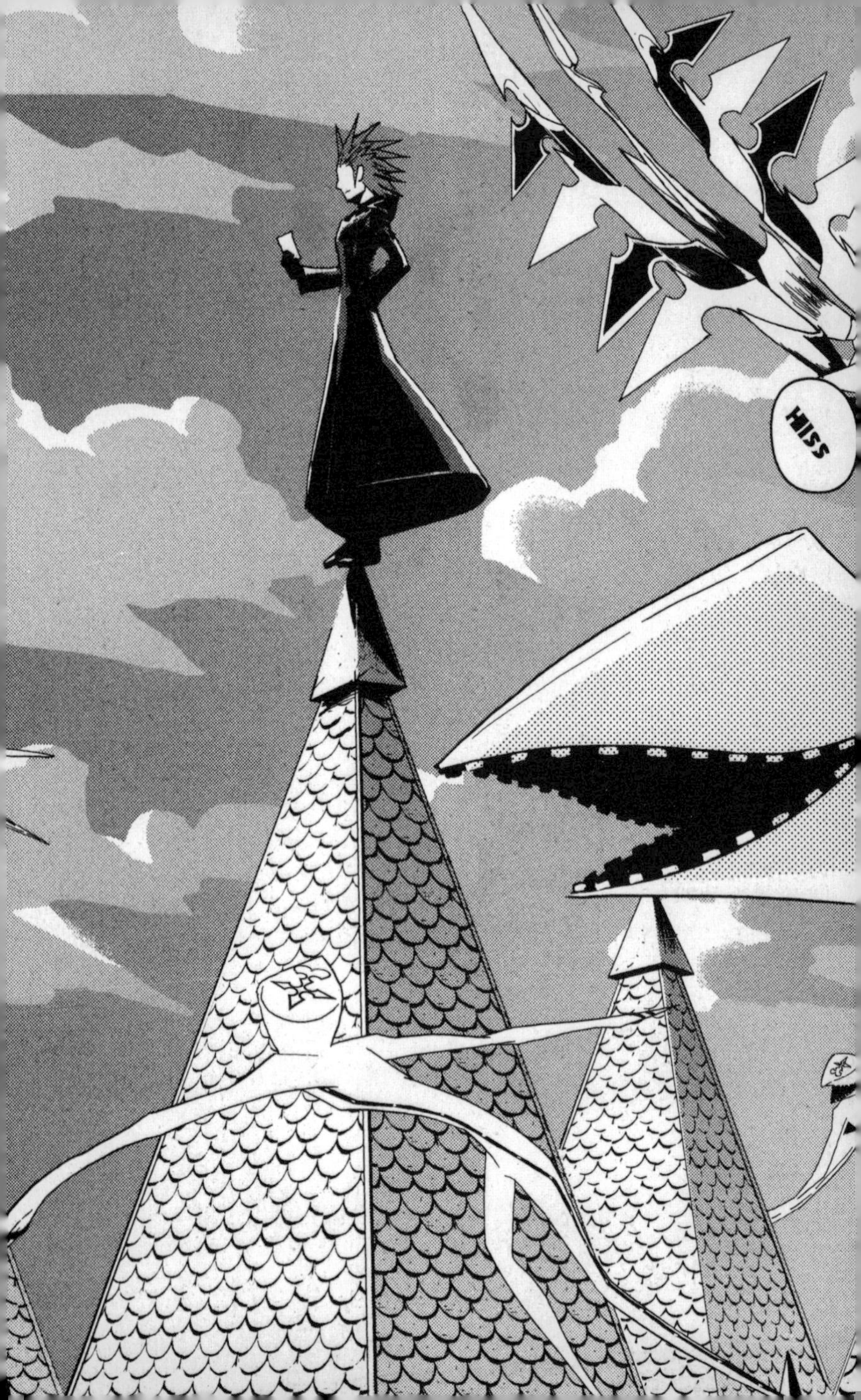
HISS

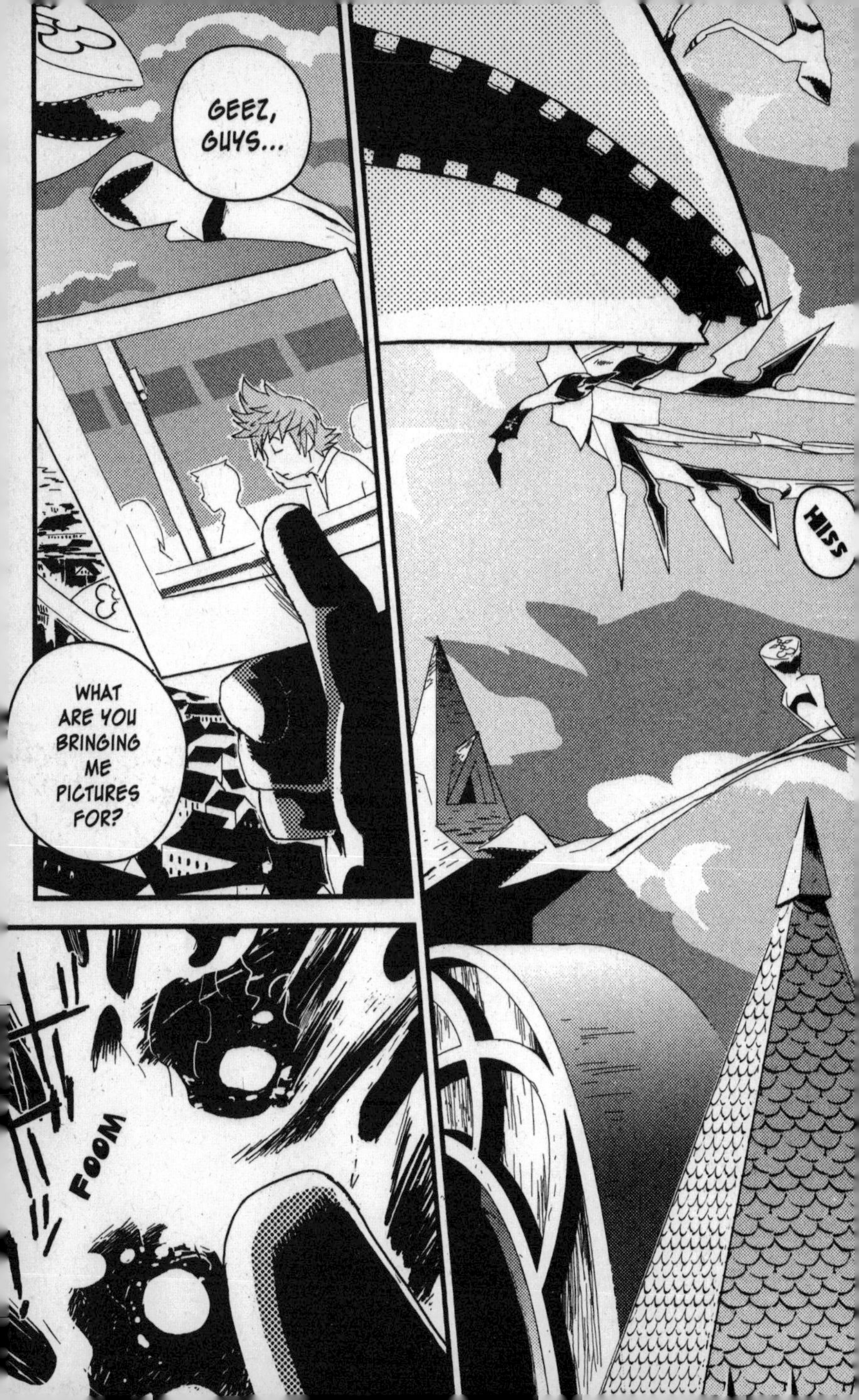
HISS
GEEZ, GUYS...
WHAT ARE YOU BRINGING ME PICTURES FOR?
FOOM

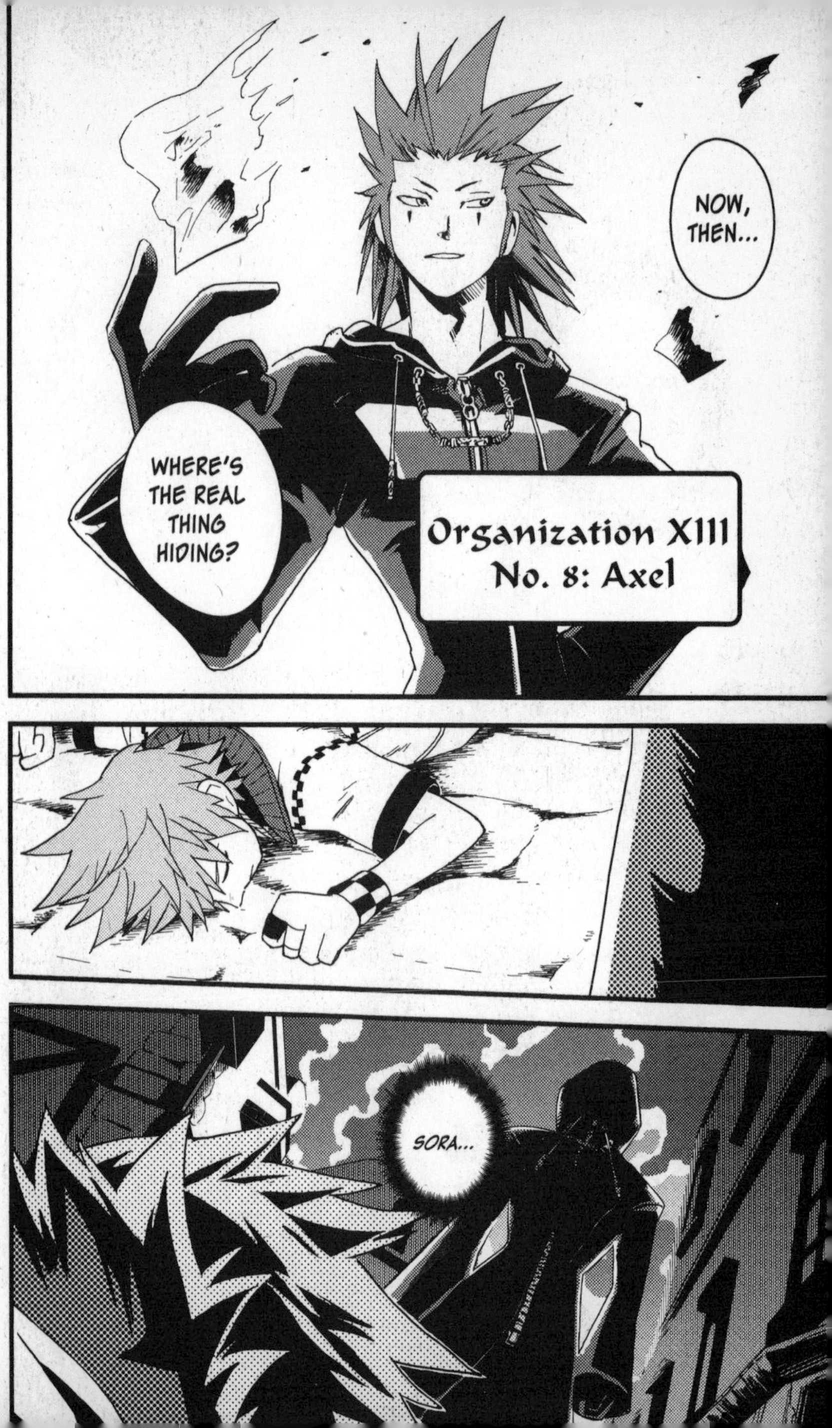
NOW, THEN...
WHERE'S THE REAL THING HIDING?
Organization XIII No. 8: Axel
SORA...

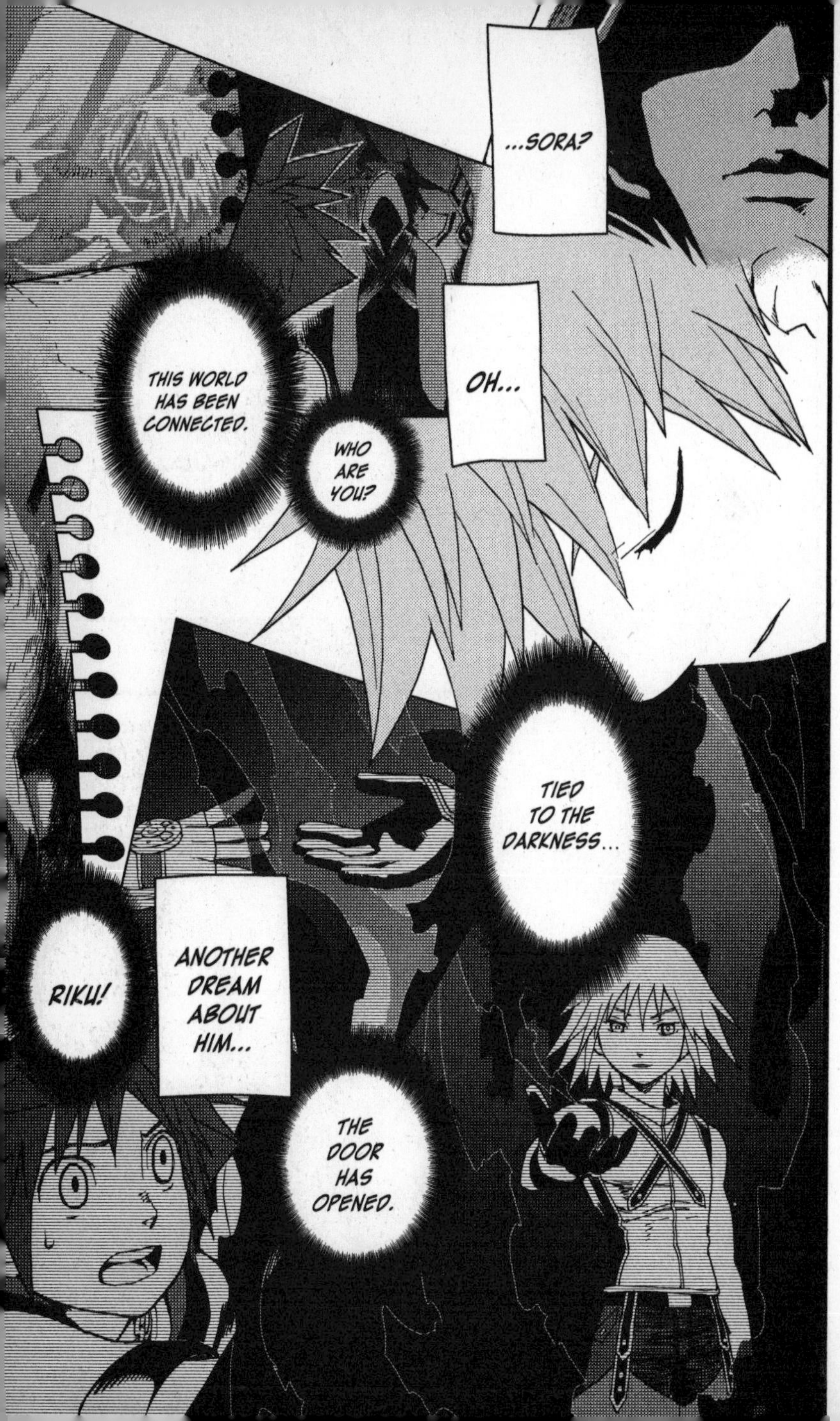
...SORA?
OH...
THIS WORLD HAS BEEN CONNECTED.
WHO ARE YOU?
TIED TO THE DARKNESS...
ANOTHER DREAM ABOUT HIM...
RIKU!
THE DOOR HAS OPENED.

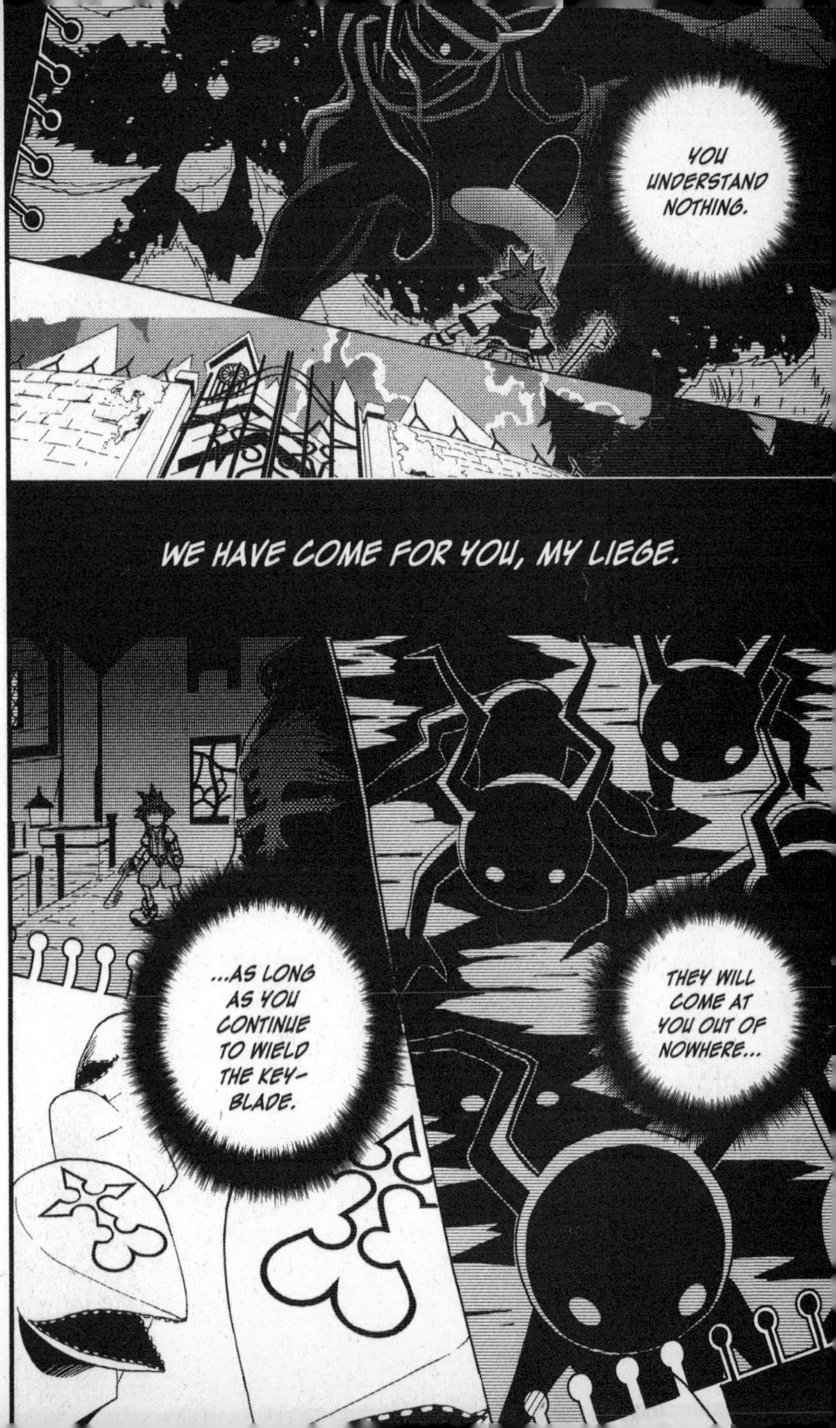
YOU UNDERSTAND NOTHING.
WE HAVE COME FOR YOU, MY LIEGE.
THEY WILL COME AT YOU OUT OF NOWHERE...
...AS LONG AS YOU CONTINUE TO WIELD THE KEY-BLADE.

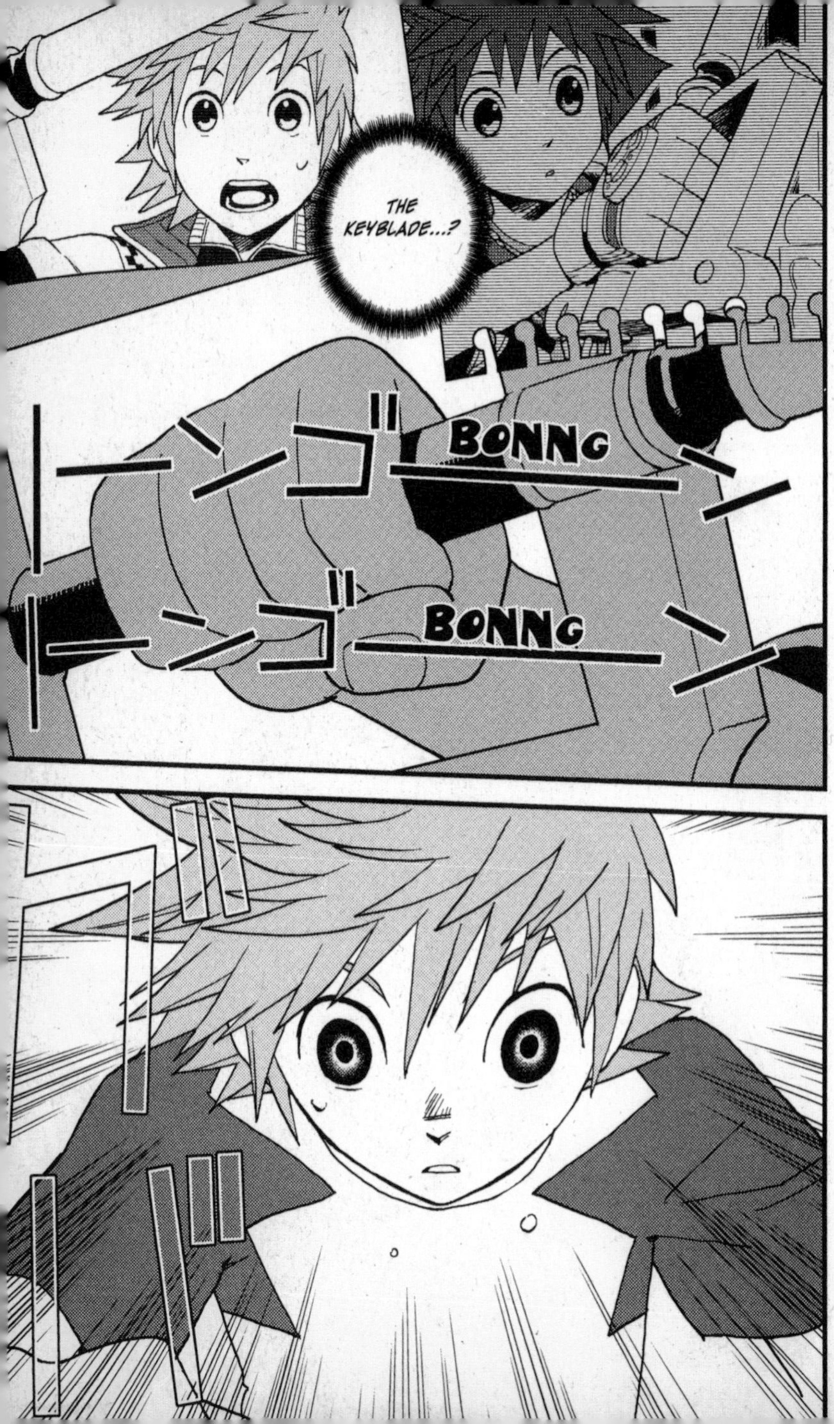
THE KEYBLADE...?
BONNG
BONNG

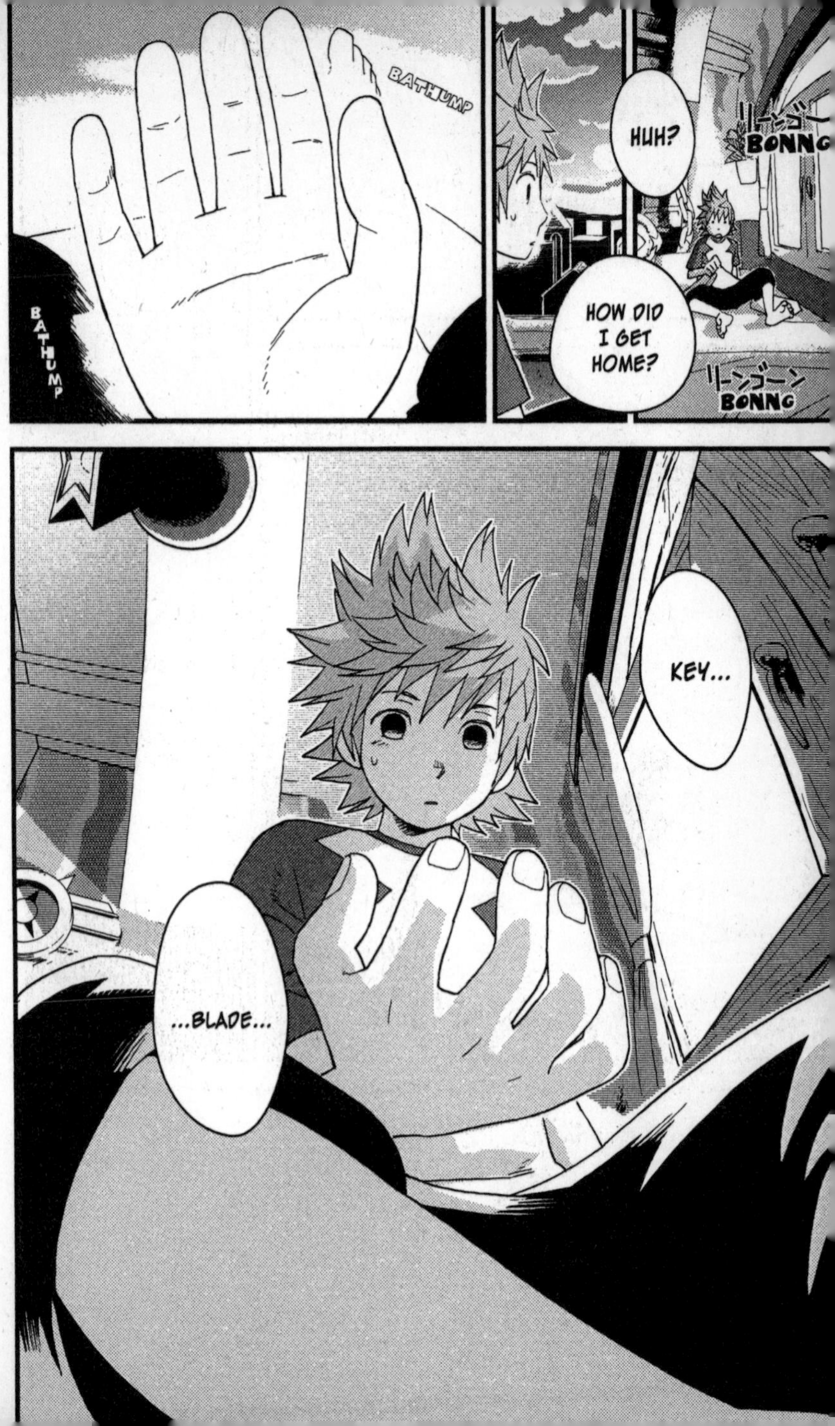
HUH?
リーンゴー
BONNG
HOW DID I GET HOME?
リーンゴーン
BONNG
BATHUMP
BATHUMP
KEY...
...BLADE...

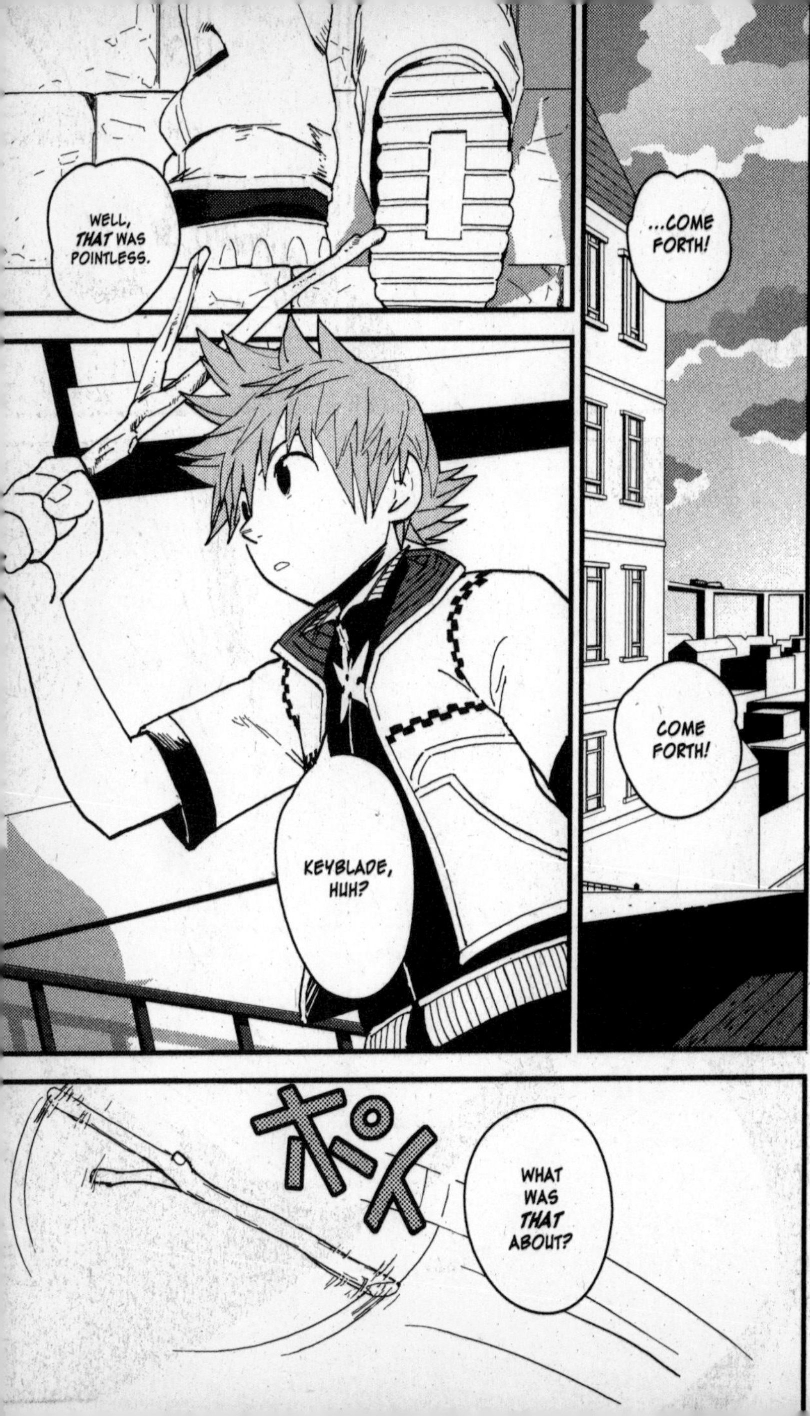
...COME FORTH!
COME FORTH!
WELL, THAT WAS POINTLESS.
KEYBLADE, HUH?
ポイ
WHAT WAS THAT ABOUT?

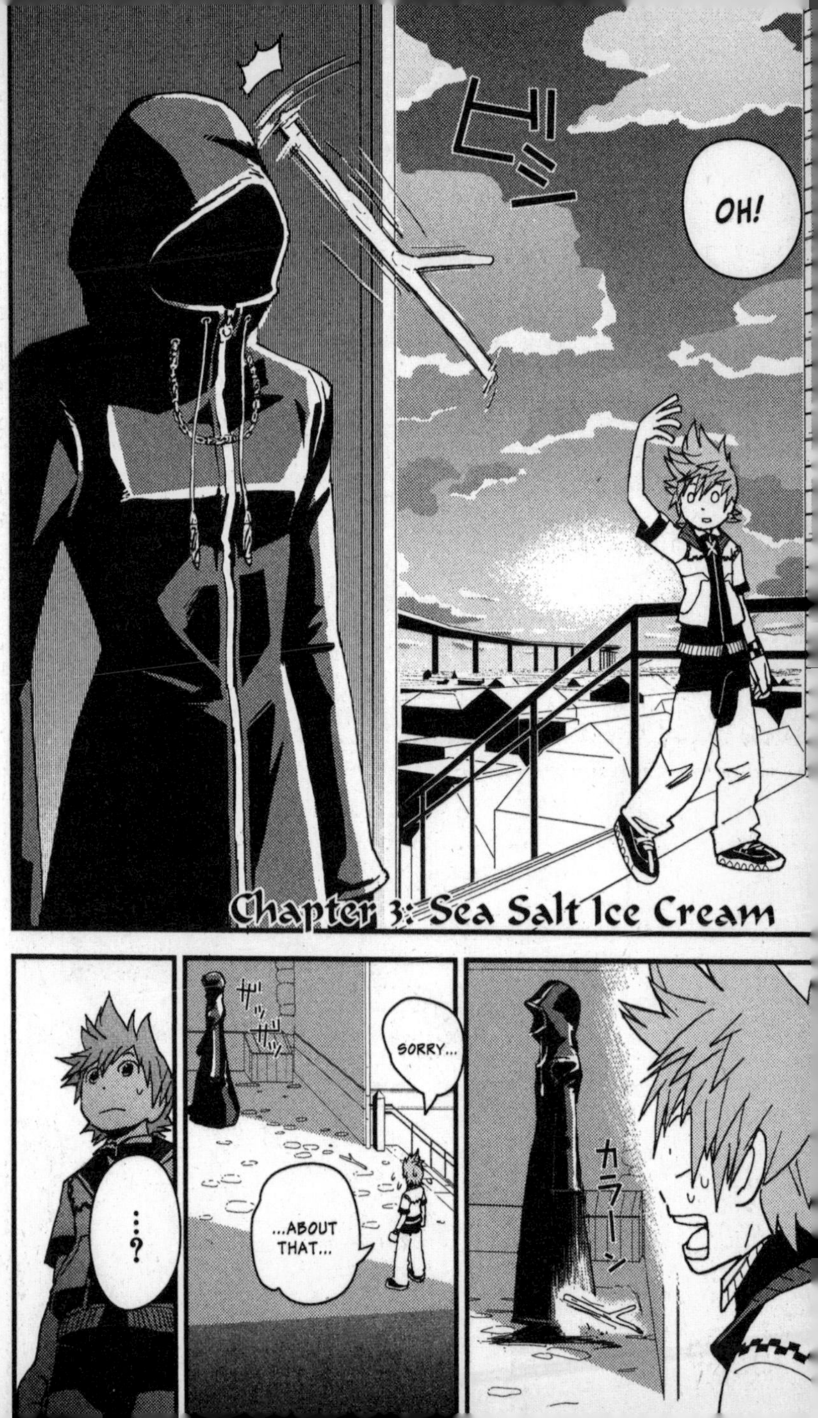
ビシー
OH!
Chapter 3: Sea Salt Ice Cream
カラーン
ザッ ザッ
SORRY...
...ABOUT THAT...
...?

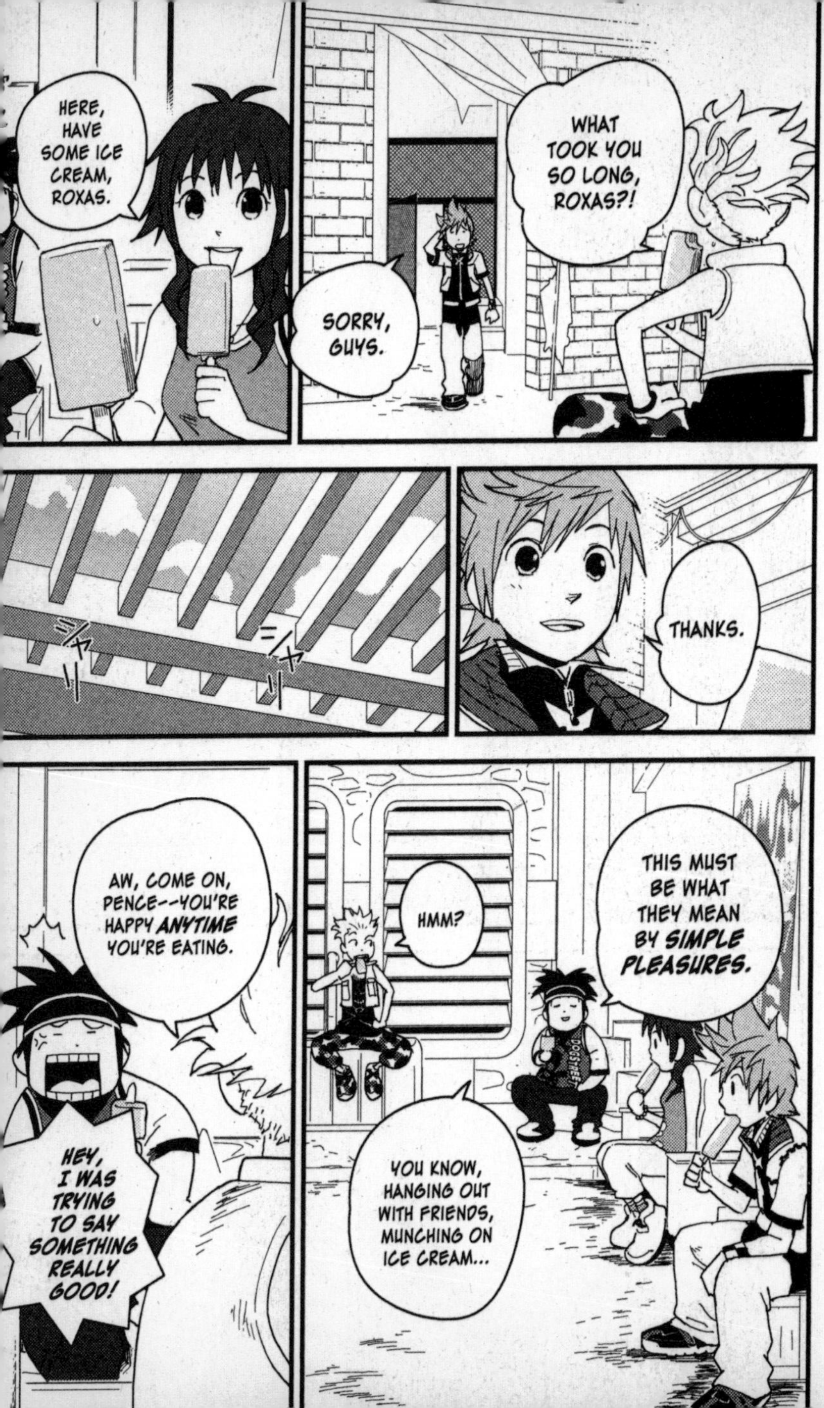
WHAT TOOK YOU SO LONG, ROXAS?!
SORRY, GUYS.
HERE, HAVE SOME ICE CREAM, ROXAS.
THANKS.
THIS MUST BE WHAT THEY MEAN BY *SIMPLE PLEASURES.*
HMM?
YOU KNOW, HANGING OUT WITH FRIENDS, MUNCHING ON ICE CREAM...
AW, COME ON, PENCE--YOU'RE HAPPY *ANYTIME* YOU'RE EATING.
*HEY, I WAS TRYING TO SAY SOMETHING REALLY GOOD!*

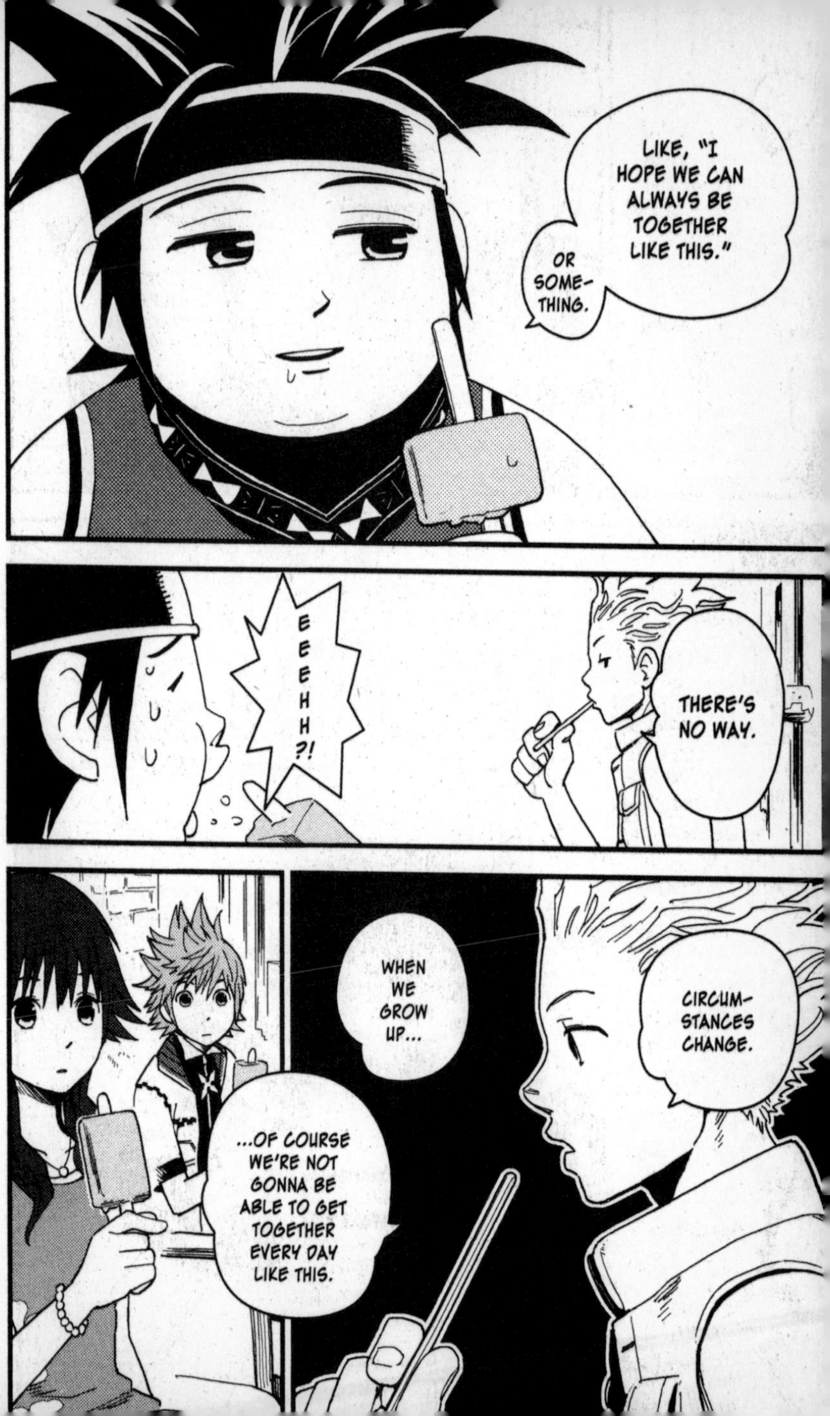
LIKE, "I HOPE WE CAN ALWAYS BE TOGETHER LIKE THIS."
OR SOMETHING.
THERE'S NO WAY.
EEEHH?!
CIRCUMSTANCES CHANGE.
WHEN WE GROW UP...
...OF COURSE WE'RE NOT GONNA BE ABLE TO GET TOGETHER EVERY DAY LIKE THIS.

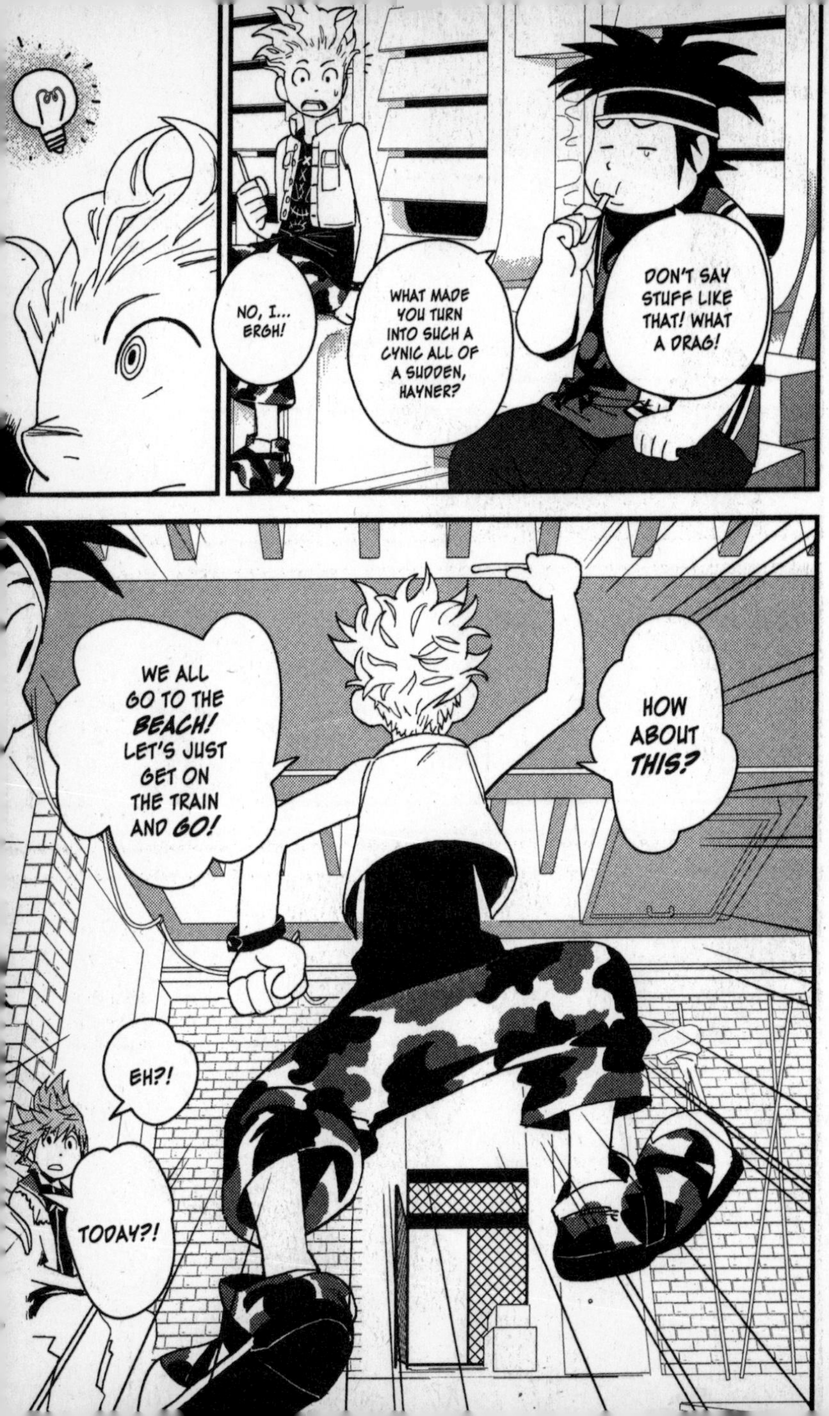
DON'T SAY STUFF LIKE THAT! WHAT A DRAG!
WHAT MADE YOU TURN INTO SUCH A CYNIC ALL OF A SUDDEN, HAYNER?
NO, I... ERGH!
HOW ABOUT *THIS?*
WE ALL GO TO THE *BEACH!* LET'S JUST GET ON THE TRAIN AND *GO!*
EH?!
TODAY?!

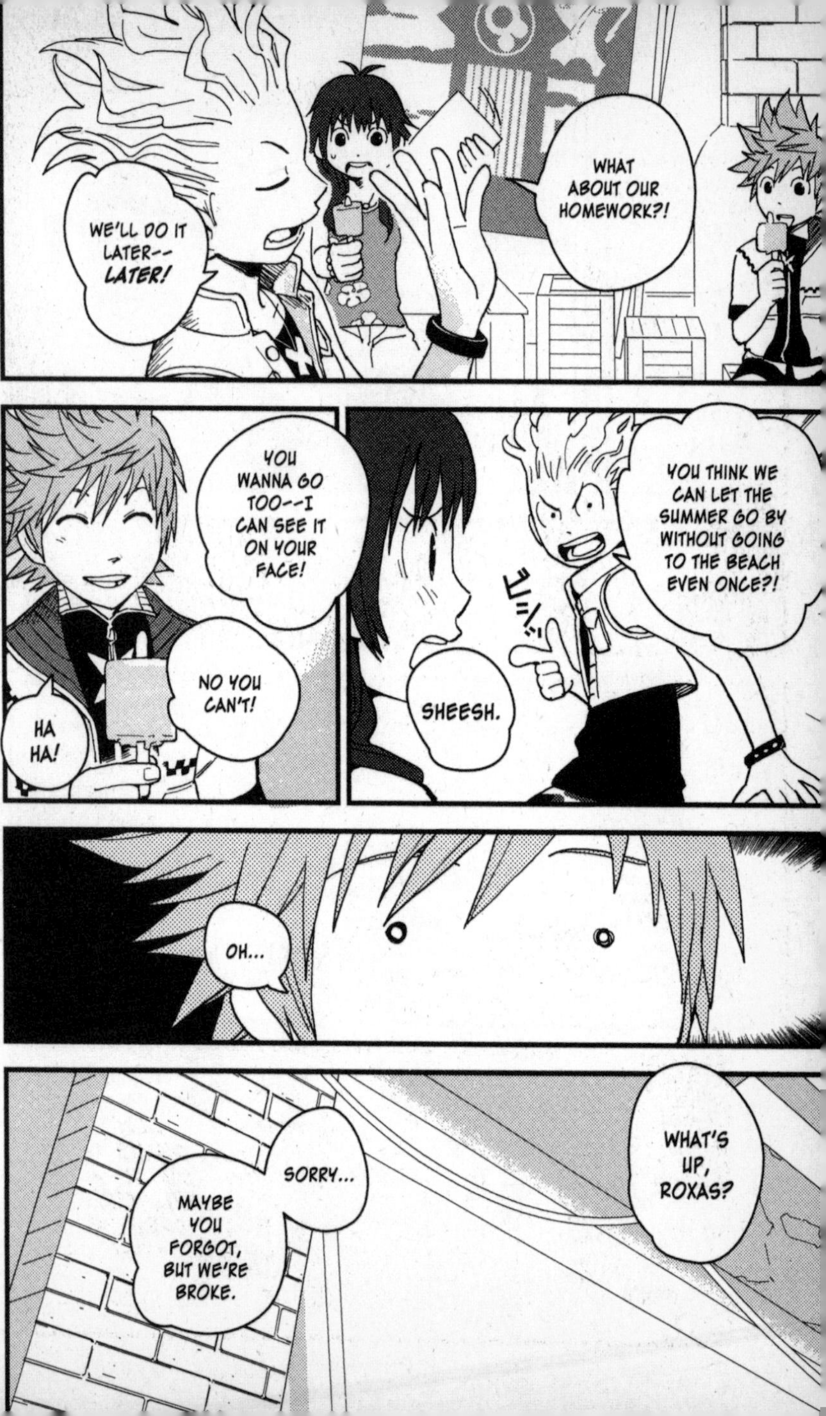
WHAT ABOUT OUR HOMEWORK?!
WE'LL DO IT LATER--LATER!
YOU THINK WE CAN LET THE SUMMER GO BY WITHOUT GOING TO THE BEACH EVEN ONCE?!
SHEESH.
YOU WANNA GO TOO--I CAN SEE IT ON YOUR FACE!
NO YOU CAN'T!
HA HA!
OH...
WHAT'S UP, ROXAS?
SORRY...
MAYBE YOU FORGOT, BUT WE'RE BROKE.

IT'S PRETTY EXPENSIVE JUST TO GET THERE...

HMM...

THAT'S TRUE.

I BOUGHT A MOAI TISSUE DISPENSER THE OTHER DAY...

THE TISSUE COMES OUT THE NOSE.

WHY IN THE WORLD DID I BUY THAT...?

...CORN ON THE COB...

AND THICK-NOODLED RAMEN...

...SHISH KEBAB...

...PLAIN CURRY RICE...

...BUTTERED BAKED POTATOES...

QUIET!

...AND THE PRICE OF THE YAKISOBA WE'LL EAT AT THE BEACH... RIGHT?

TRAIN FARE TO THE BEACH...

?

JUST GIMME A MINUTE-- I'LL TAKE CARE OF THIS!

YOU AND I HAVE TO MAKE IT TO THE FINALS!

THAT WAY, NO MATTER WHO WINS, THE FOUR OF US SPLIT THE PRIZE!

YOU CAN'T LET SEIFER AND HIS GANG BEAT YOU, OKAY?

THERE'S KIND OF A LOT.

NO WAY WE'LL LOSE! RIGHT, ROXAS?!!

YOU AND ME.

WE CAN DO IT, RIGHT?

YOU SURE ARE CONFIDENT.

GO GET 'EM!

IT'S A PROMISE!

ALL RIGHT!

YOU'RE ON.

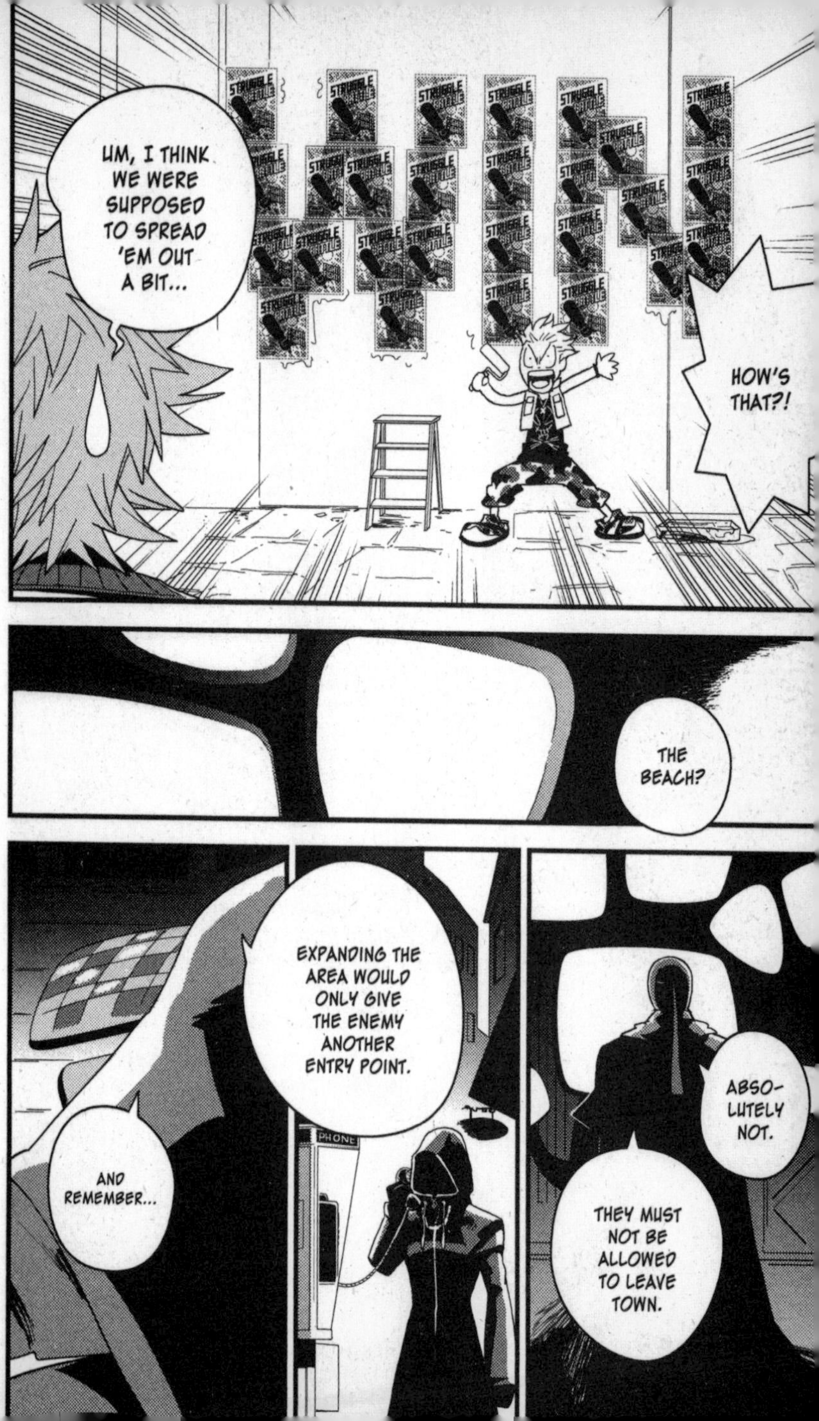
HOW'S THAT?!
UM, I THINK WE WERE SUPPOSED TO SPREAD 'EM OUT A BIT...
THE BEACH?
ABSO-LUTELY NOT.
THEY MUST NOT BE ALLOWED TO LEAVE TOWN.
EXPANDING THE AREA WOULD ONLY GIVE THE ENEMY ANOTHER ENTRY POINT.
PHONE
AND REMEMBER...

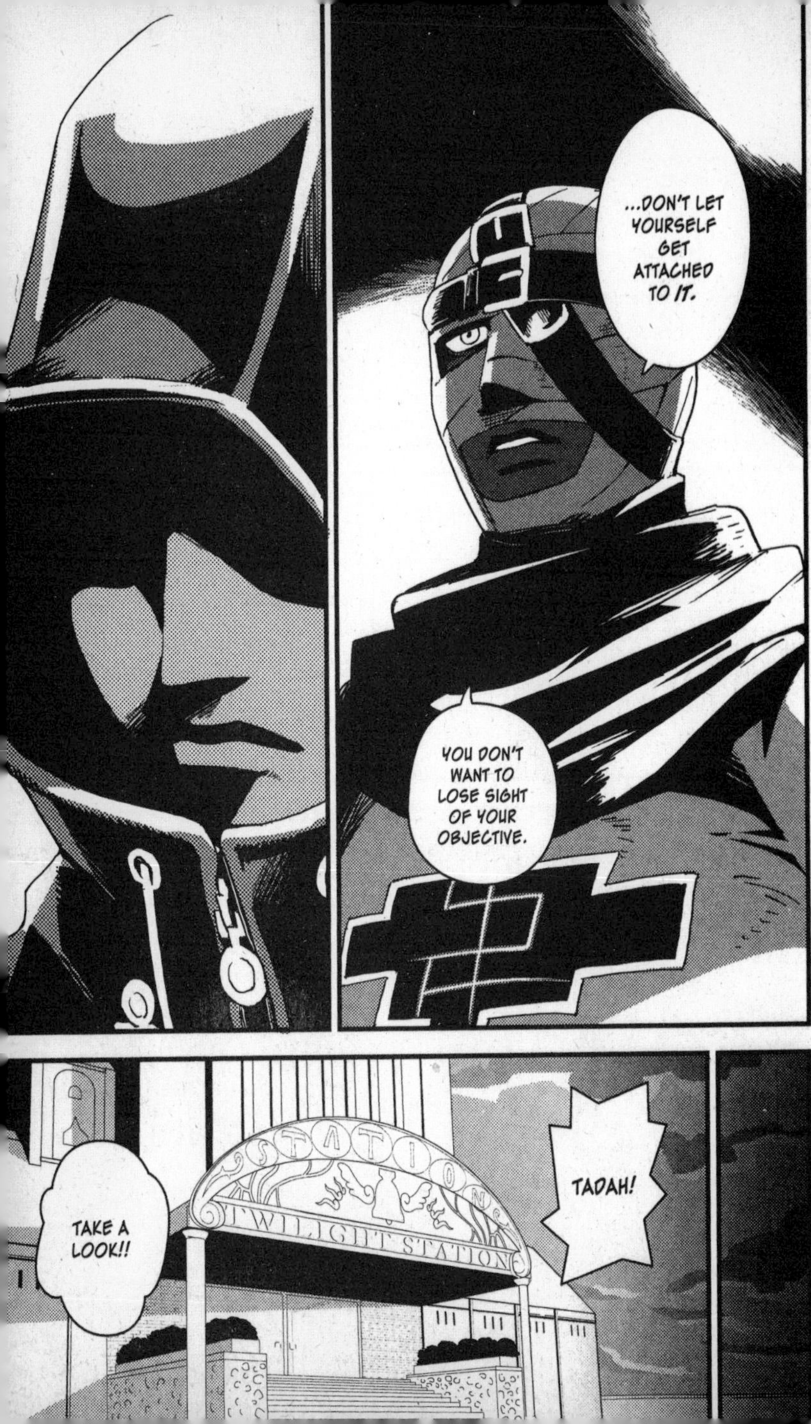
...DON'T LET YOURSELF GET ATTACHED TO *IT*.
YOU DON'T WANT TO LOSE SIGHT OF YOUR OBJECTIVE.
STATION
TWILIGHT STATION
TADAH!
TAKE A LOOK!!

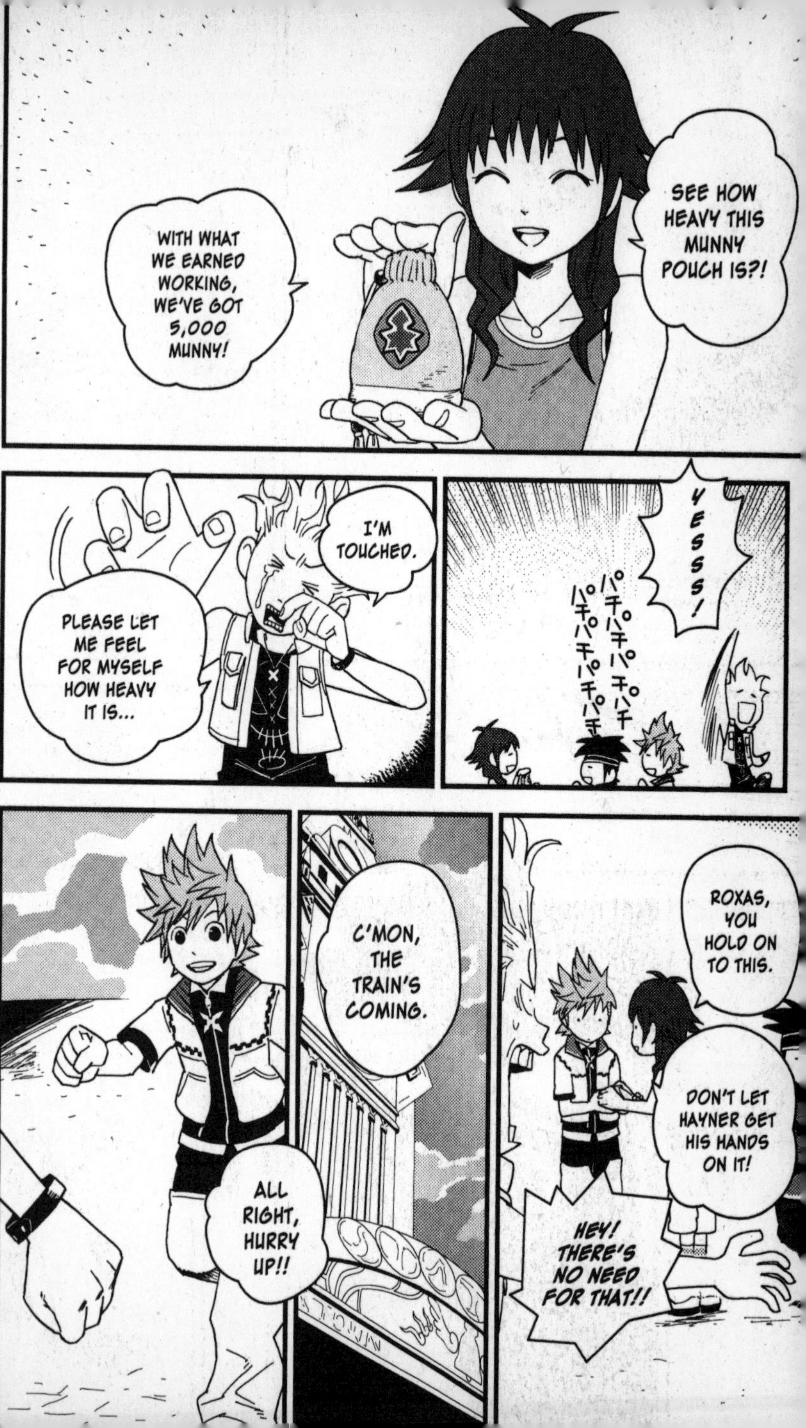
SEE HOW HEAVY THIS MUNNY POUCH IS?!
WITH WHAT WE EARNED WORKING, WE'VE GOT 5,000 MUNNY!
YESSS!
パチパチパチパチ
パチパチパチパチ
I'M TOUCHED.
PLEASE LET ME FEEL FOR MYSELF HOW HEAVY IT IS...
ROXAS, YOU HOLD ON TO THIS.
DON'T LET HAYNER GET HIS HANDS ON IT!
HEY! THERE'S NO NEED FOR THAT!!
C'MON, THE TRAIN'S COMING.
ALL RIGHT, HURRY UP!!

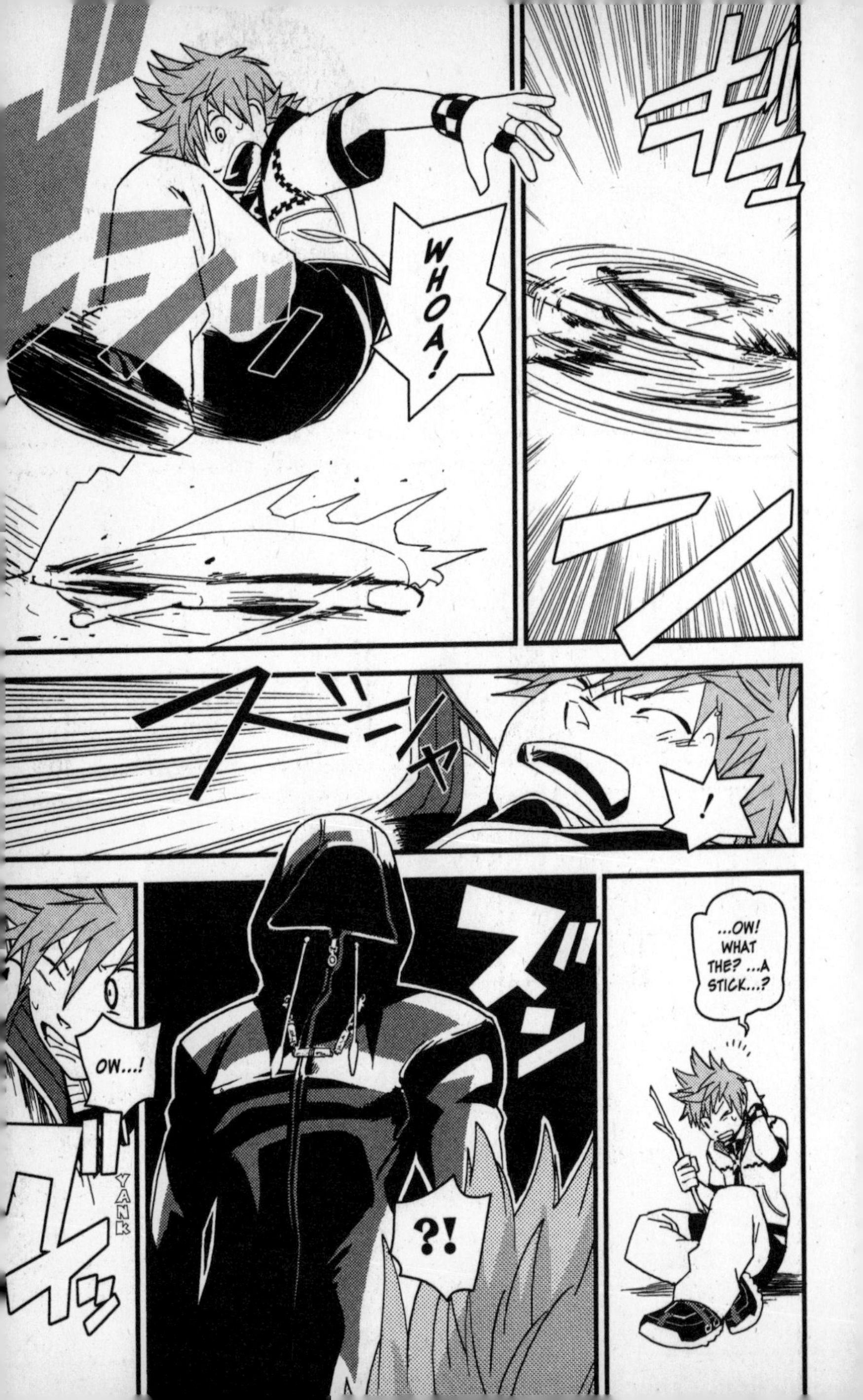
WHOA!
!
...OW! WHAT THE? ...A STICK...?
?!
OW...!
YANK

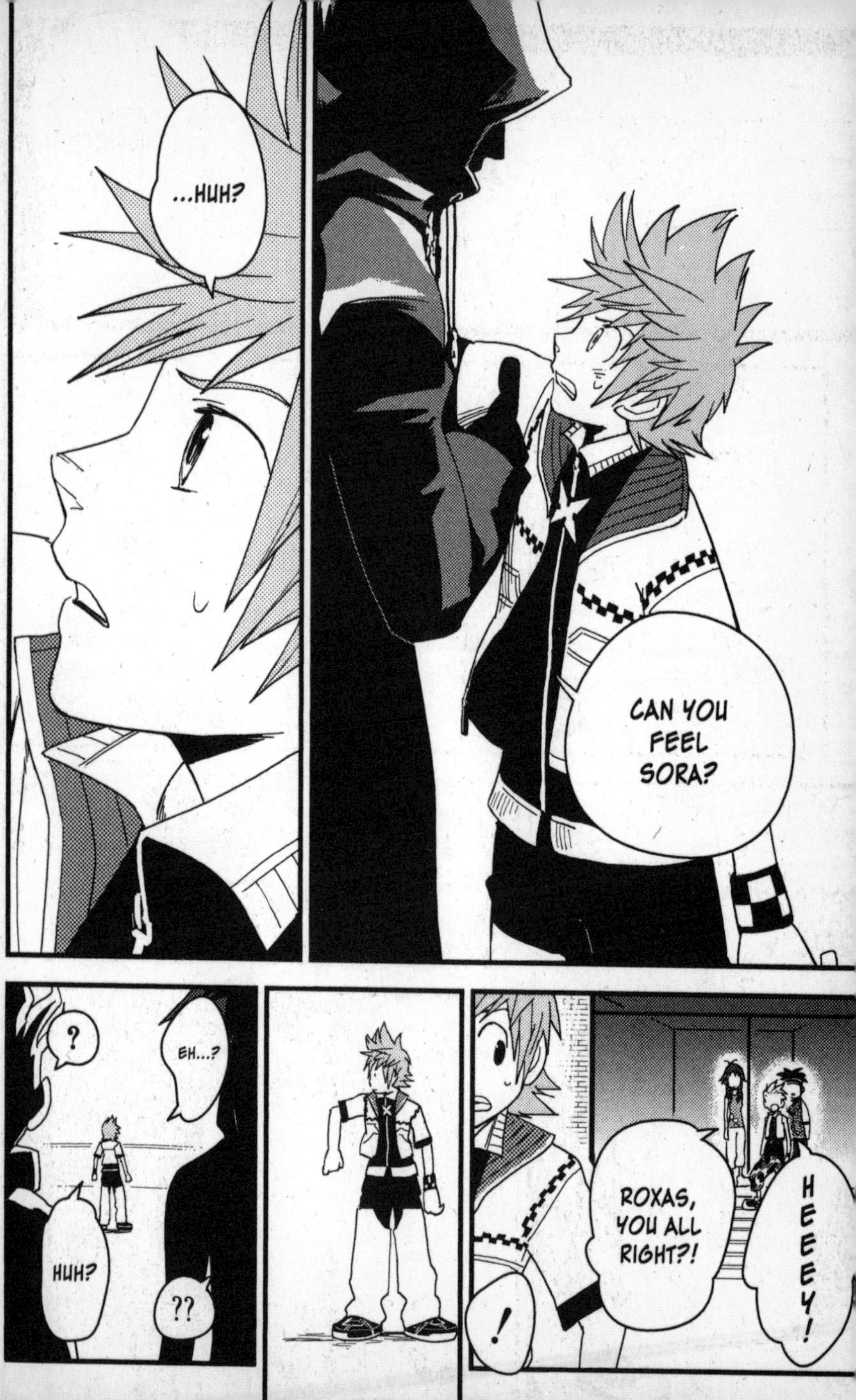
CAN YOU FEEL SORA?
...HUH?
HEEEY!
ROXAS, YOU ALL RIGHT?!
!
EH...?
?
??
HUH?

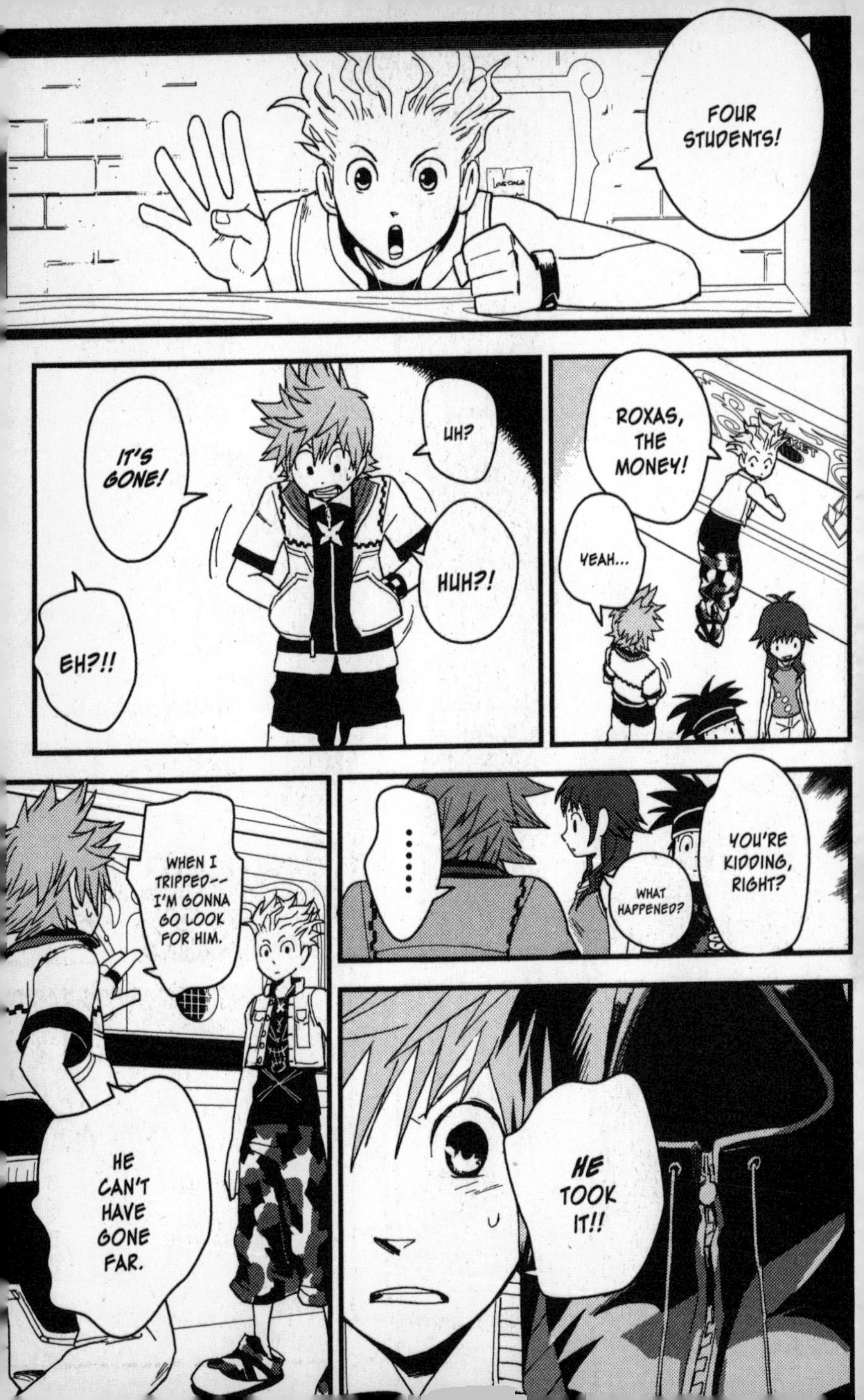
FOUR STUDENTS!
ROXAS, THE MONEY!
YEAH...
IT'S GONE!
UH?
HUH?!
EH?!!
YOU'RE KIDDING, RIGHT?
WHAT HAPPENED?
......
HE TOOK IT!!
WHEN I TRIPPED-- I'M GONNA GO LOOK FOR HIM.
HE CAN'T HAVE GONE FAR.

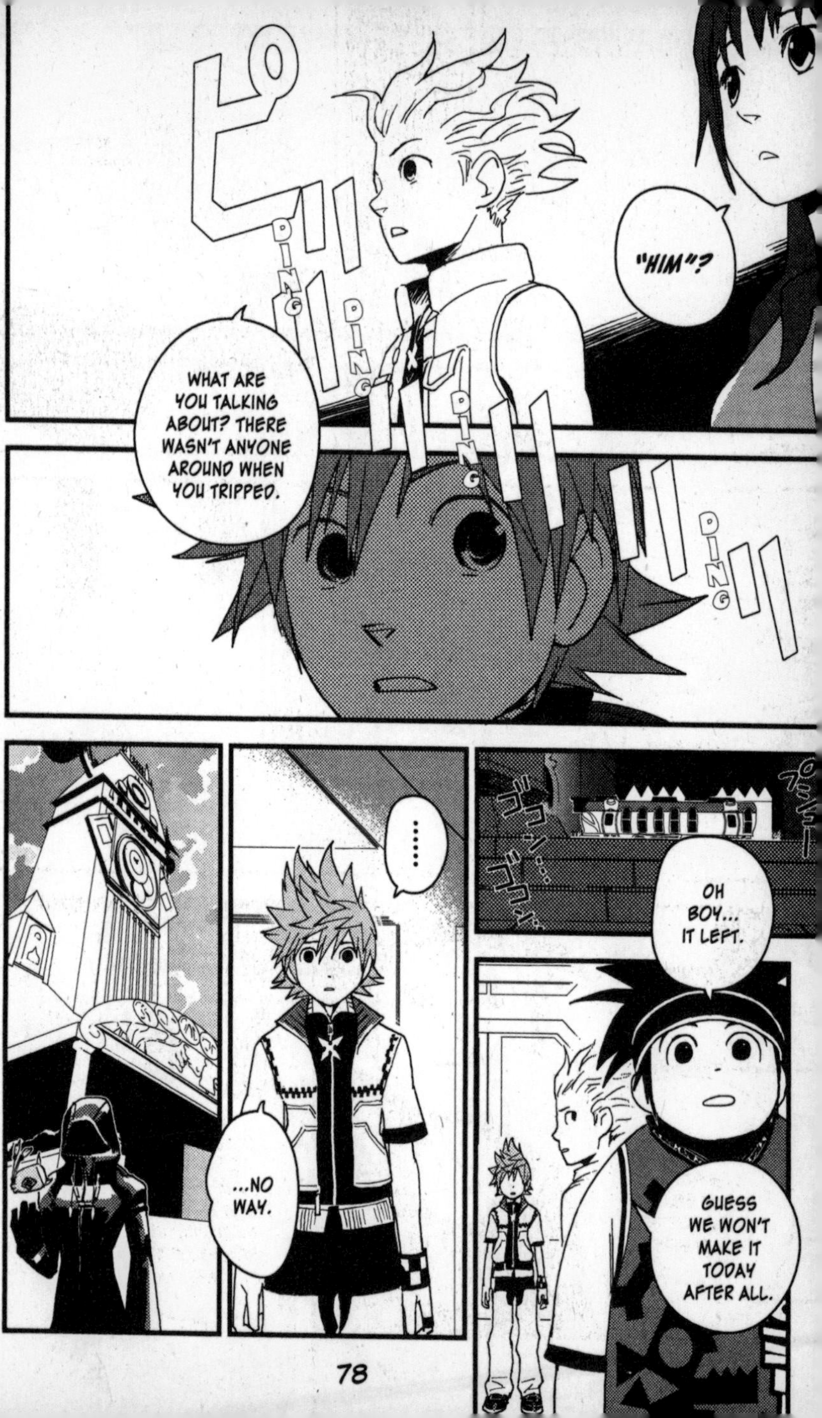
"HIM"?
WHAT ARE YOU TALKING ABOUT? THERE WASN'T ANYONE AROUND WHEN YOU TRIPPED.
DING
DING
DING
DING
OH BOY... IT LEFT.
GUESS WE WON'T MAKE IT TODAY AFTER ALL.
......
...NO WAY.

79

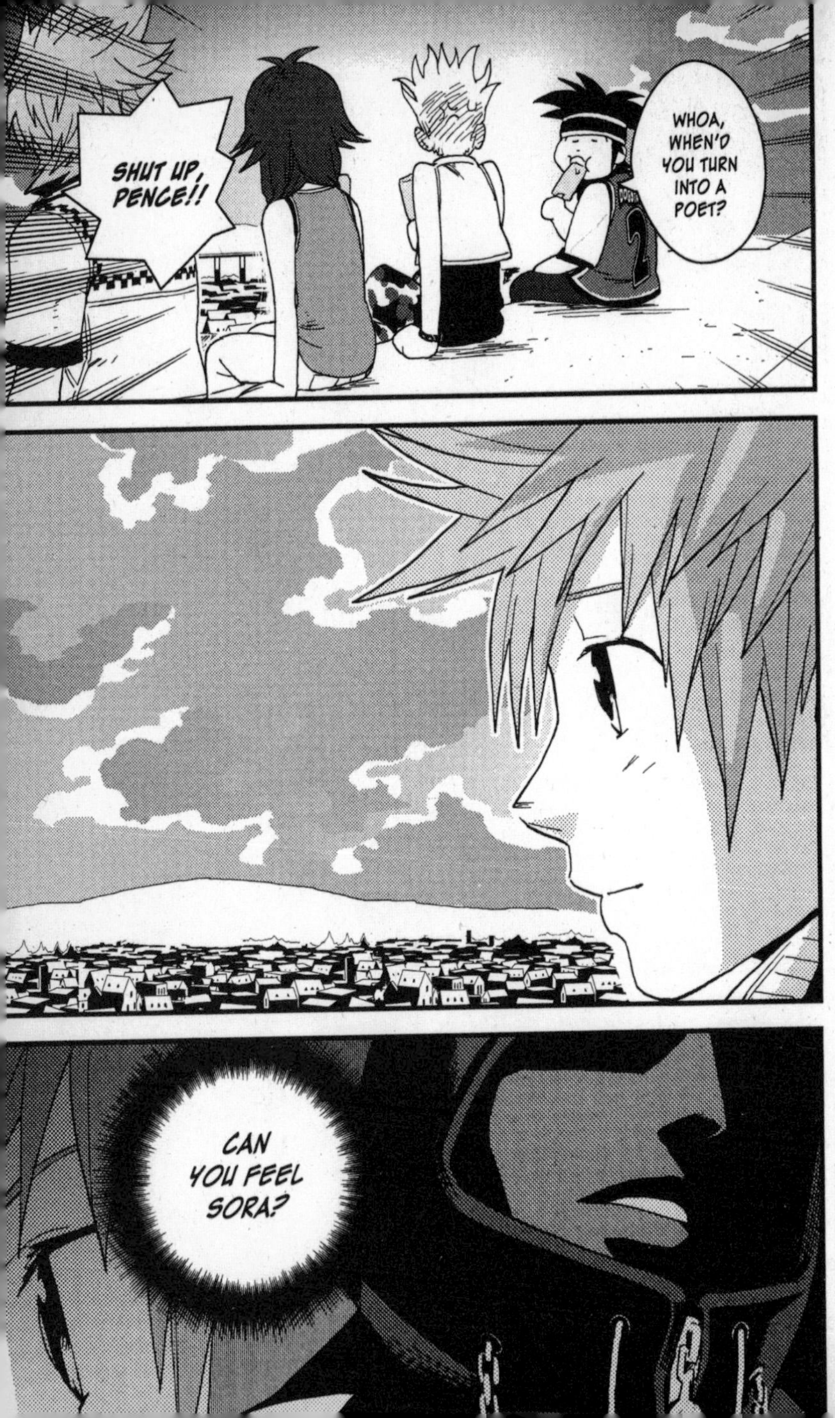
WHOA, WHEN'D YOU TURN INTO A POET?
SHUT UP, PENCE!!
CAN YOU FEEL SORA?

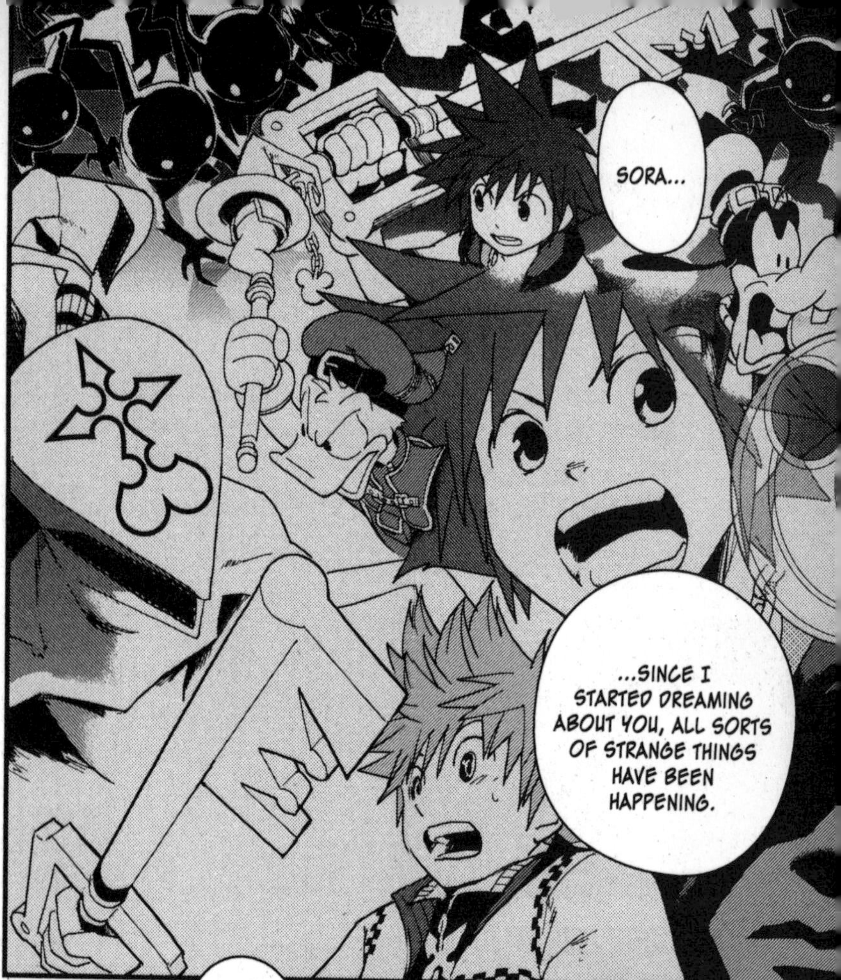
SORA...
...SINCE I STARTED DREAMING ABOUT YOU, ALL SORTS OF STRANGE THINGS HAVE BEEN HAPPENING.
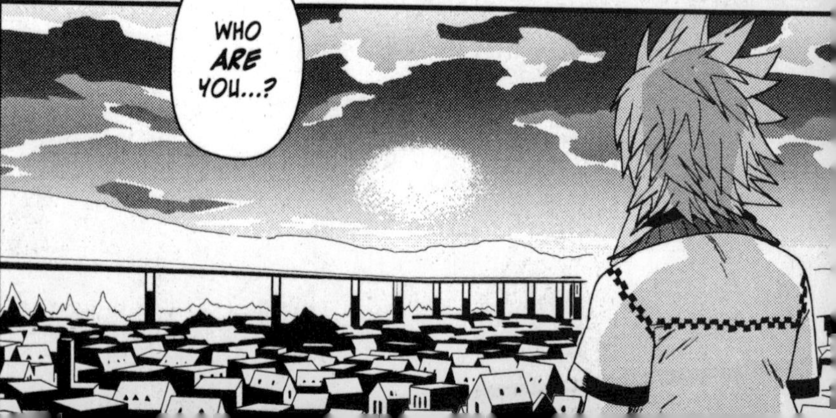
WHO **ARE** YOU...?

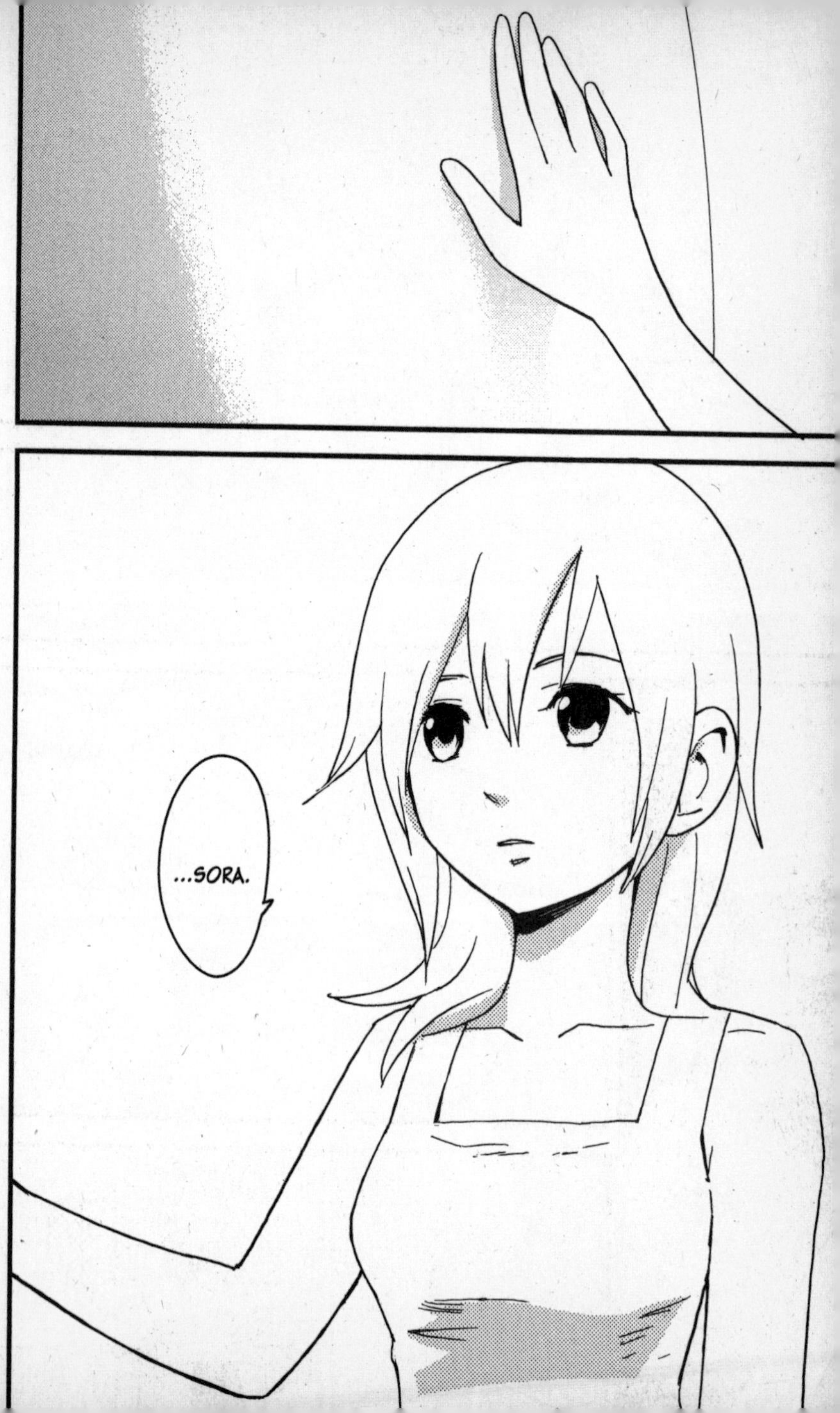
...SORA.

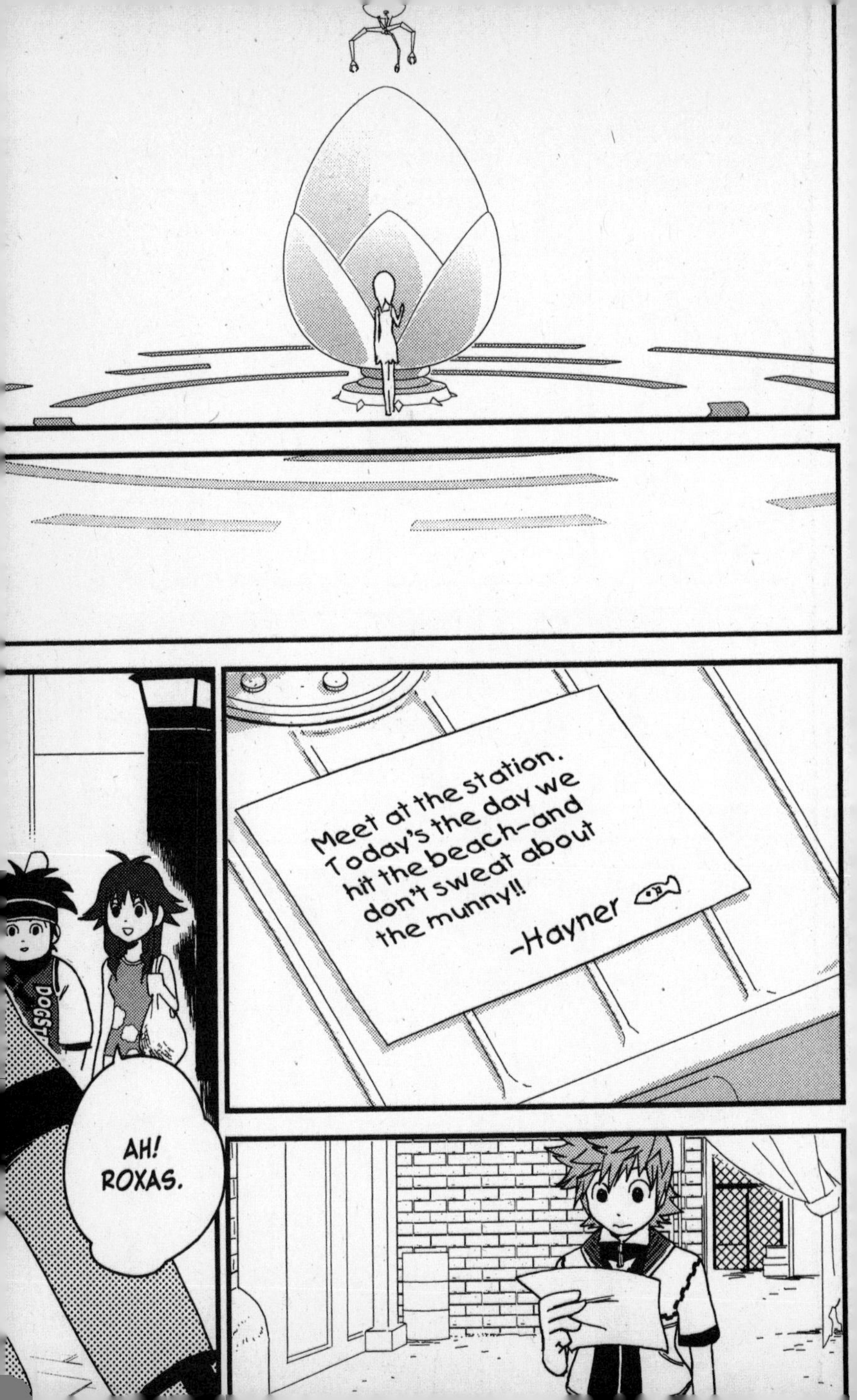
Meet at the station. Today's the day we hit the beach—and don't sweat about the munny!!
-Hayner
DOGST
AH! ROXAS.

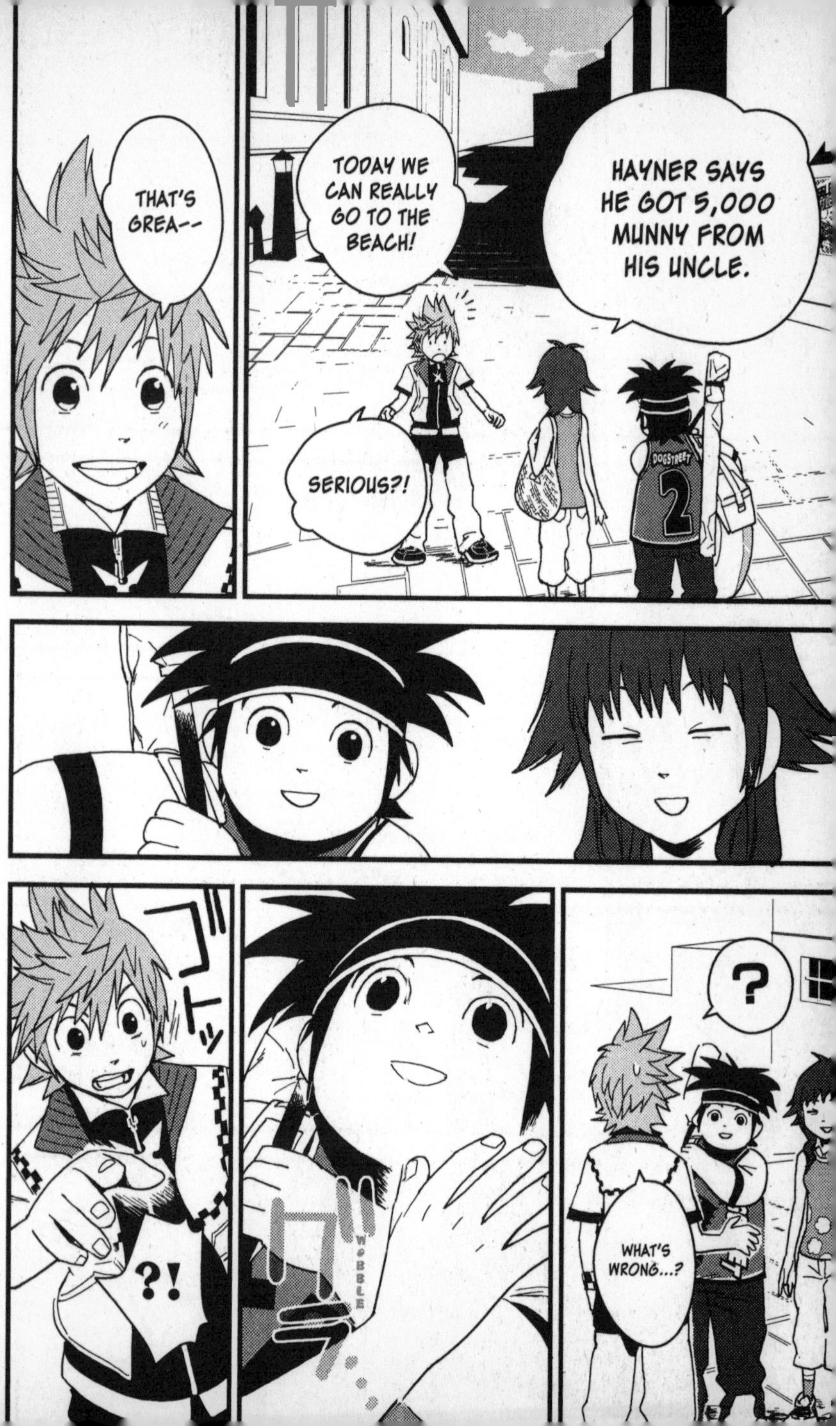
HAYNER SAYS HE GOT 5,000 MUNNY FROM HIS UNCLE.
TODAY WE CAN REALLY GO TO THE BEACH!
SERIOUS?!
THAT'S GREA--
?
WHAT'S WRONG...?
WOBBLE
ゴトッ
?!

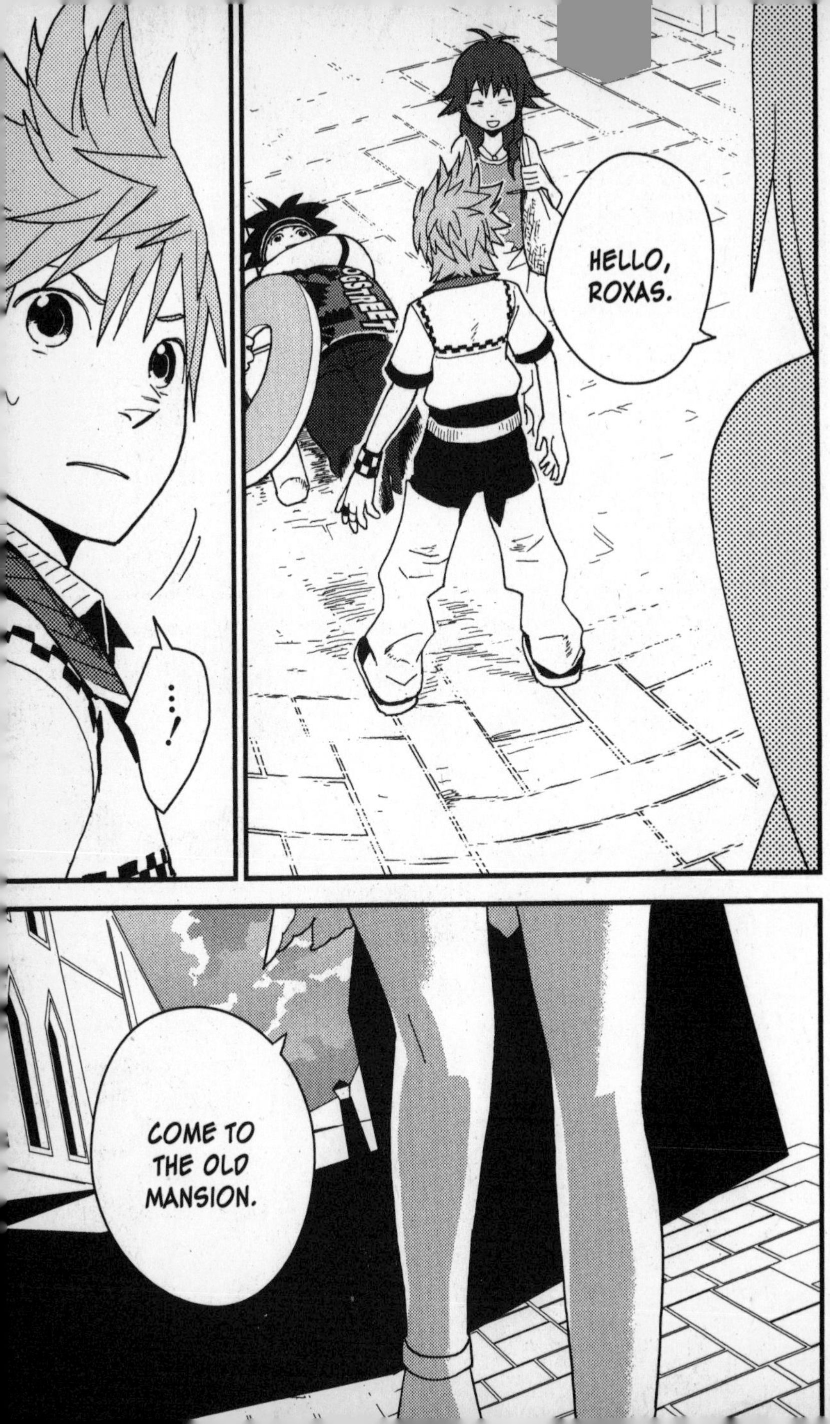
HELLO, ROXAS.
...!
COME TO THE OLD MANSION.

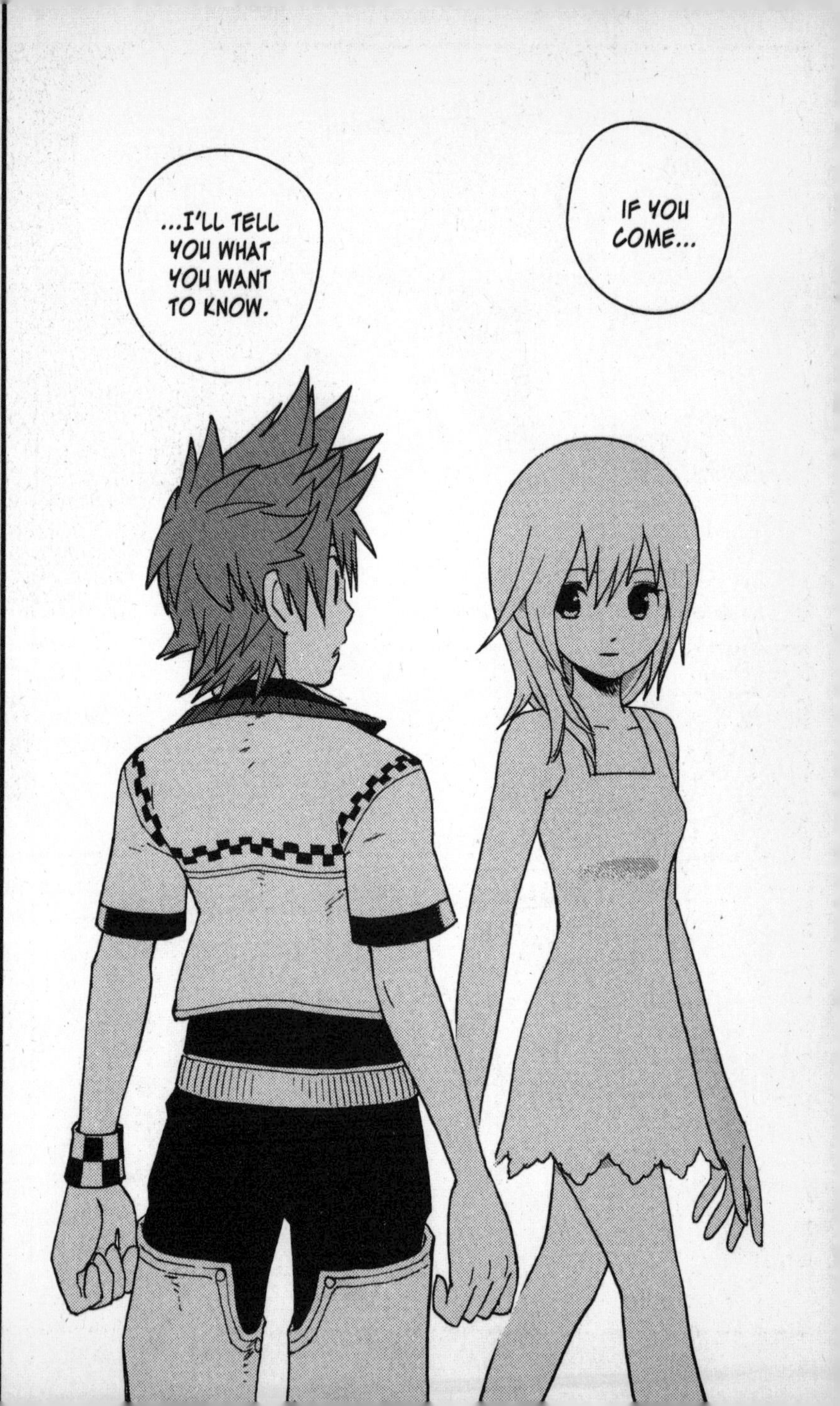
IF YOU COME...
...I'LL TELL YOU WHAT YOU WANT TO KNOW.

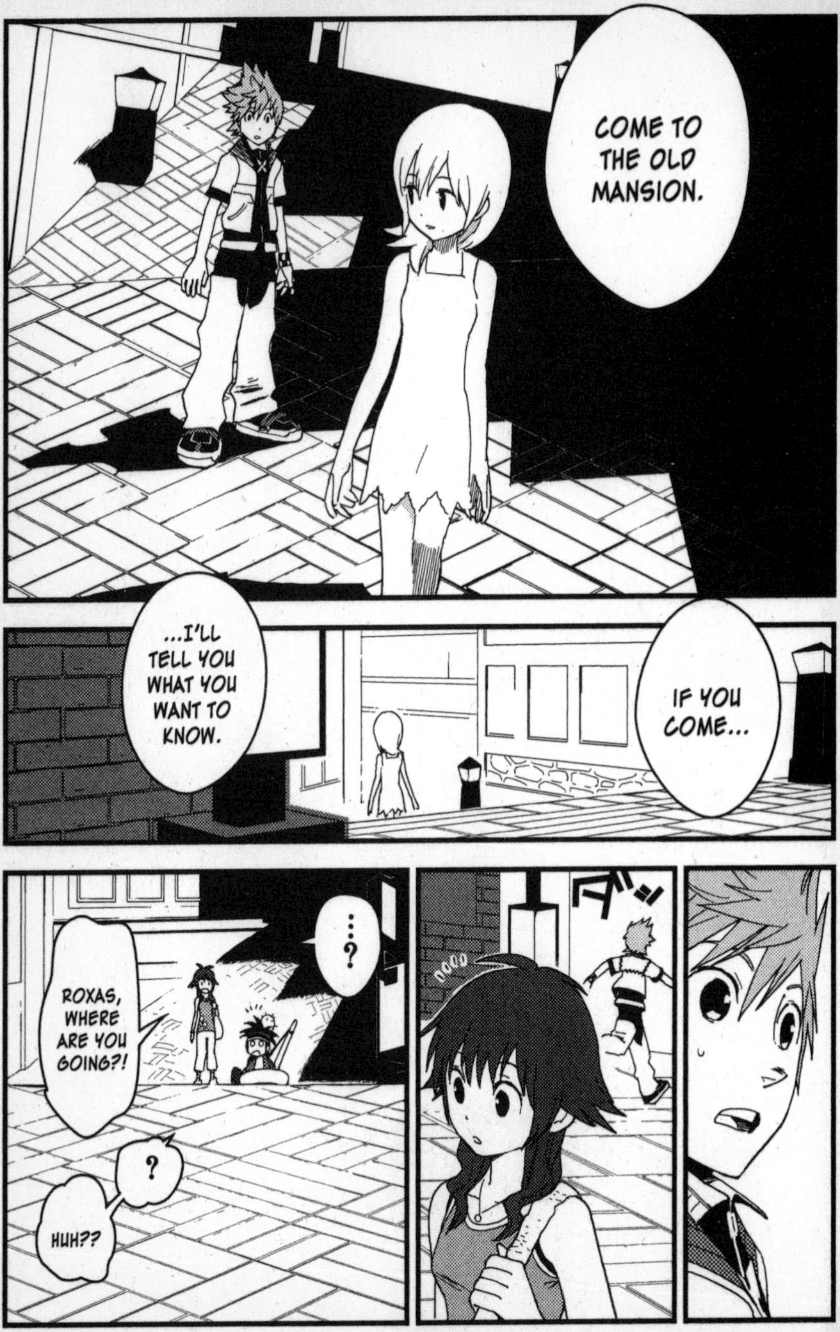
COME TO THE OLD MANSION.
IF YOU COME...
...I'LL TELL YOU WHAT YOU WANT TO KNOW.
...?
ROXAS, WHERE ARE YOU GOING?!
?
HUH??

# Chapter 4: The Distant Sound of Waves

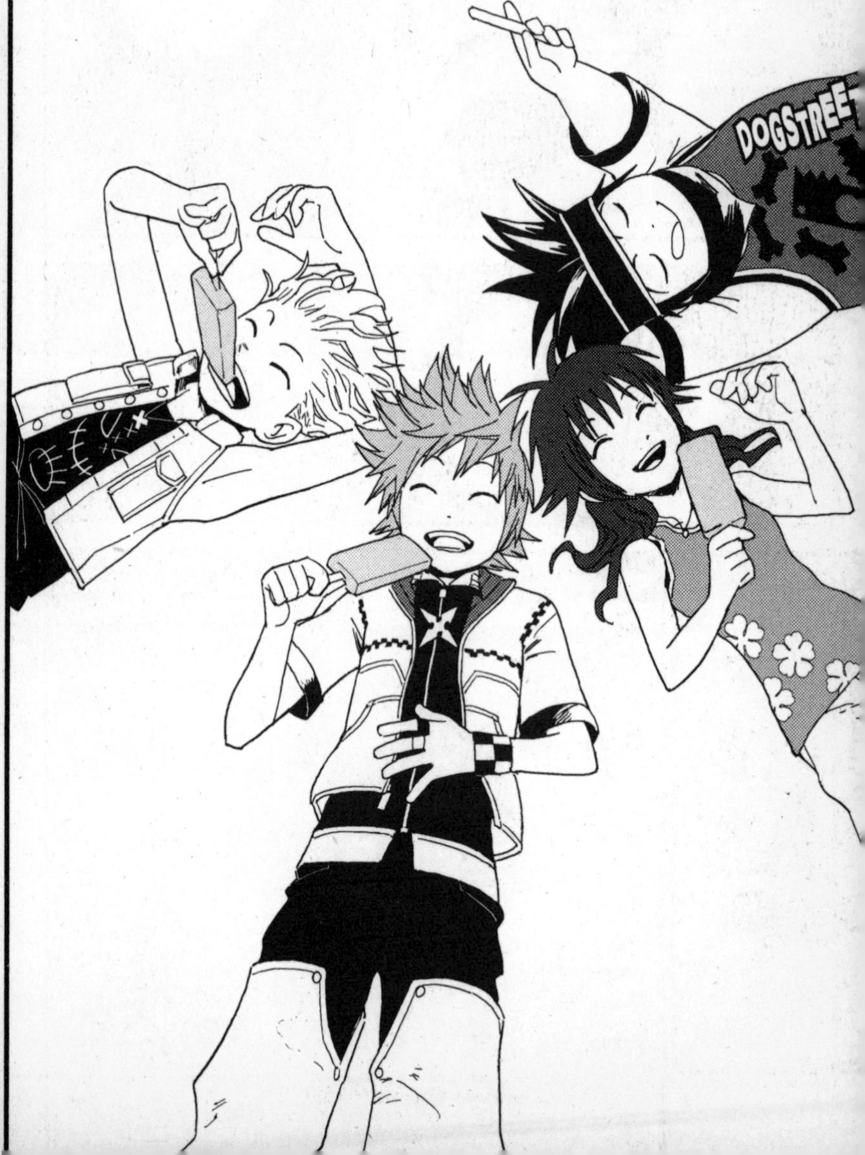
DOGSTREET

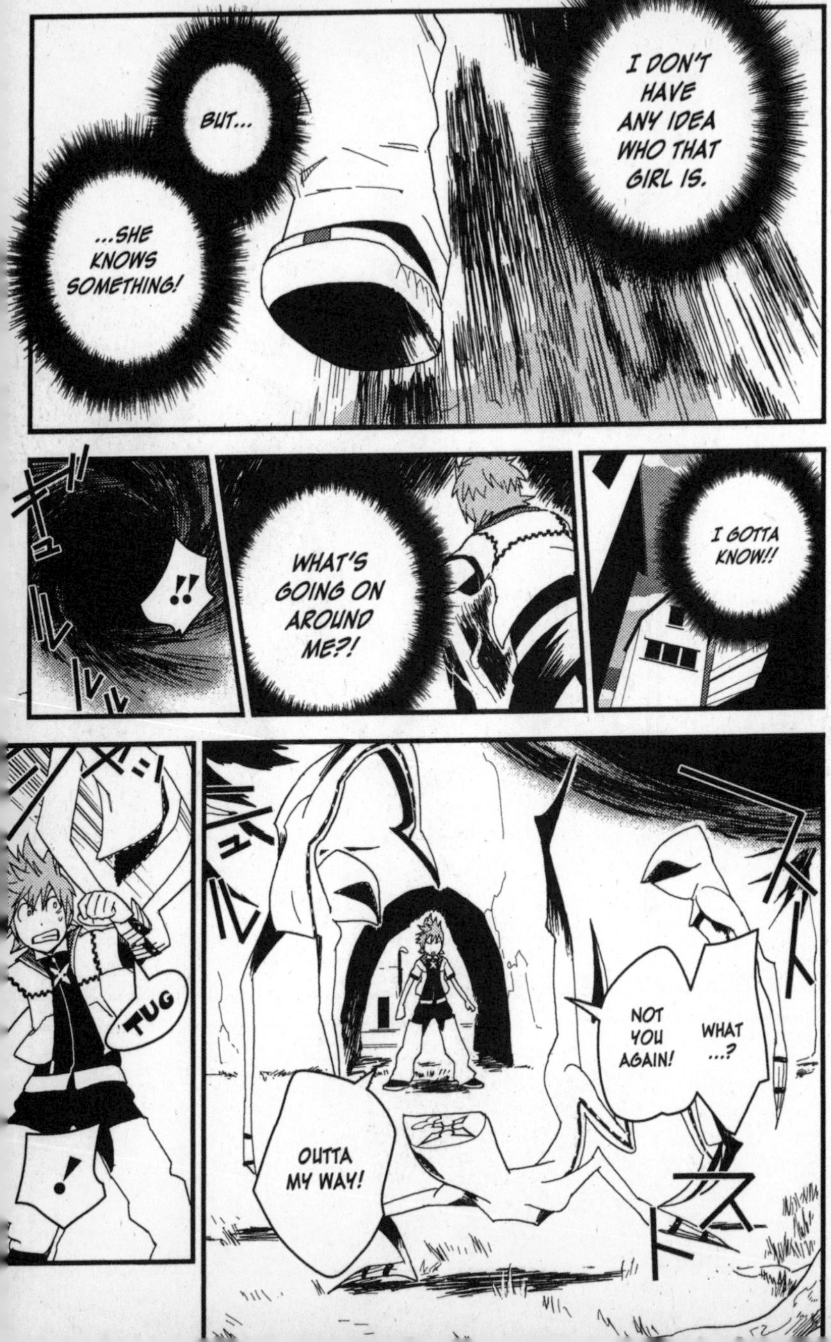
I DON'T HAVE ANY IDEA WHO THAT GIRL IS.
BUT...
...SHE KNOWS SOMETHING!
I GOTTA KNOW!!
WHAT'S GOING ON AROUND ME?!
!!
WHAT ...?
NOT YOU AGAIN!
OUTTA MY WAY!
TUG
!

OUT FOR A JOG?!

HEY, CHICKEN-WUSS!

A WEAPON...

IF ONLY I HAD THE KEYBLADE...

LET GO OF ME!!

HEH.

VICTORY IMMINENT.

SEIFER'LL BE THE WINNER, Y'KNOW?!

NO CHICKENING OUT OF THE TOURNAMENT TOMORROW!

HUFF WHEEZE

HUFF WHEEZE

STRUGGLE BATTLE

FIGHT! FIGHT!

PRESENTS

CLINK CLINK

KRAANG KRAANG

HEY! DON'T YOU IGNORE ME!

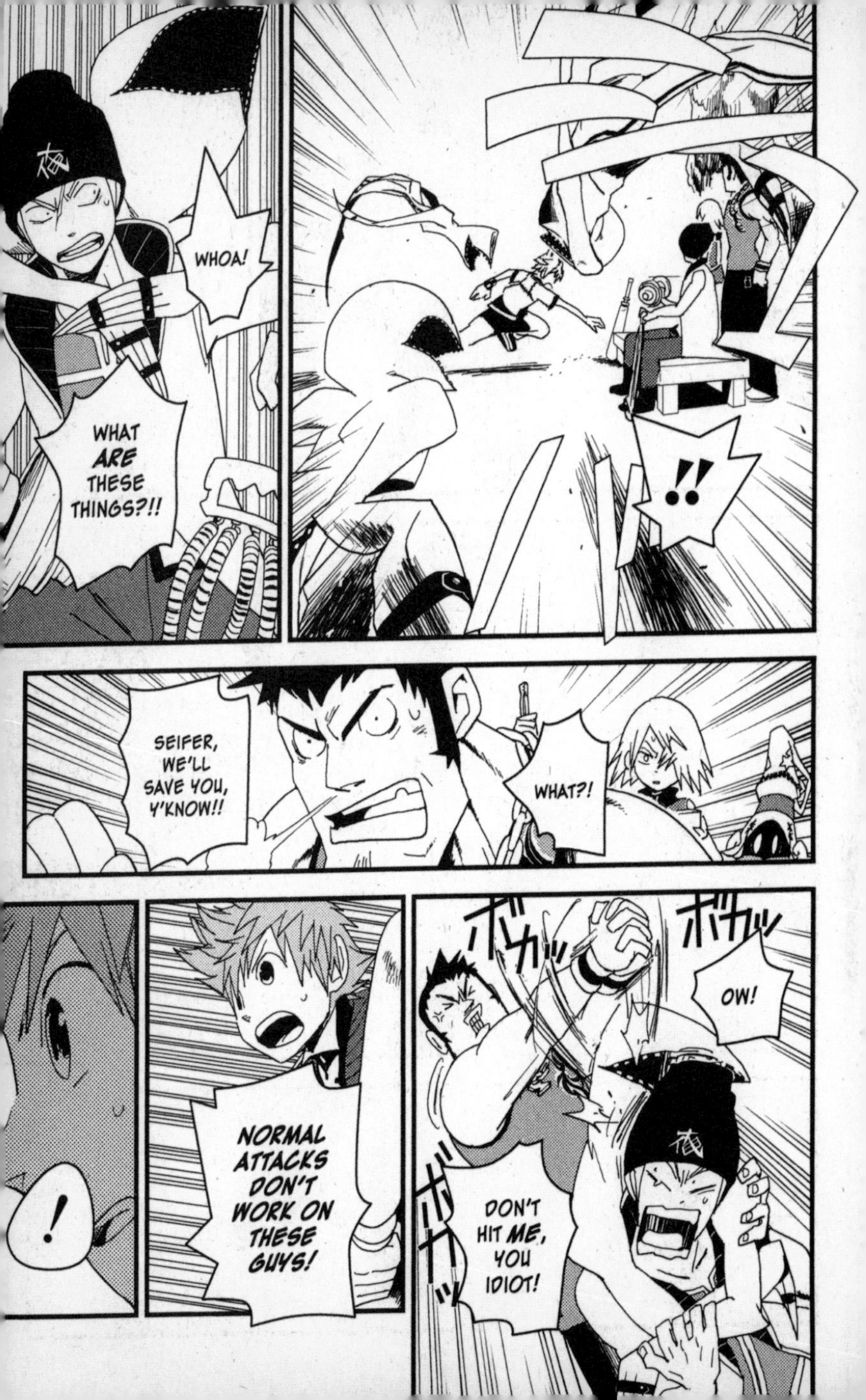
!!
WHOA!
WHAT *ARE* THESE THINGS?!!
WHAT?!
SEIFER, WE'LL SAVE YOU, Y'KNOW!!
ボカッ
ボカッ
OW!
ボカッ
DON'T HIT *ME*, YOU IDIOT!
NORMAL ATTACKS DON'T WORK ON THESE GUYS!
!

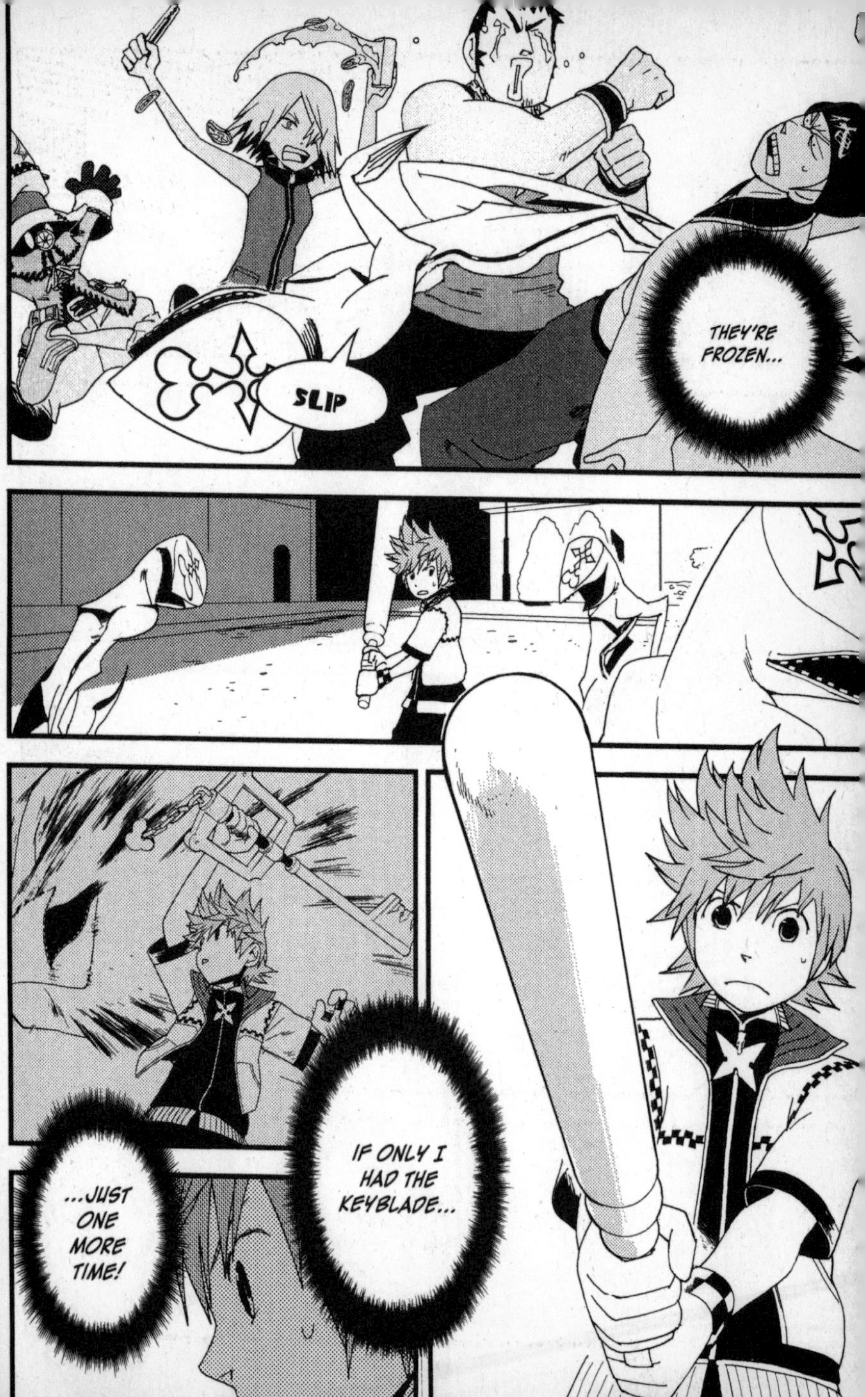
THEY'RE FROZEN...
SLIP
IF ONLY I HAD THE KEYBLADE...
...JUST ONE MORE TIME!

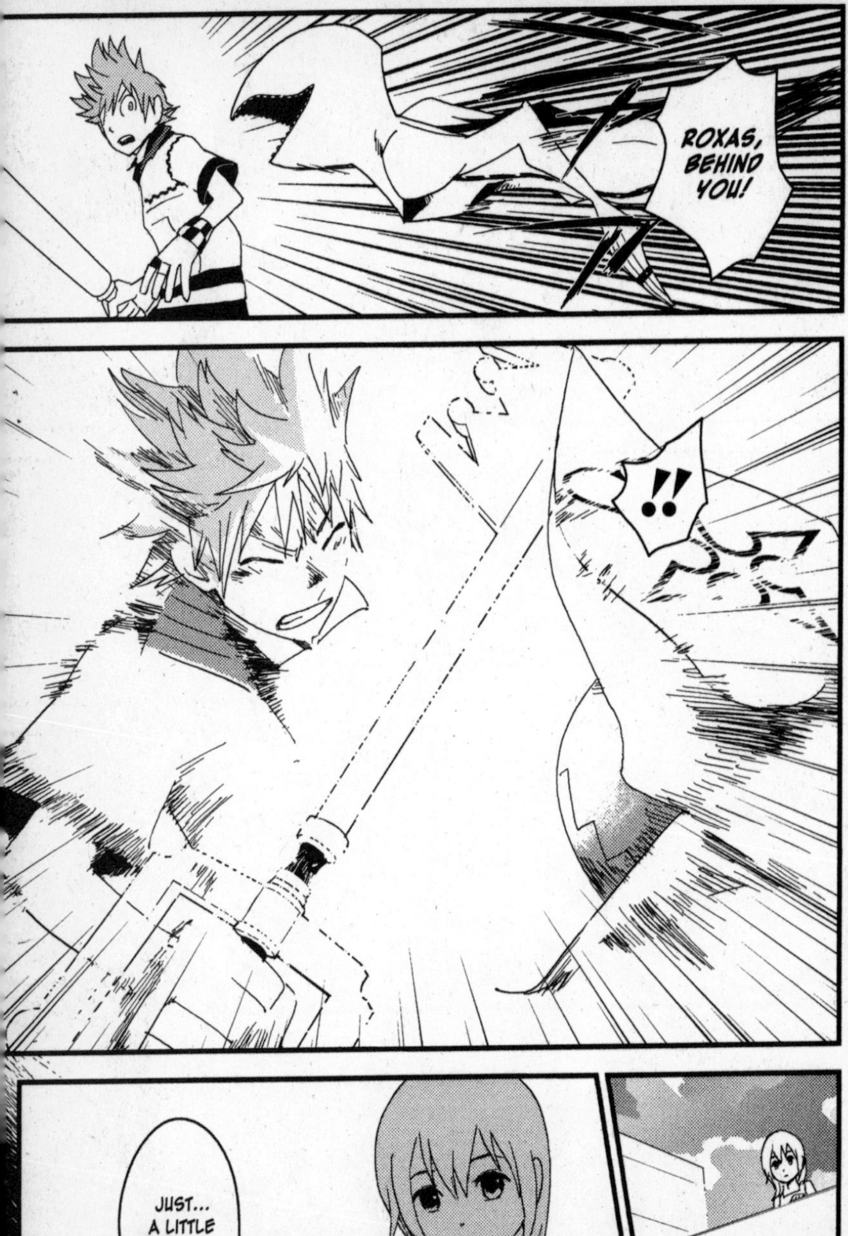
ROXAS, BEHIND YOU!
!!
JUST... A LITTLE LONGER...

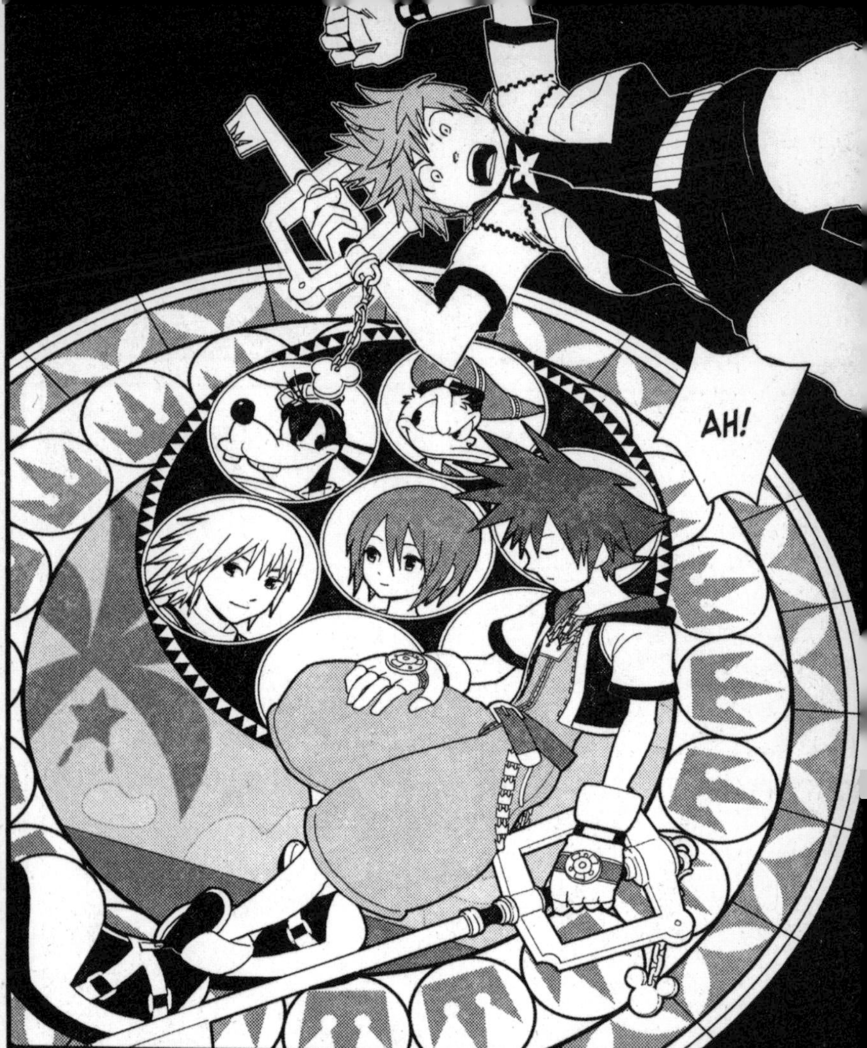
AH!

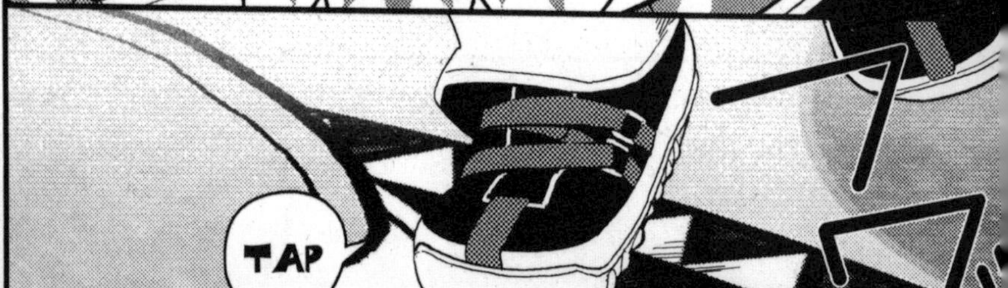
TAP

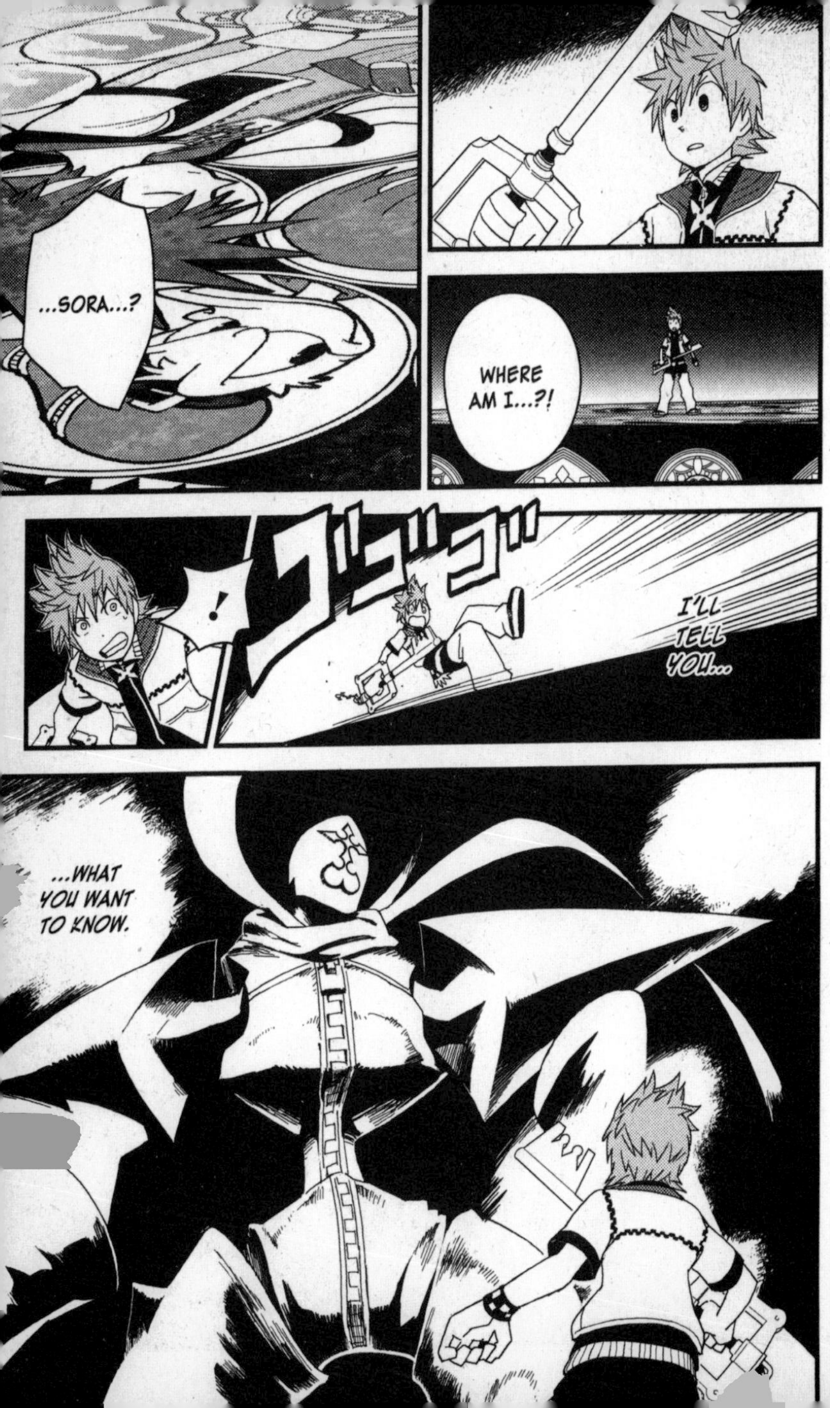
WHERE AM I...?!
...SORA...?
I'LL TELL YOU...
ゴゴゴ
!
...WHAT YOU WANT TO KNOW.

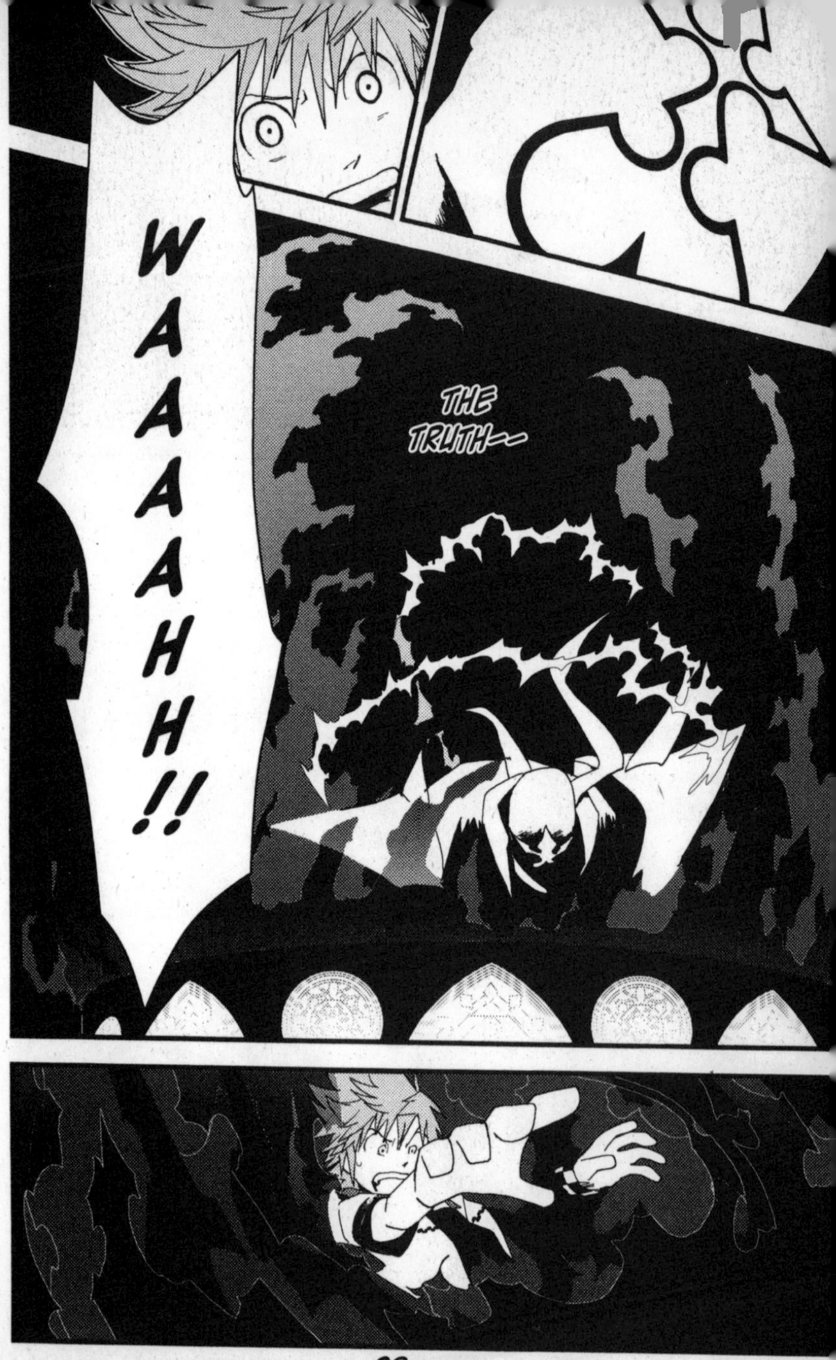
WAAAAHH!!
THE TRUTH--

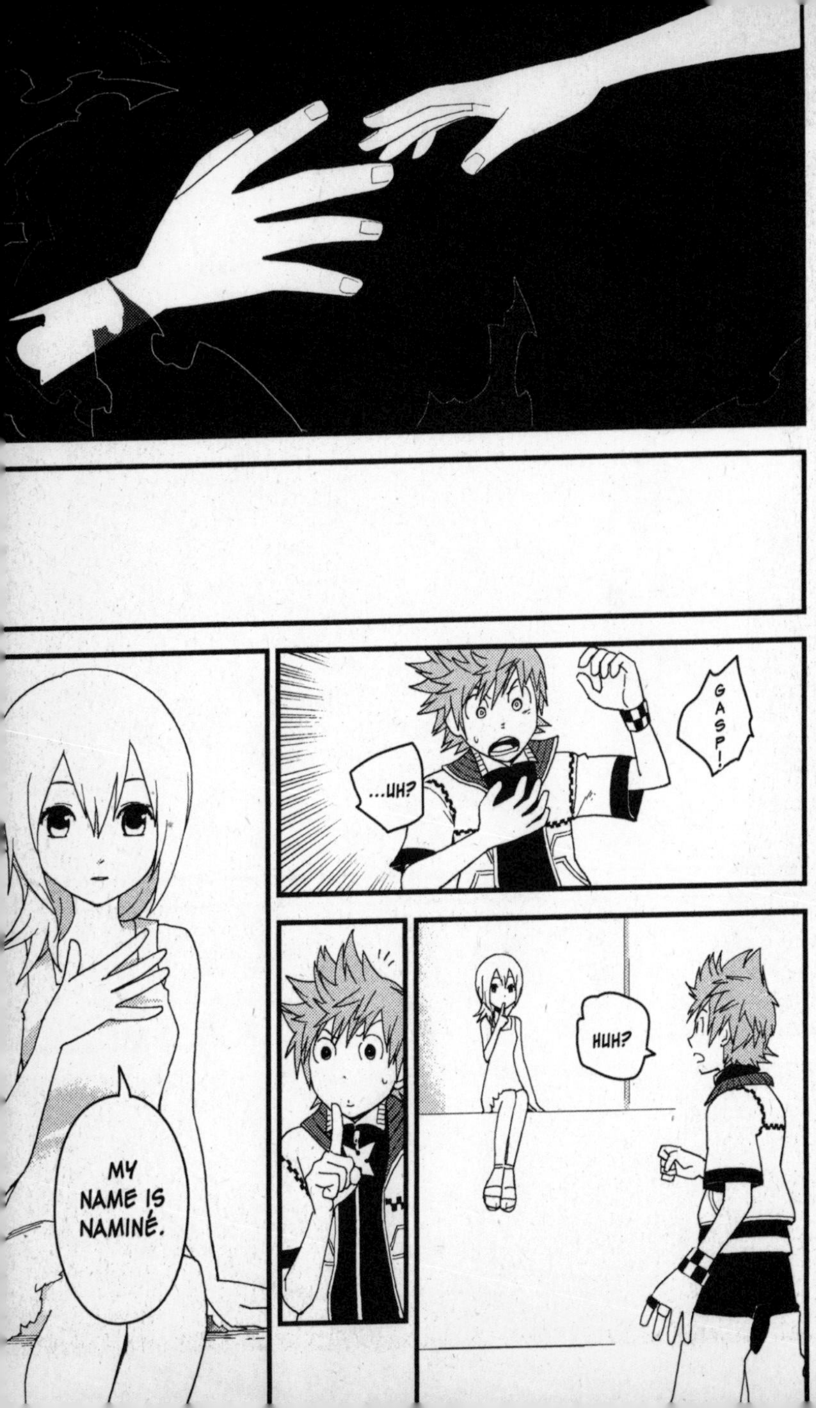
GASP!
...UH?
HUH?
MY NAME IS NAMINÉ.

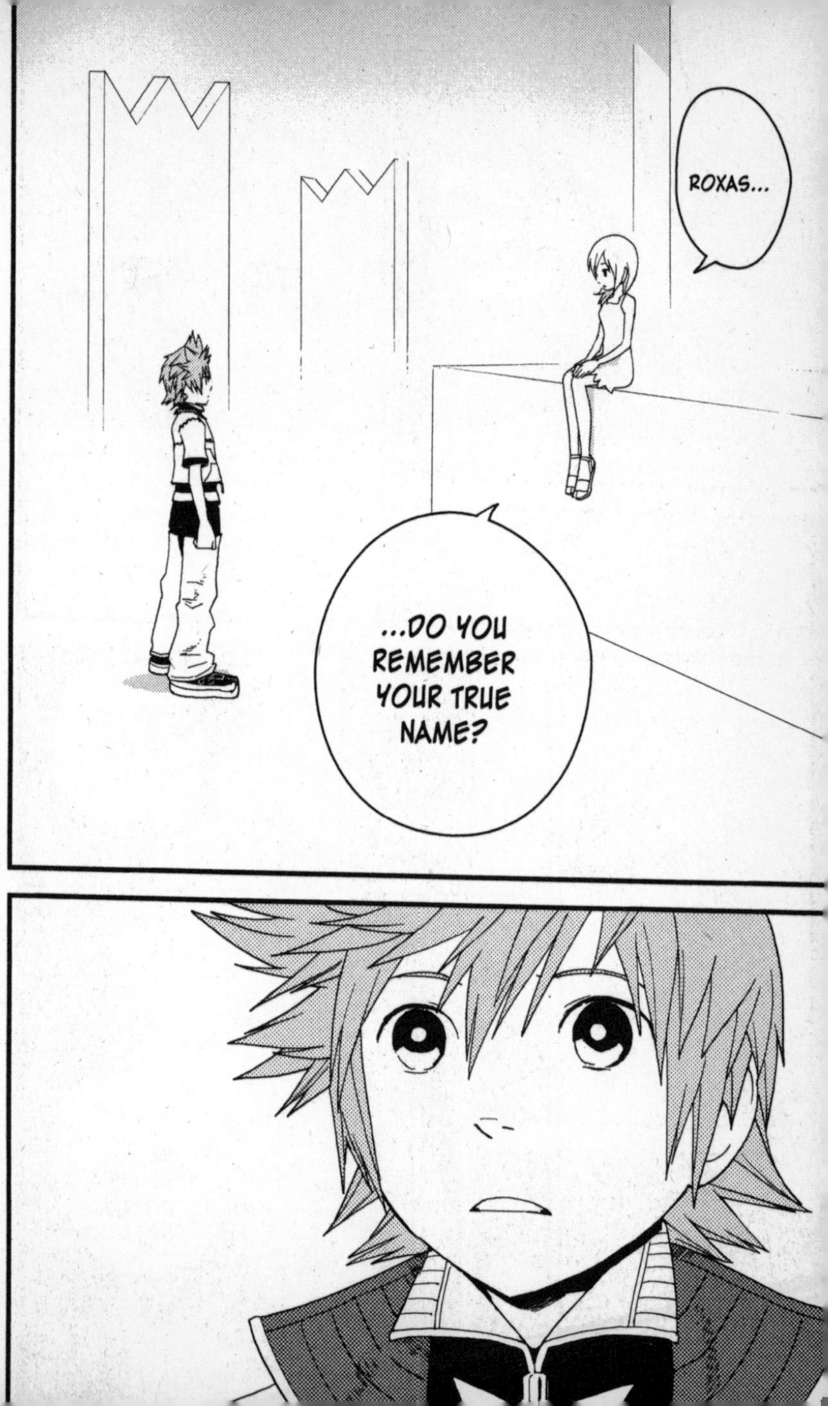
ROXAS...
...DO YOU REMEMBER YOUR TRUE NAME?

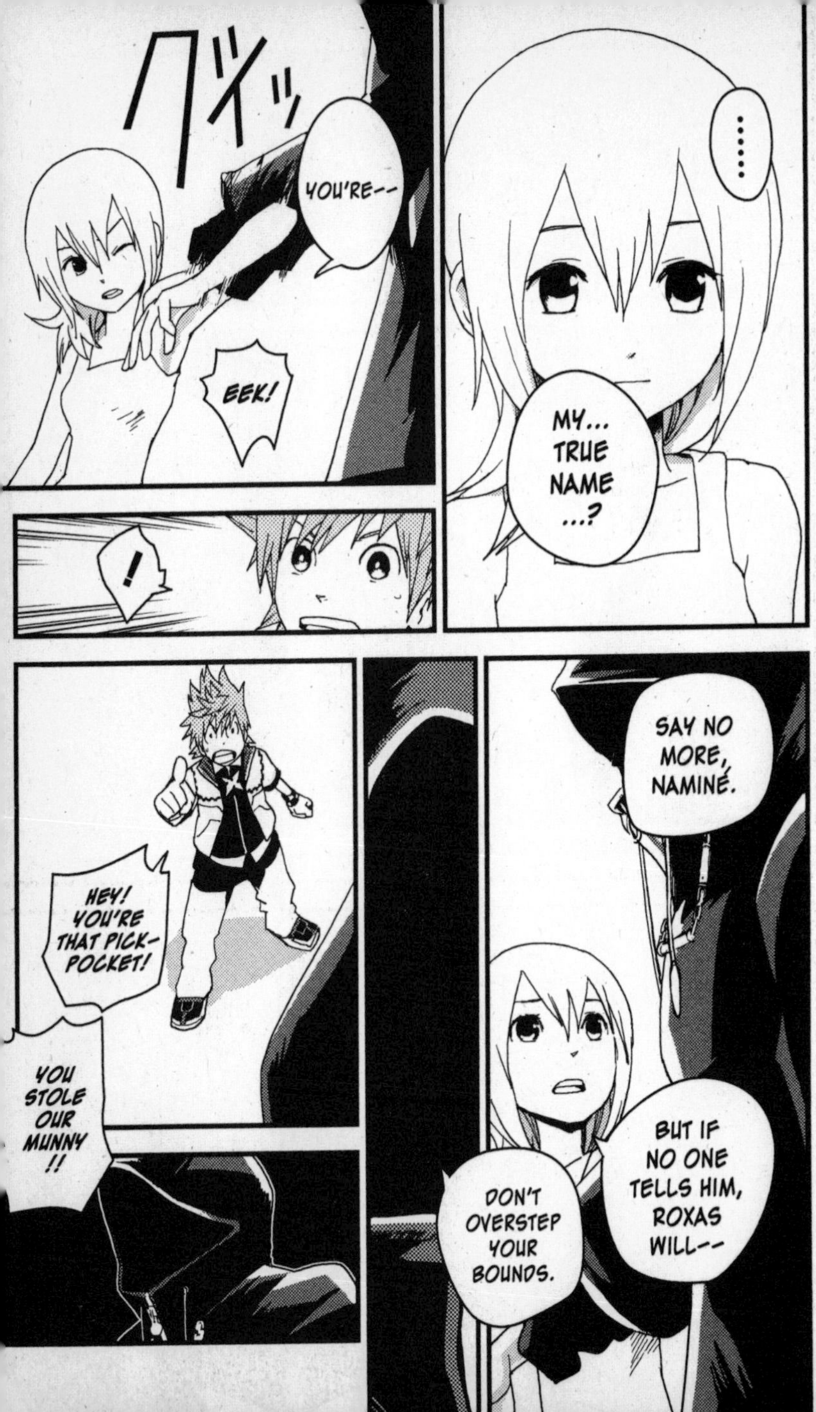
......
MY... TRUE NAME ...?
ヴィッ
YOU'RE--
EEK!
!
SAY NO MORE, NAMINÉ.
BUT IF NO ONE TELLS HIM, ROXAS WILL--
DON'T OVERSTEP YOUR BOUNDS.
HEY! YOU'RE THAT PICK-POCKET!
YOU STOLE OUR MUNNY !!

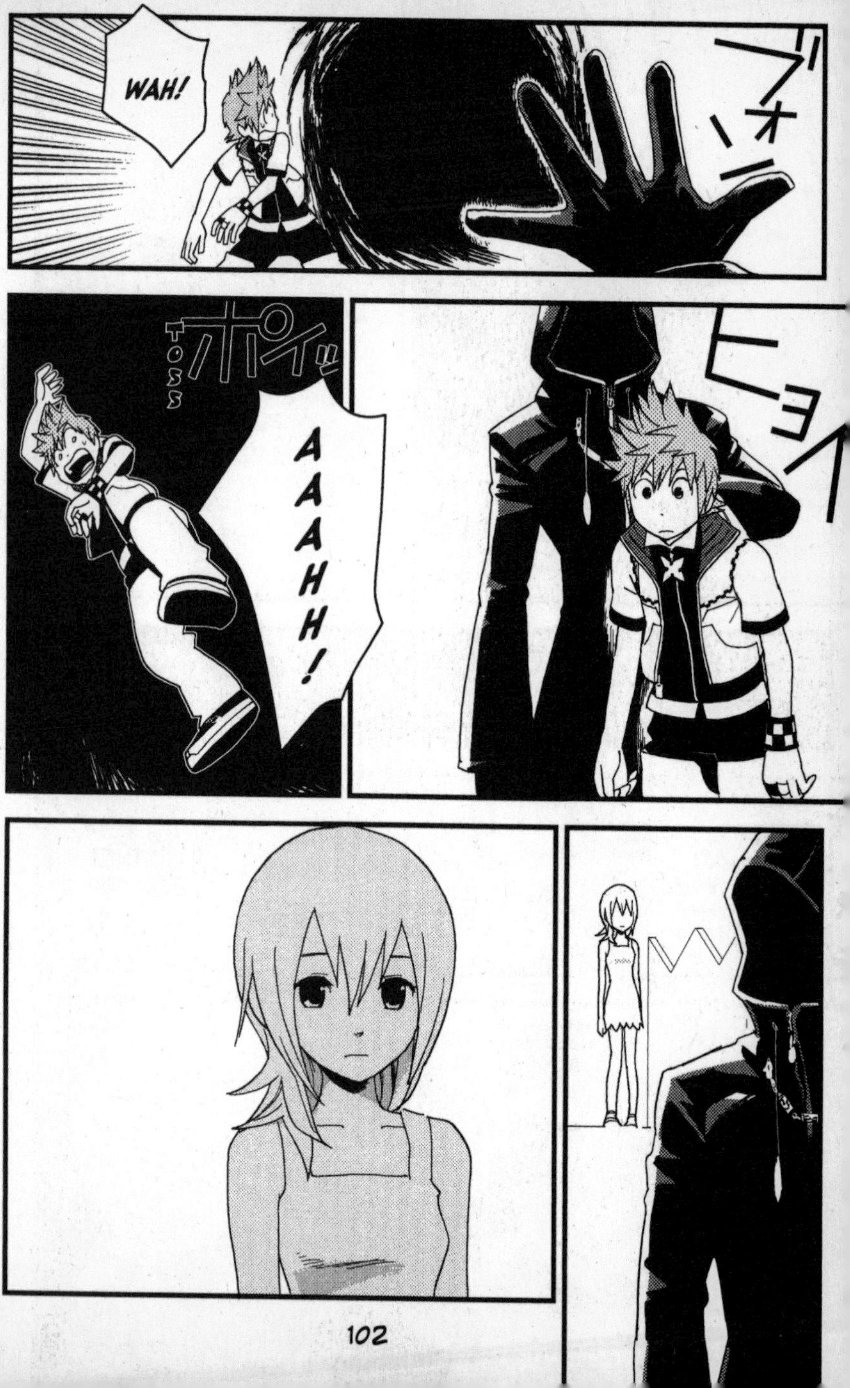
ブォン
WAH!
ヒョイ
ポイッ
TOSS
AAAAHH!

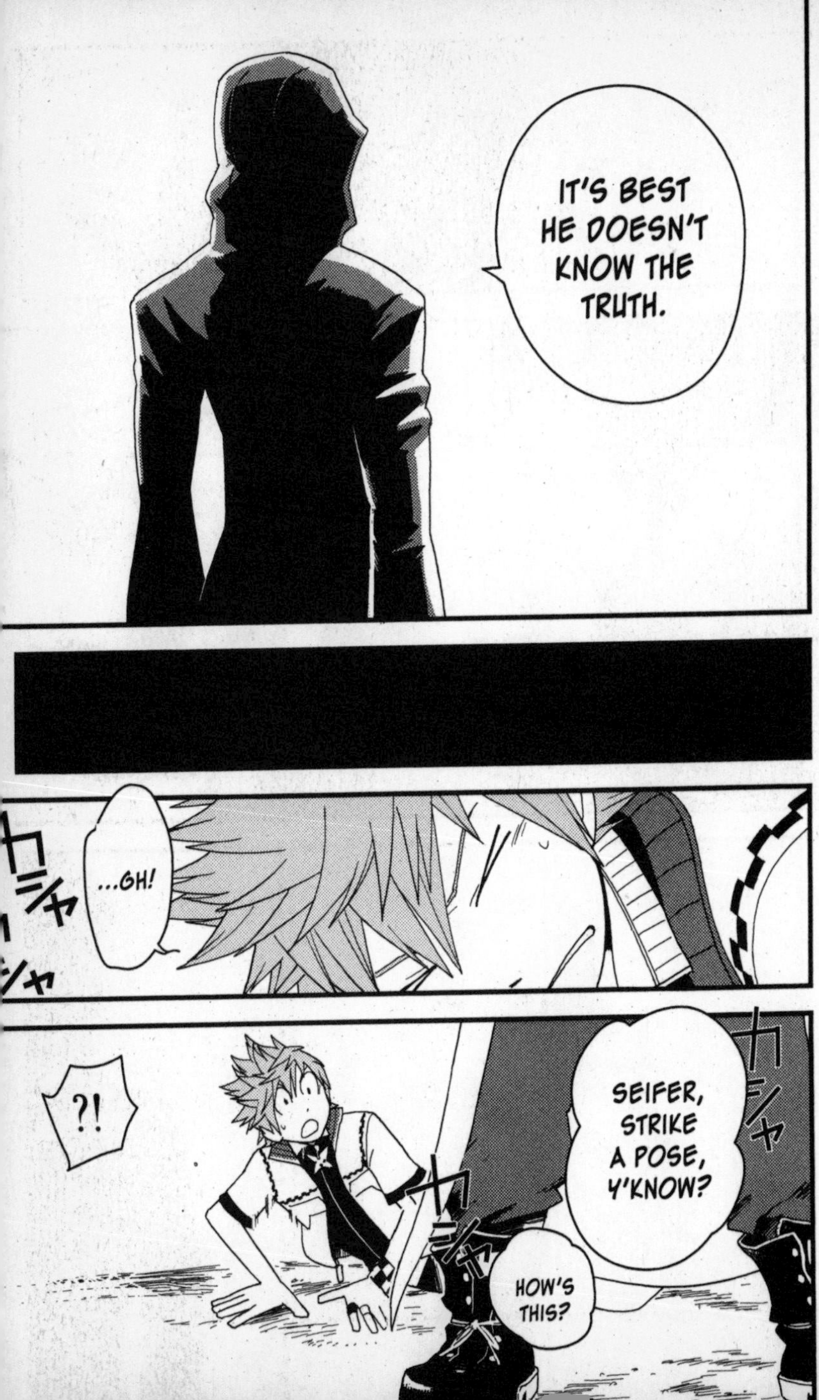
IT'S BEST HE DOESN'T KNOW THE TRUTH.
...GH!
カシャ
カシャ
SEIFER, STRIKE A POSE, Y'KNOW?
カシャ
HOW'S THIS?
?!

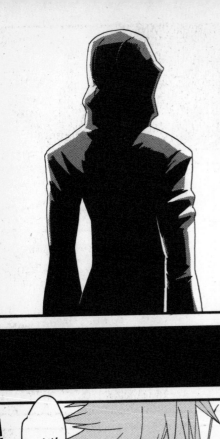

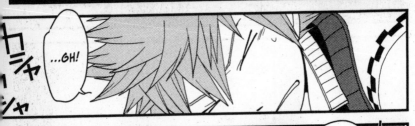

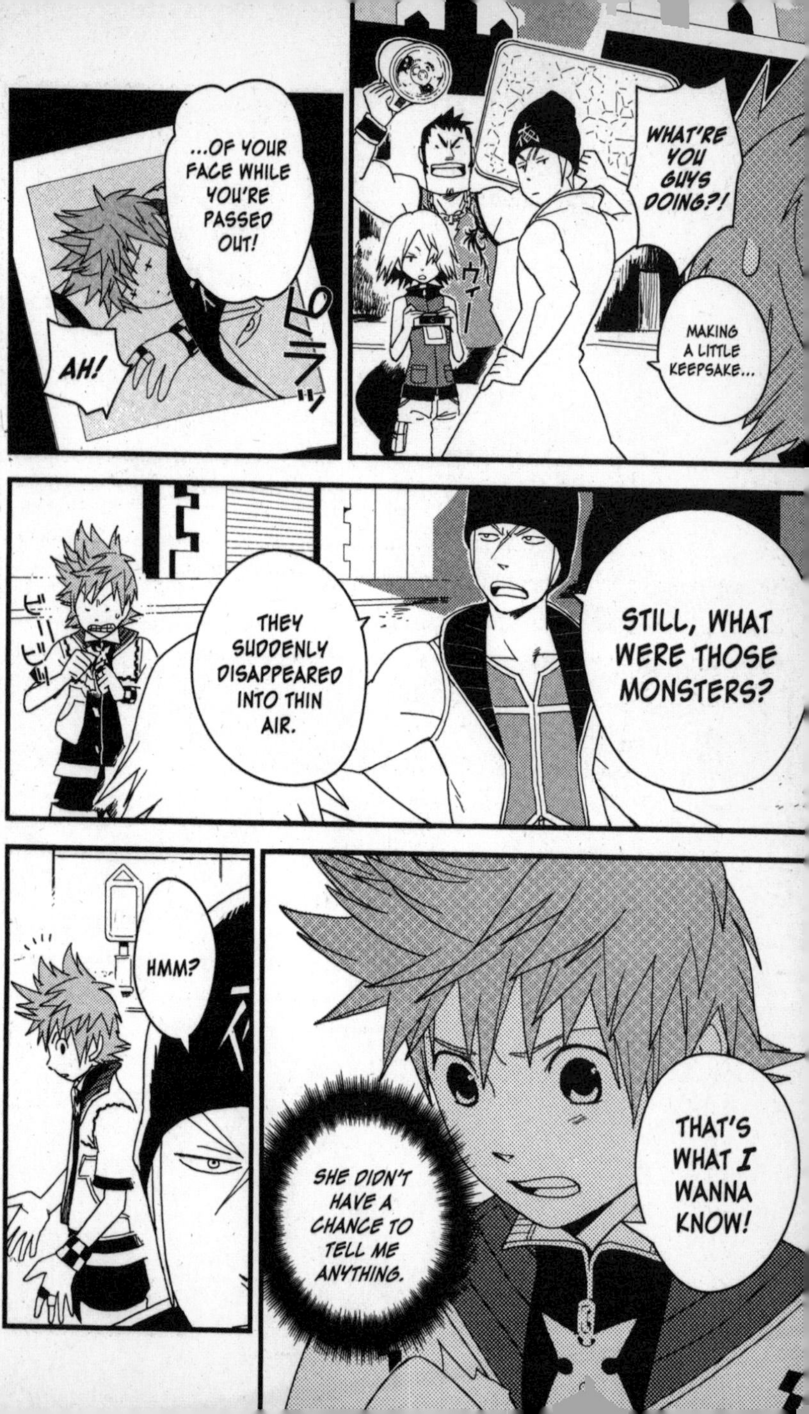
WHAT'RE YOU GUYS DOING?!
MAKING A LITTLE KEEPSAKE...
...OF YOUR FACE WHILE YOU'RE PASSED OUT!
AH!
STILL, WHAT WERE THOSE MONSTERS?
THEY SUDDENLY DISAPPEARED INTO THIN AIR.
THAT'S WHAT I WANNA KNOW!
SHE DIDN'T HAVE A CHANCE TO TELL ME ANYTHING.
HMM?

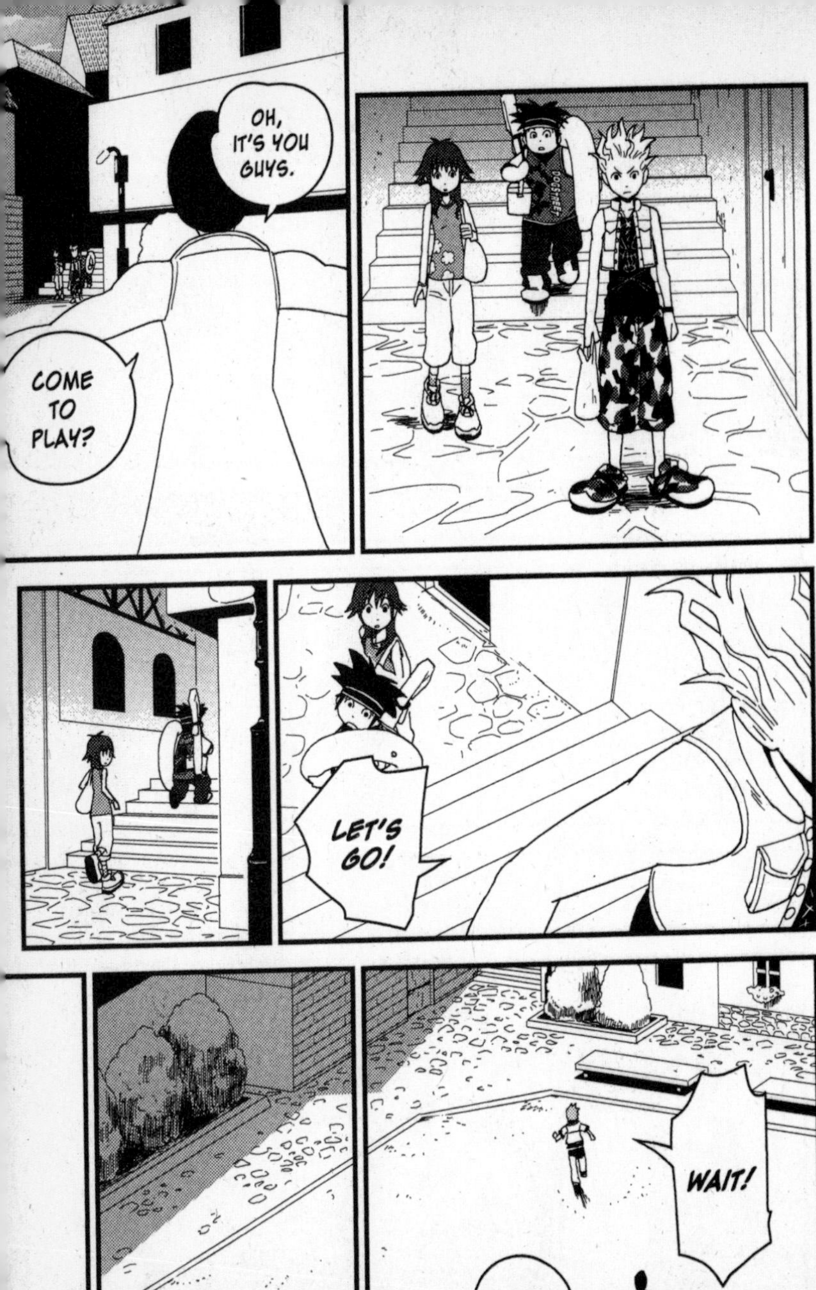
OH, IT'S YOU GUYS.
COME TO PLAY?
LET'S GO!
WAIT!
HMPH.

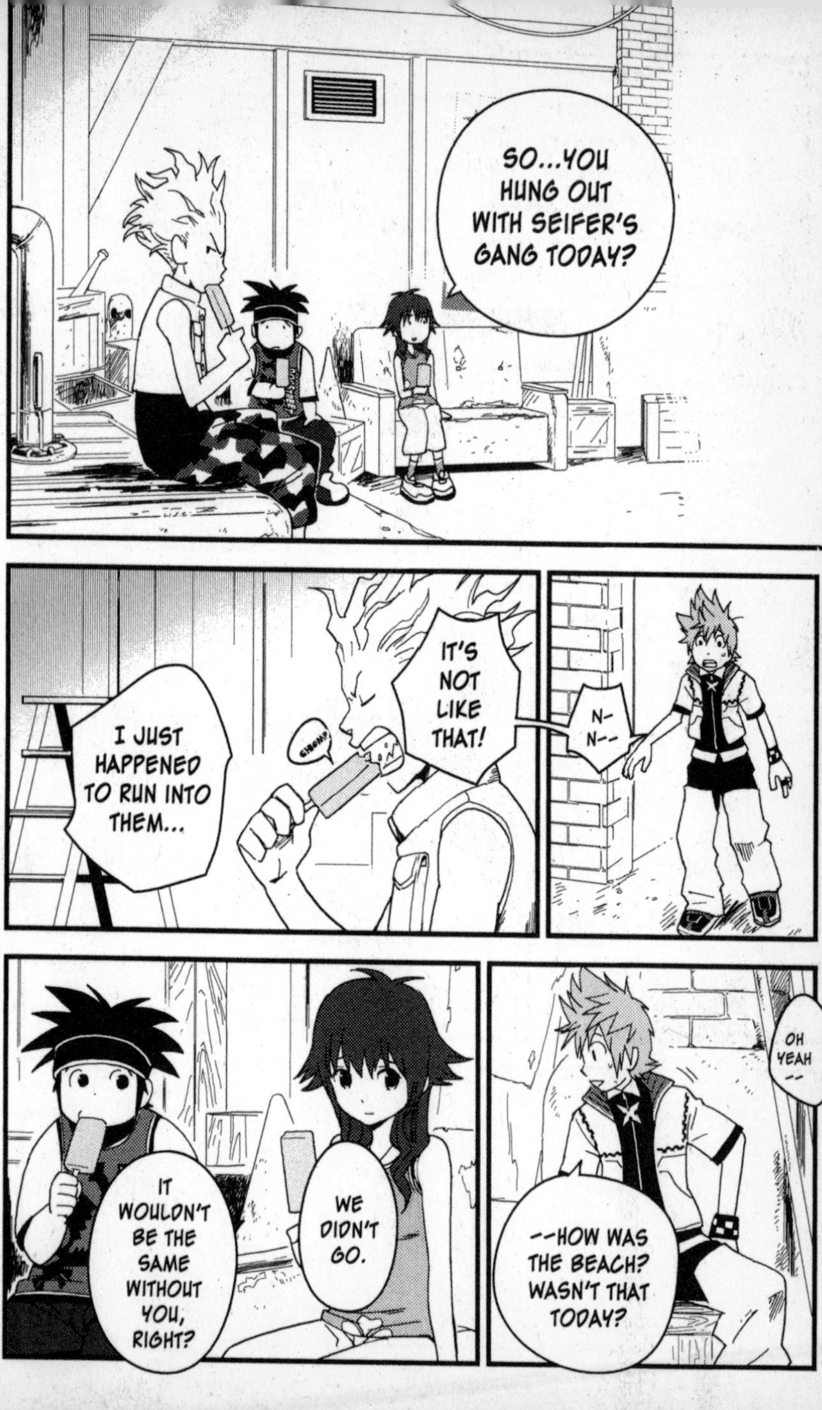
SO...YOU HUNG OUT WITH SEIFER'S GANG TODAY?
N- N--
IT'S NOT LIKE THAT!
CHOMP
I JUST HAPPENED TO RUN INTO THEM...
OH YEAH --
--HOW WAS THE BEACH? WASN'T THAT TODAY?
WE DIDN'T GO.
IT WOULDN'T BE THE SAME WITHOUT YOU, RIGHT?

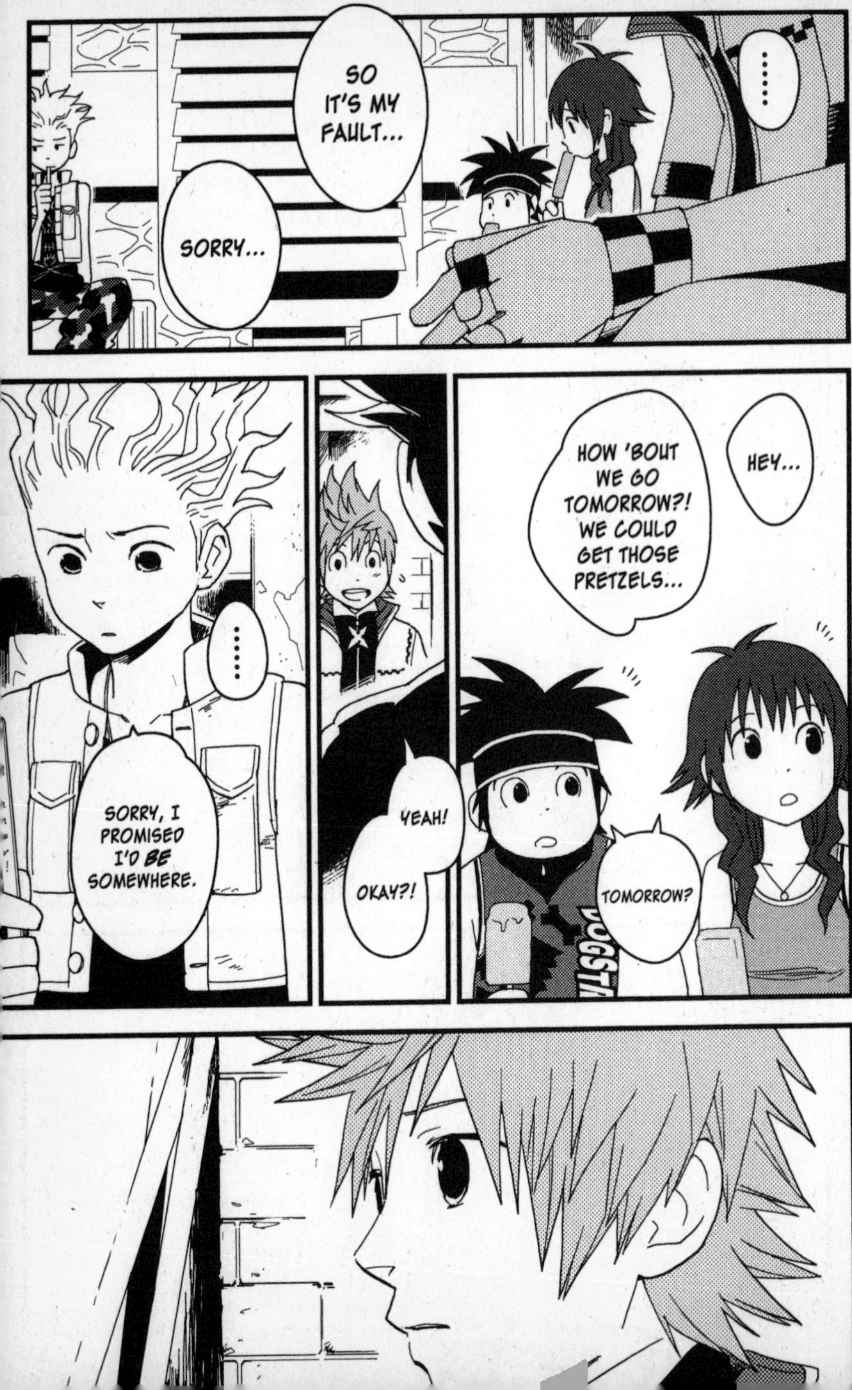
......
SO IT'S MY FAULT...
SORRY...
HEY...
HOW 'BOUT WE GO TOMORROW?! WE COULD GET THOSE PRETZELS...
TOMORROW?
YEAH! OKAY?!
......
SORRY, I PROMISED I'D *BE* SOMEWHERE.

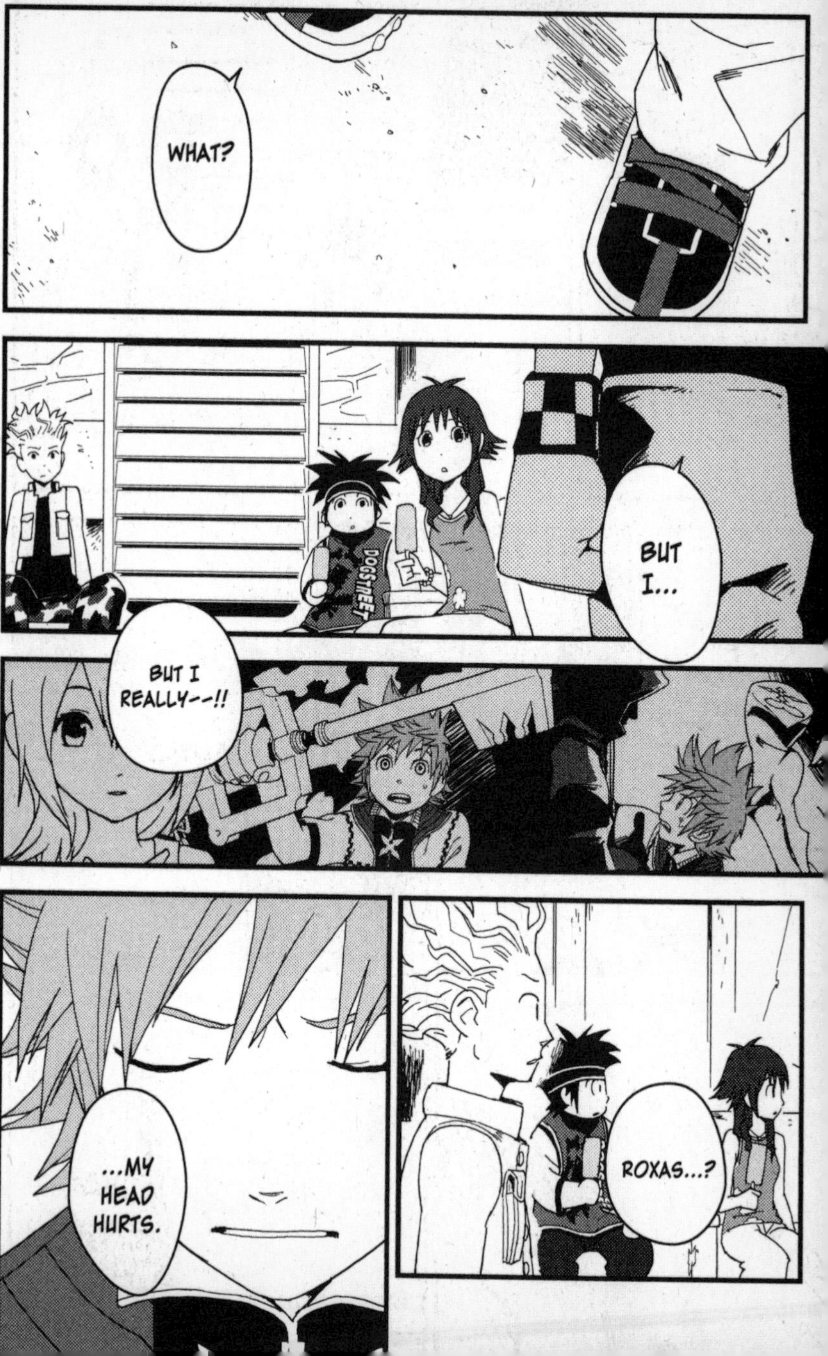
WHAT?
BUT I...
DOGSTREET
BUT I REALLY--!!
ROXAS...?
...MY HEAD HURTS.

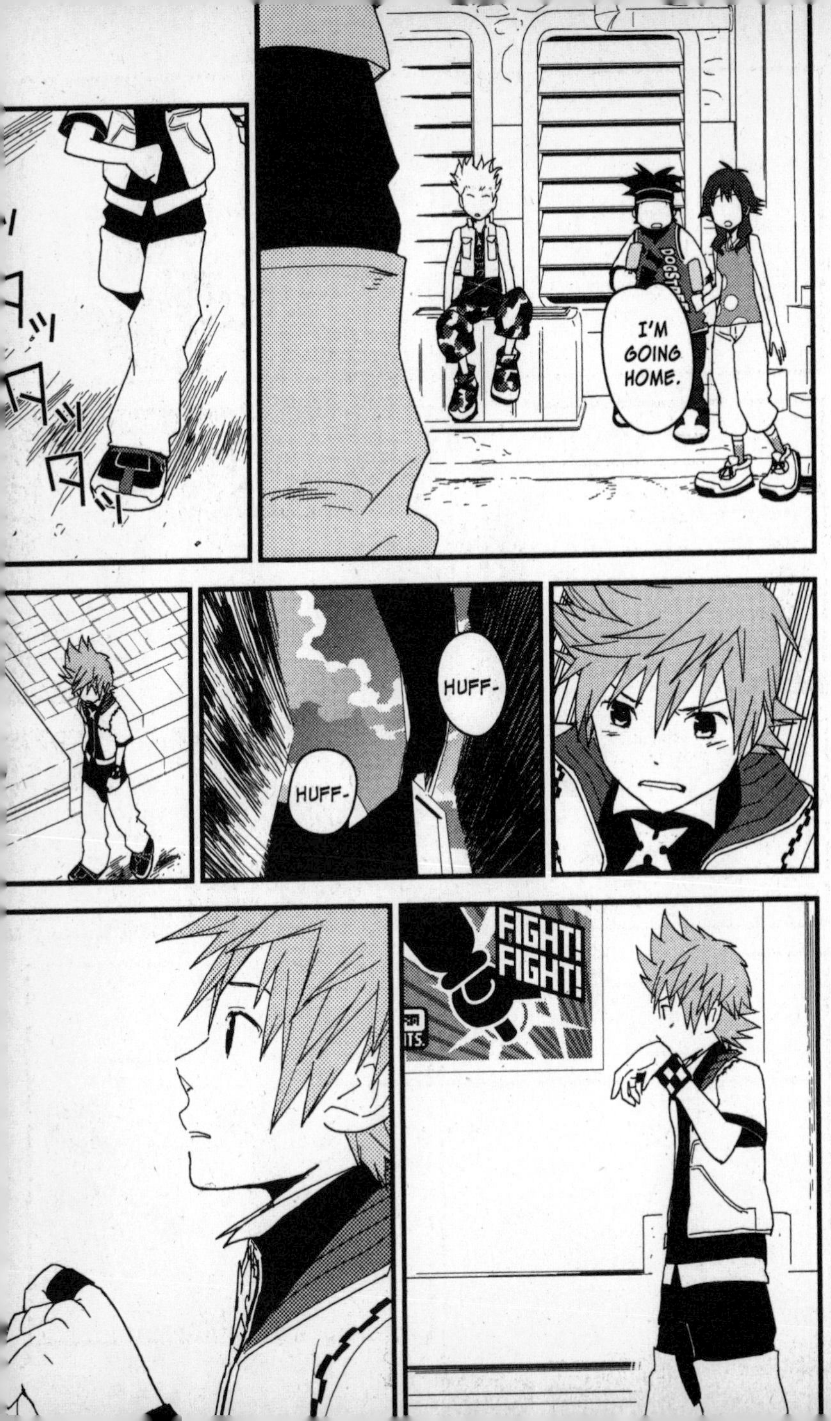
I'M GOING HOME.
HUFF-
HUFF-
FIGHT! FIGHT!

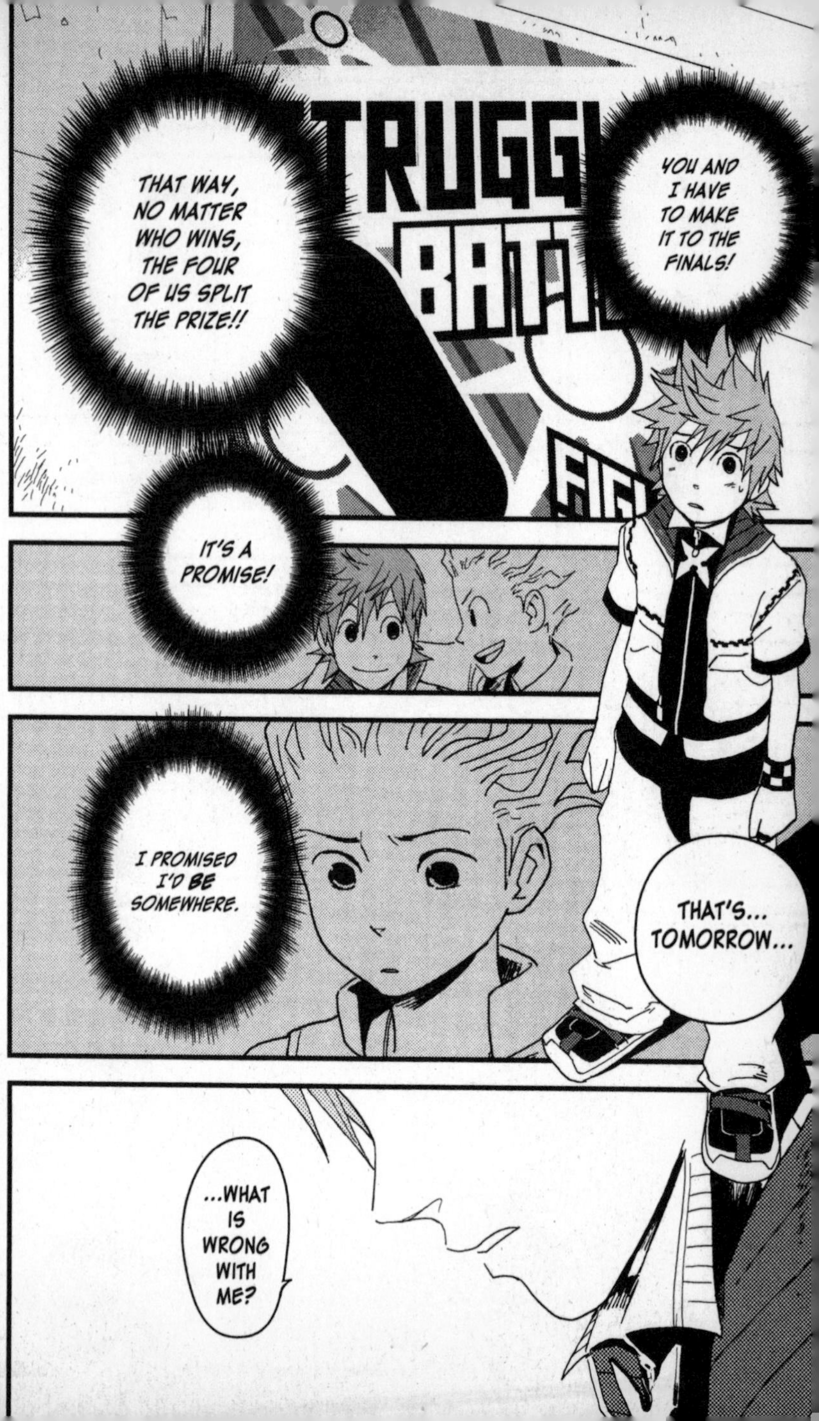
YOU AND I HAVE TO MAKE IT TO THE FINALS!
THAT WAY, NO MATTER WHO WINS, THE FOUR OF US SPLIT THE PRIZE!!
IT'S A PROMISE!
I PROMISED I'D BE SOMEWHERE.
THAT'S... TOMORROW...
...WHAT IS WRONG WITH ME?

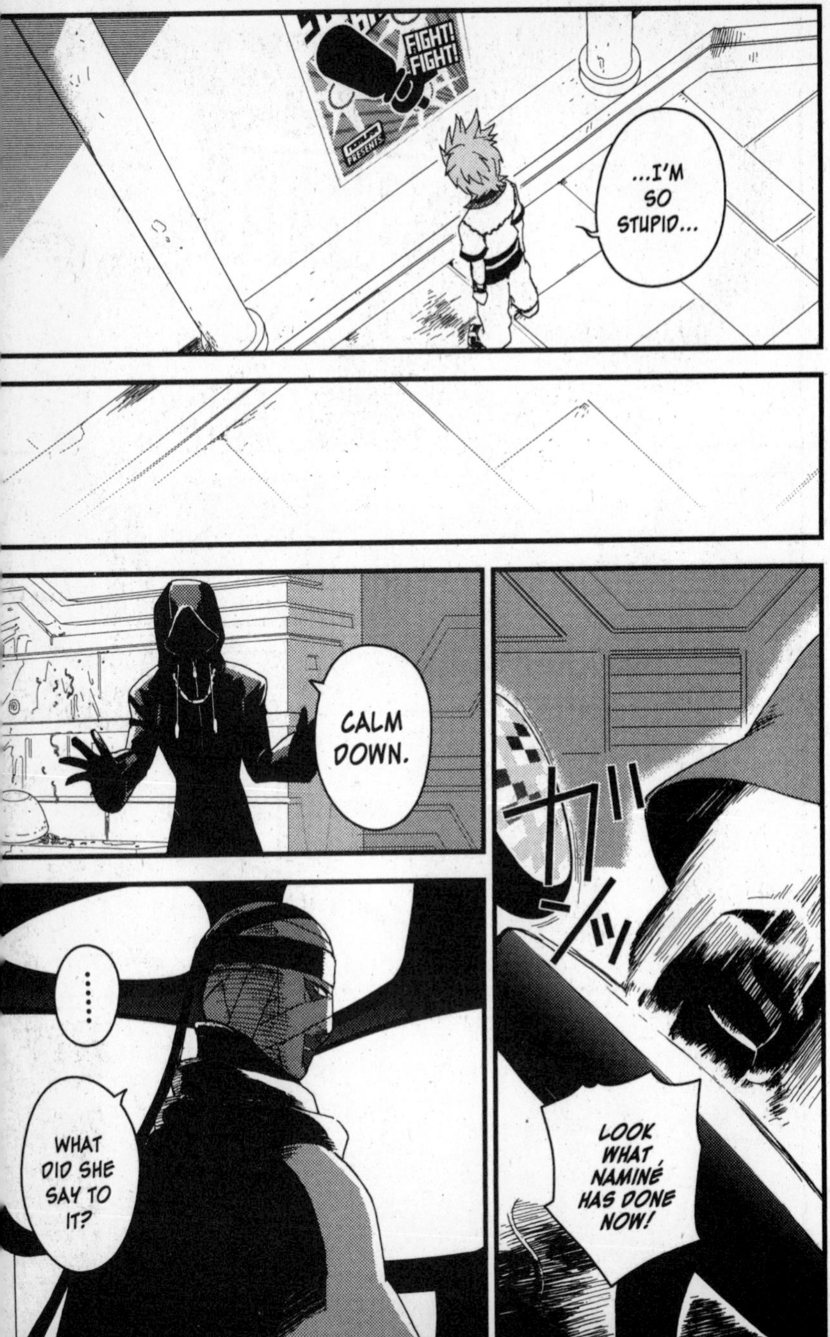
FIGHT! FIGHT!
...I'M SO STUPID...
LOOK WHAT NAMINÉ HAS DONE NOW!
CALM DOWN.
......
WHAT DID SHE SAY TO IT?

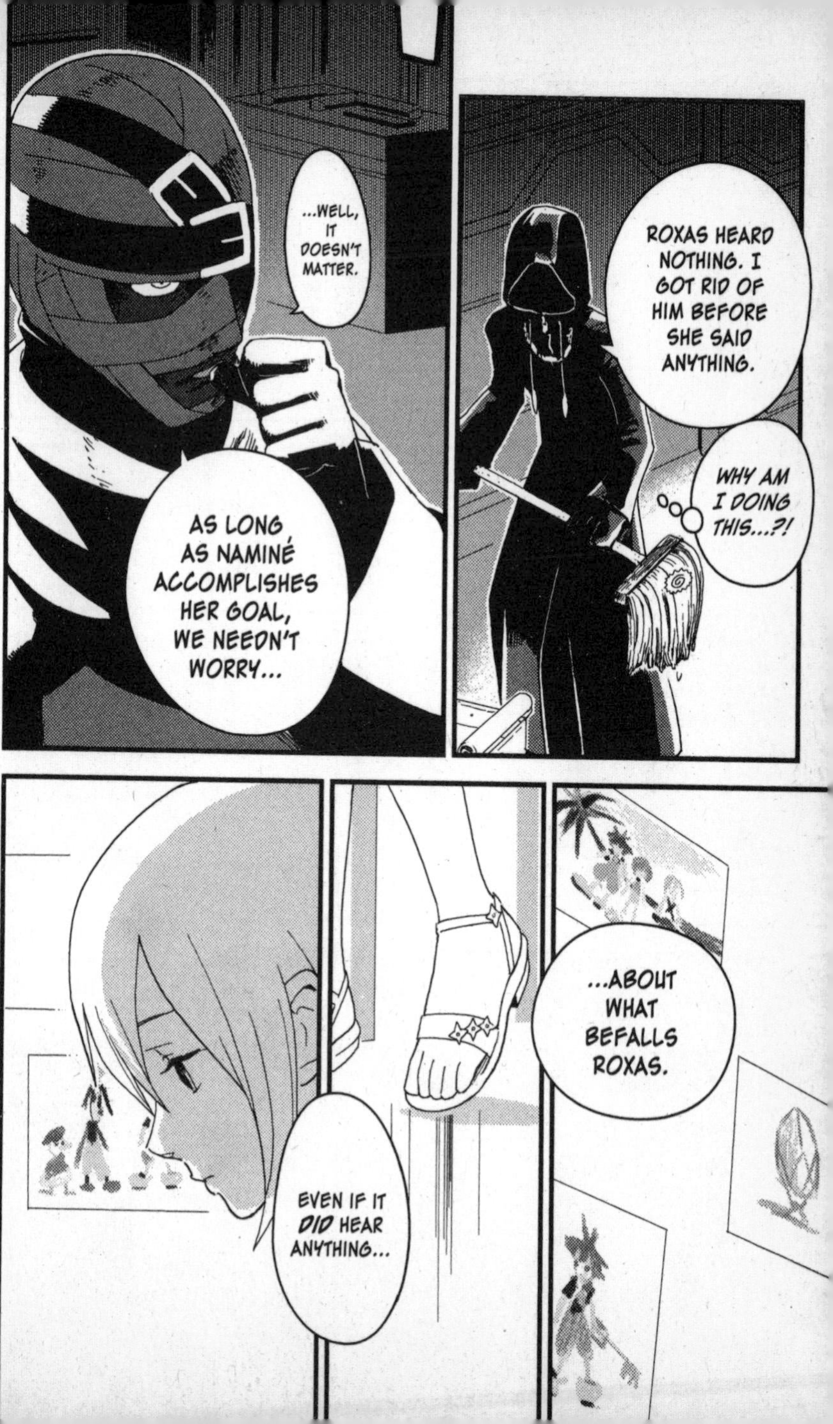
ROXAS HEARD NOTHING. I GOT RID OF HIM BEFORE SHE SAID ANYTHING.
WHY AM I DOING THIS...?!
...WELL, IT DOESN'T MATTER.
AS LONG AS NAMINÉ ACCOMPLISHES HER GOAL, WE NEEDN'T WORRY...
...ABOUT WHAT BEFALLS ROXAS.
EVEN IF IT DID HEAR ANYTHING...

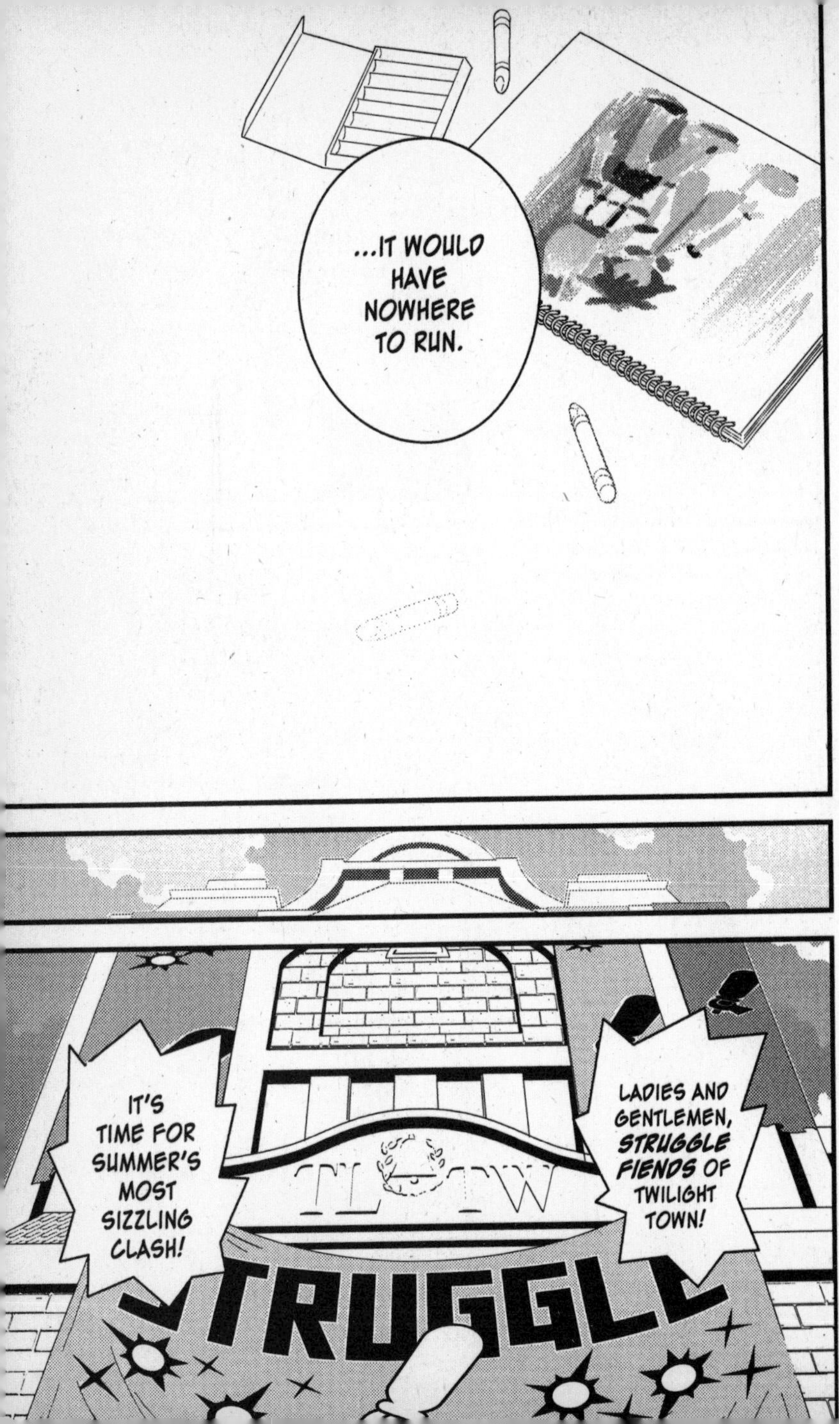
...IT WOULD HAVE NOWHERE TO RUN.
LADIES AND GENTLEMEN, ***STRUGGLE FIENDS*** OF TWILIGHT TOWN!
IT'S TIME FOR SUMMER'S MOST SIZZLING CLASH!

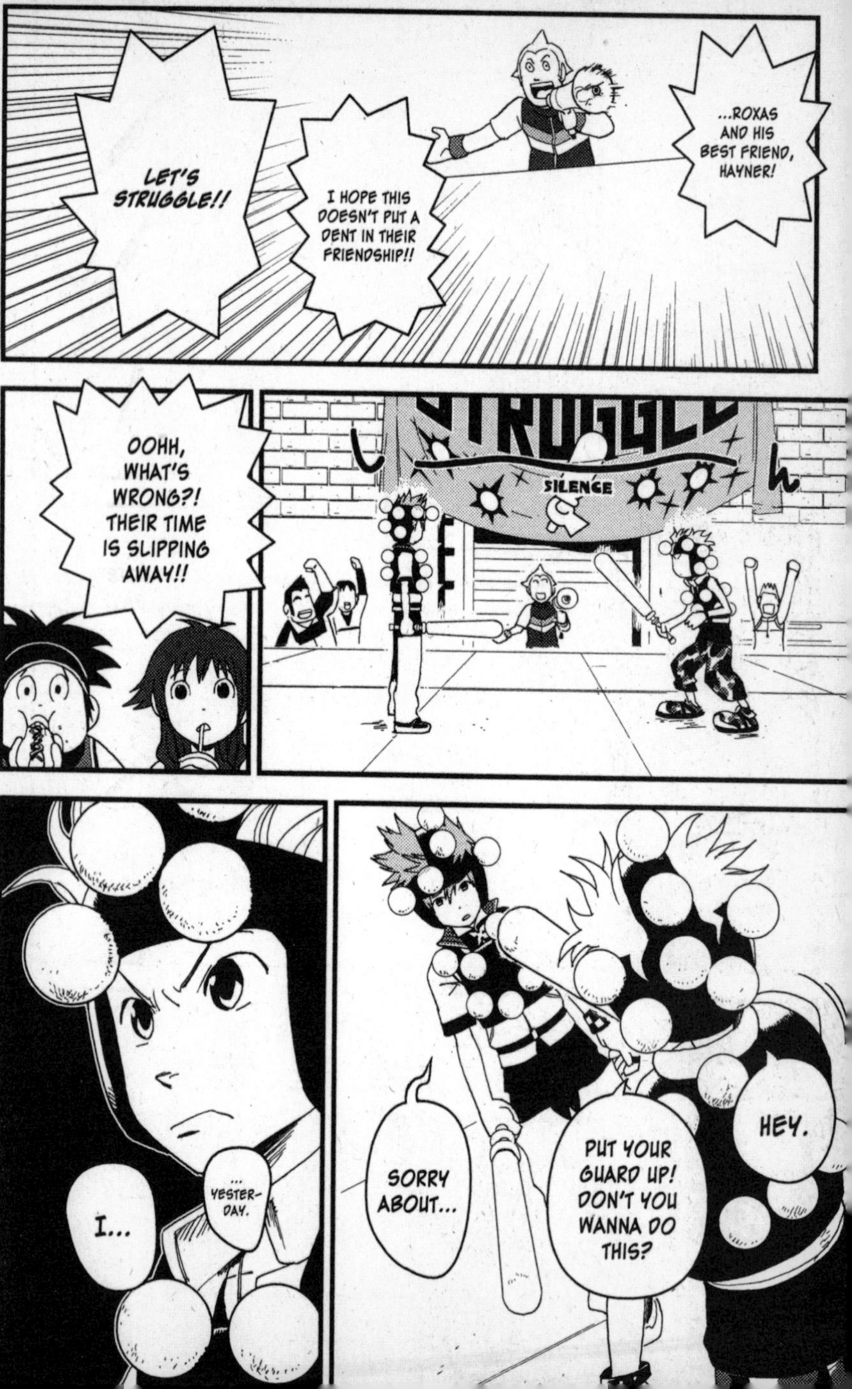
...ROXAS AND HIS BEST FRIEND, HAYNER!
I HOPE THIS DOESN'T PUT A DENT IN THEIR FRIENDSHIP!!
LET'S STRUGGLE!!
SILENCE
OOHH, WHAT'S WRONG?! THEIR TIME IS SLIPPING AWAY!!
HEY.
PUT YOUR GUARD UP! DON'T YOU WANNA DO THIS?
SORRY ABOUT...
...YESTER-DAY.
I...

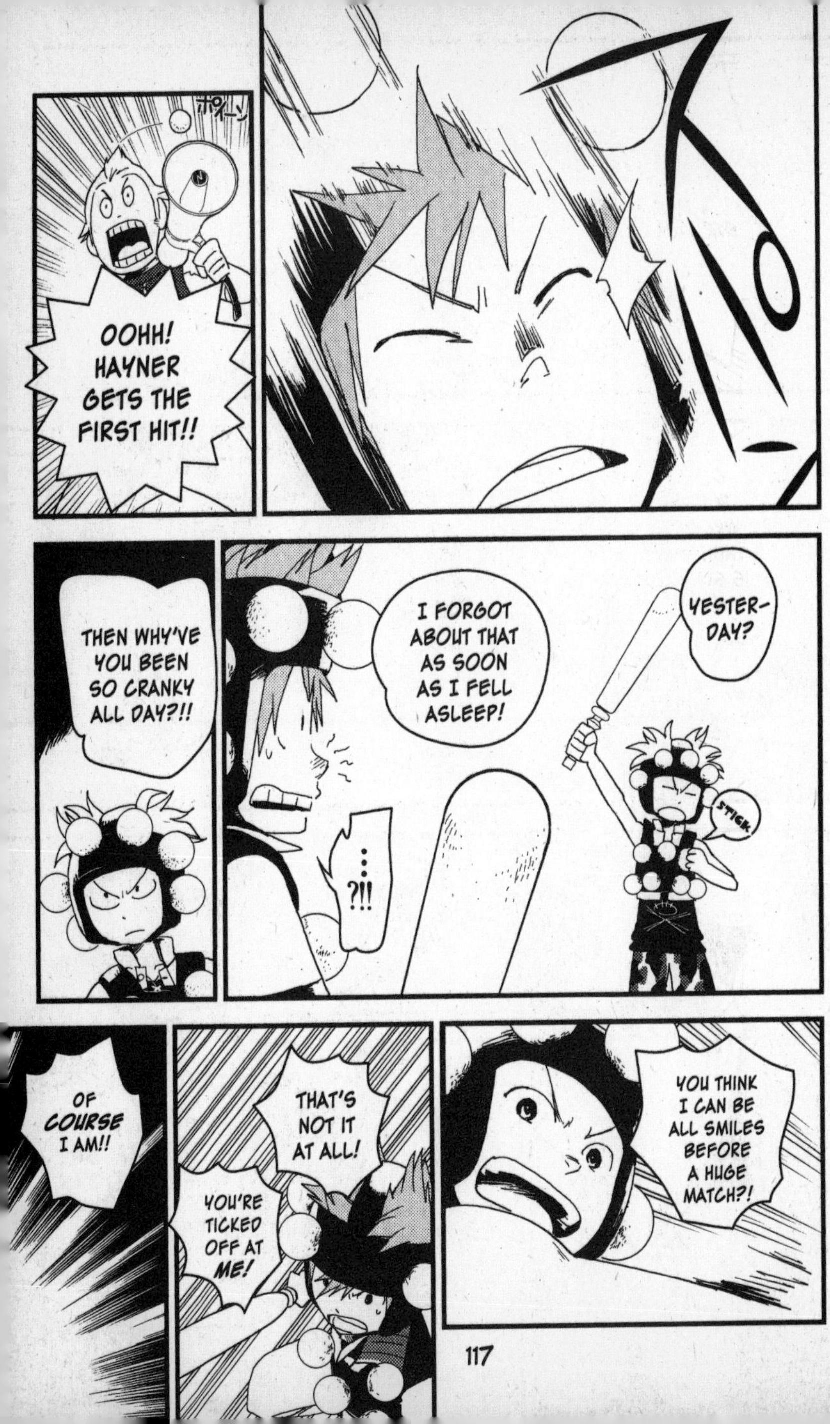
OOHH! HAYNER GETS THE FIRST HIT!!
YESTER-DAY?
STICK
I FORGOT ABOUT THAT AS SOON AS I FELL ASLEEP!
...?!!
THEN WHY'VE YOU BEEN SO CRANKY ALL DAY?!!
YOU THINK I CAN BE ALL SMILES BEFORE A HUGE MATCH?!
THAT'S NOT IT AT ALL!
YOU'RE TICKED OFF AT ME!
OF COURSE I AM!!

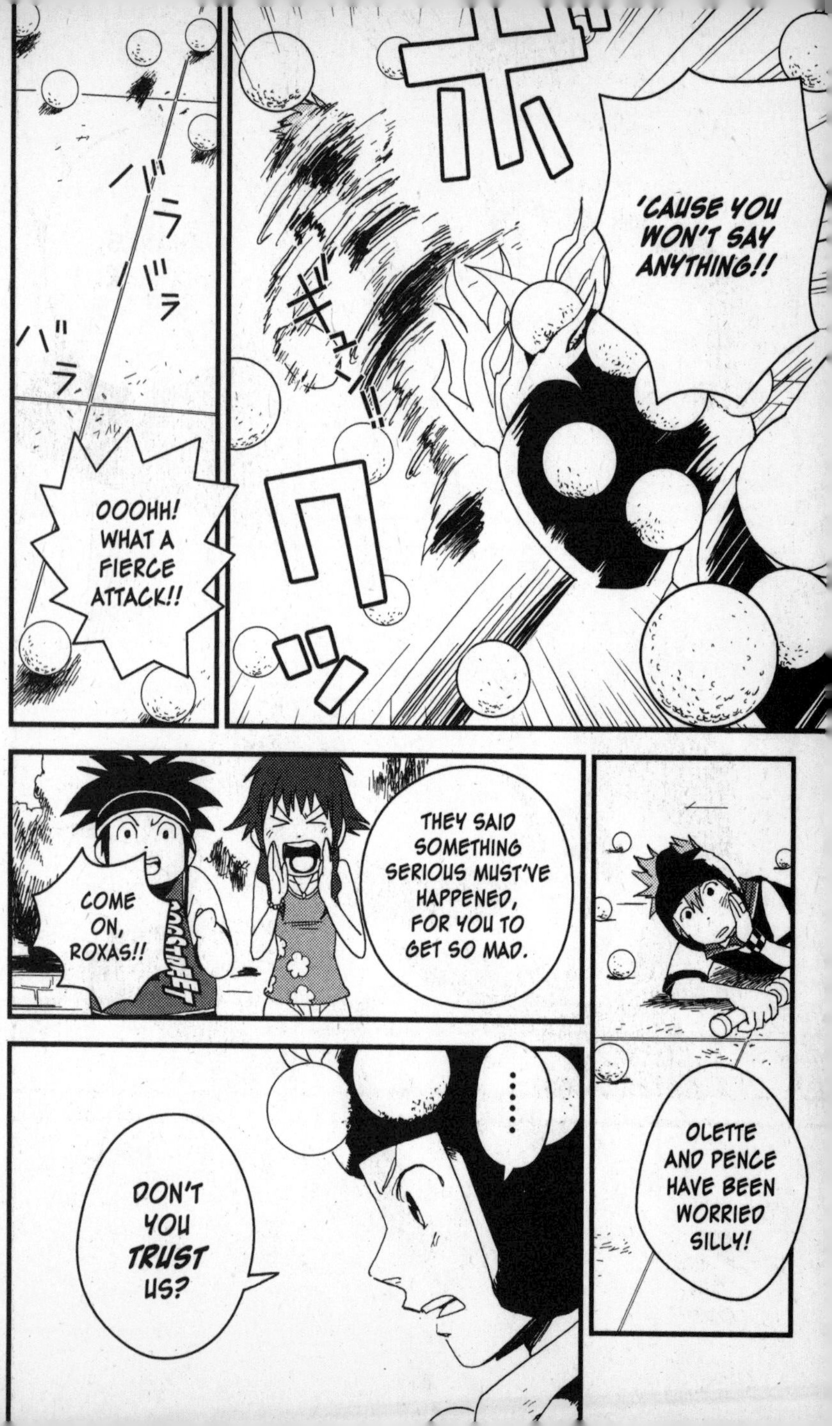
'CAUSE YOU WON'T SAY ANYTHING!!
OOOHH! WHAT A FIERCE ATTACK!!
OLETTE AND PENCE HAVE BEEN WORRIED SILLY!
THEY SAID SOMETHING SERIOUS MUST'VE HAPPENED, FOR YOU TO GET SO MAD.
COME ON, ROXAS!!
......
DON'T YOU TRUST US?

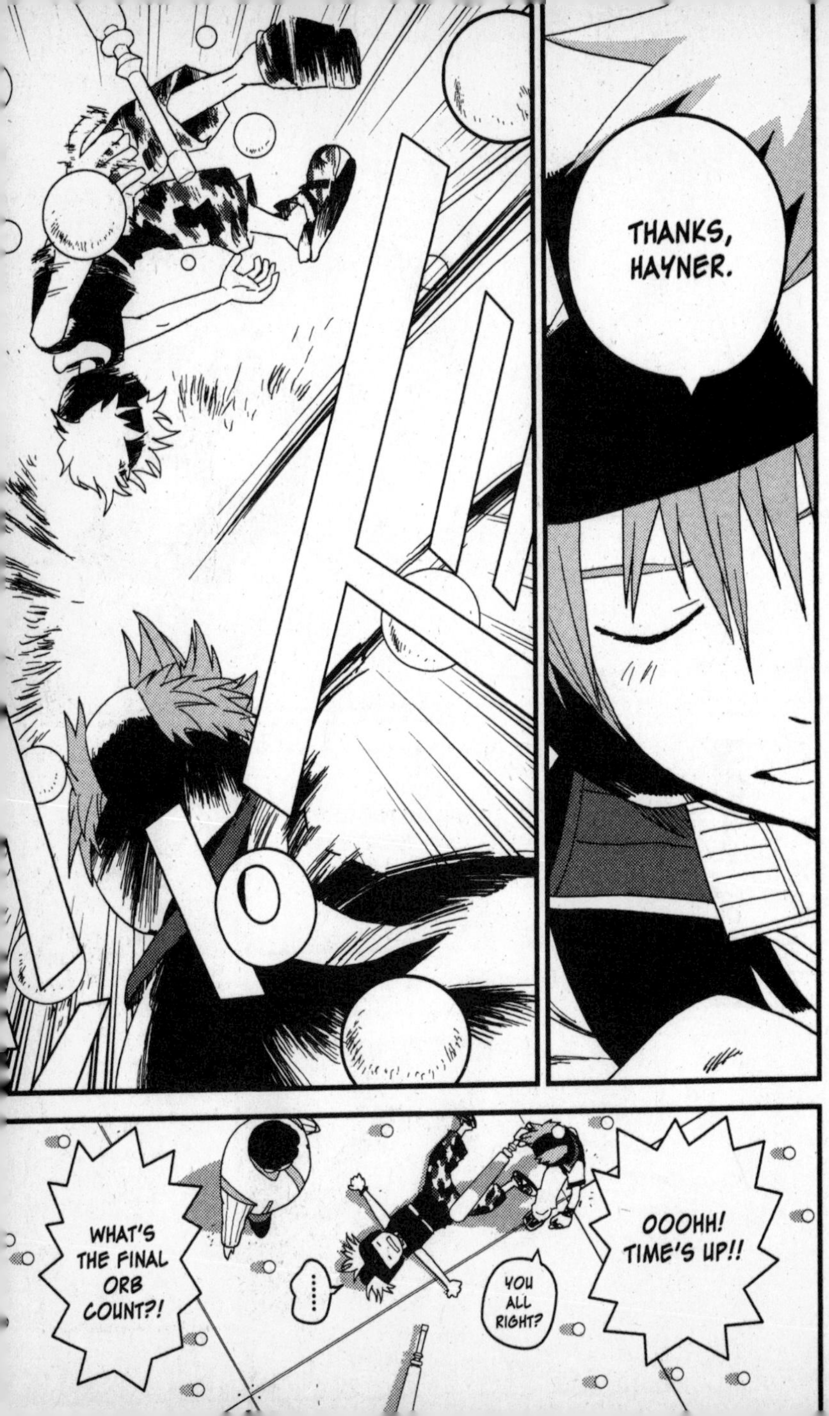
THANKS, HAYNER.
OOOHH! TIME'S UP!!
YOU ALL RIGHT?
......
WHAT'S THE FINAL ORB COUNT?!

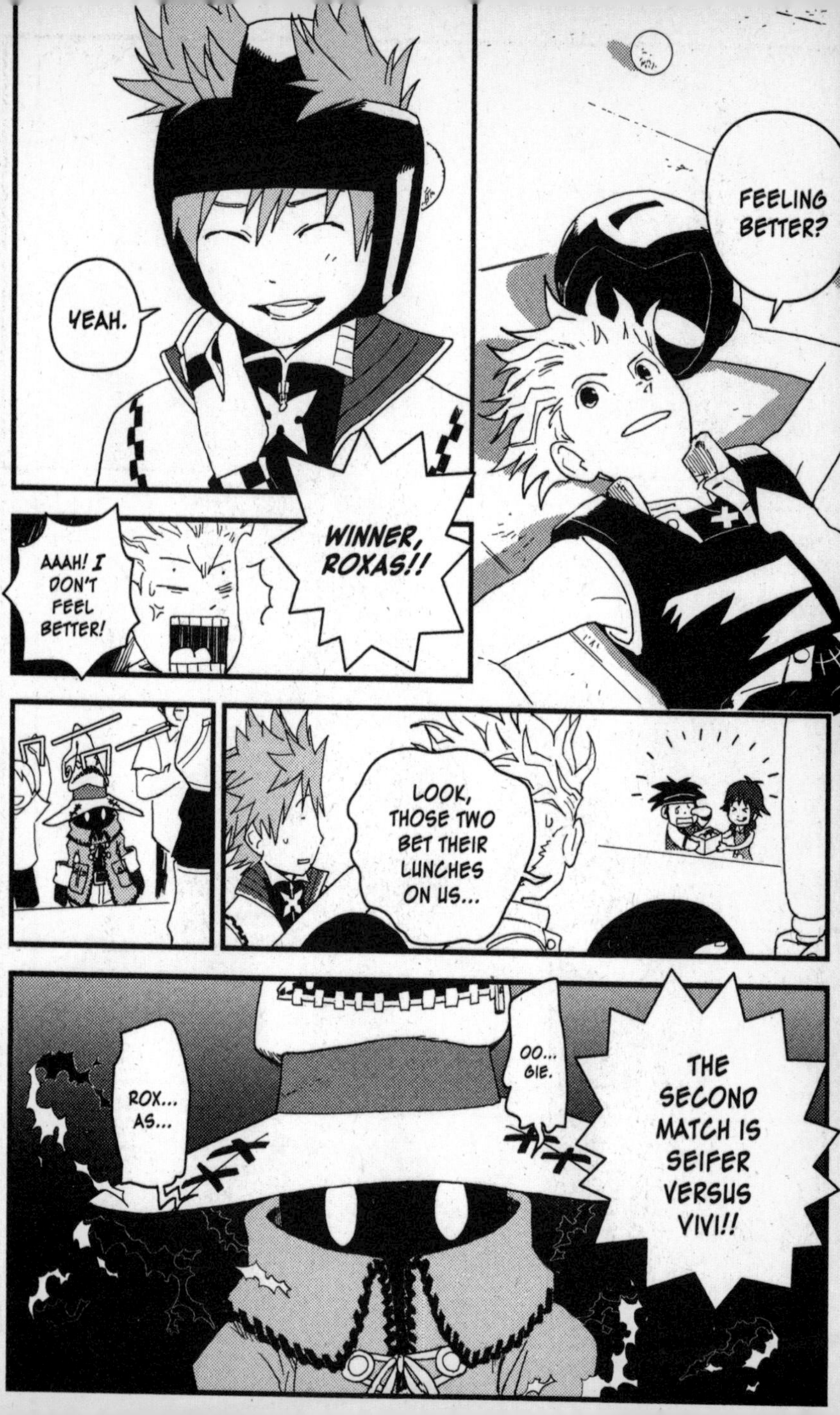
FEELING BETTER?
YEAH.
WINNER, ROXAS!!
AAAH! I DON'T FEEL BETTER!
LOOK, THOSE TWO BET THEIR LUNCHES ON US...
THE SECOND MATCH IS SEIFER VERSUS VIVI!!
OO... GIE.
ROX... AS...

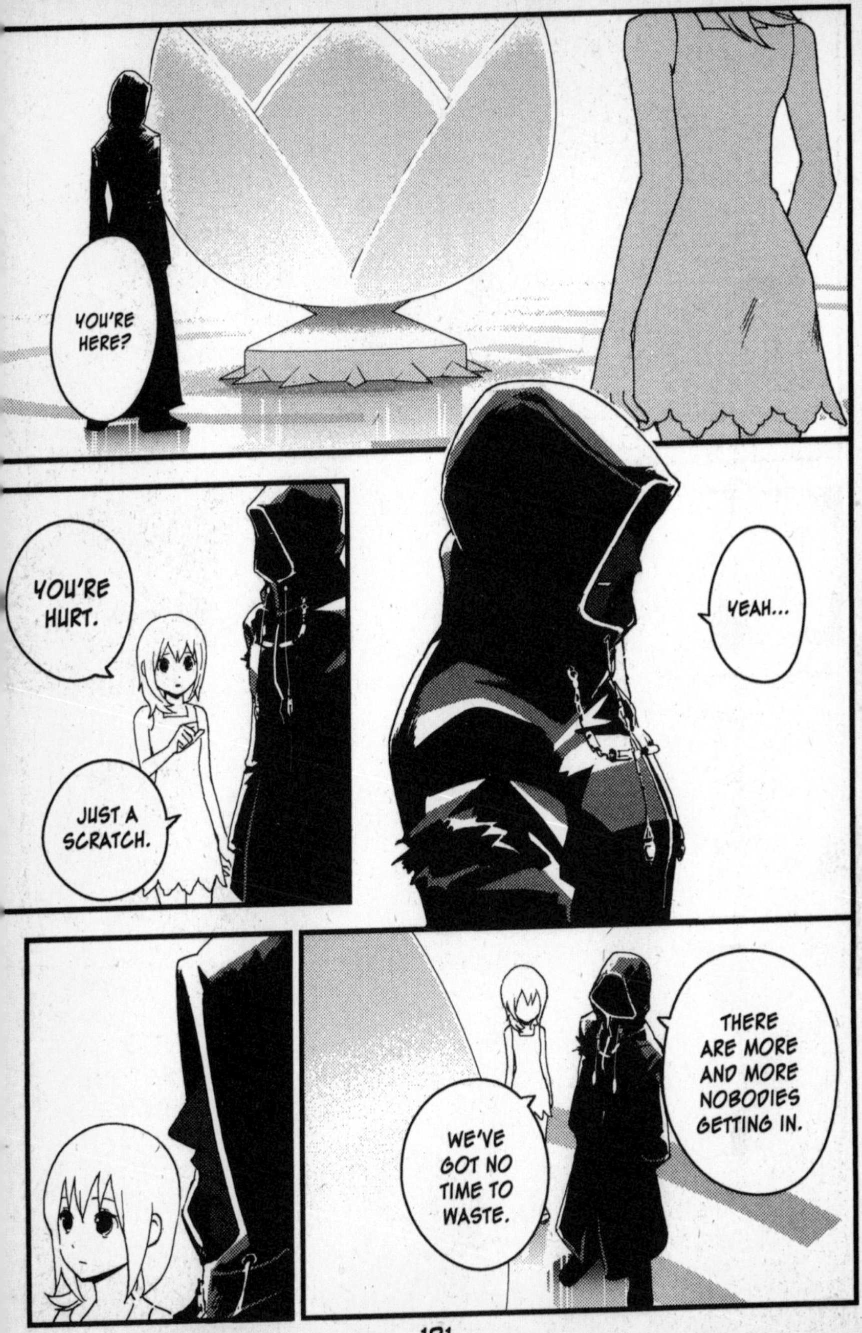
YOU'RE HERE?
YEAH...
YOU'RE HURT.
JUST A SCRATCH.
THERE ARE MORE AND MORE NOBODIES GETTING IN.
WE'VE GOT NO TIME TO WASTE.

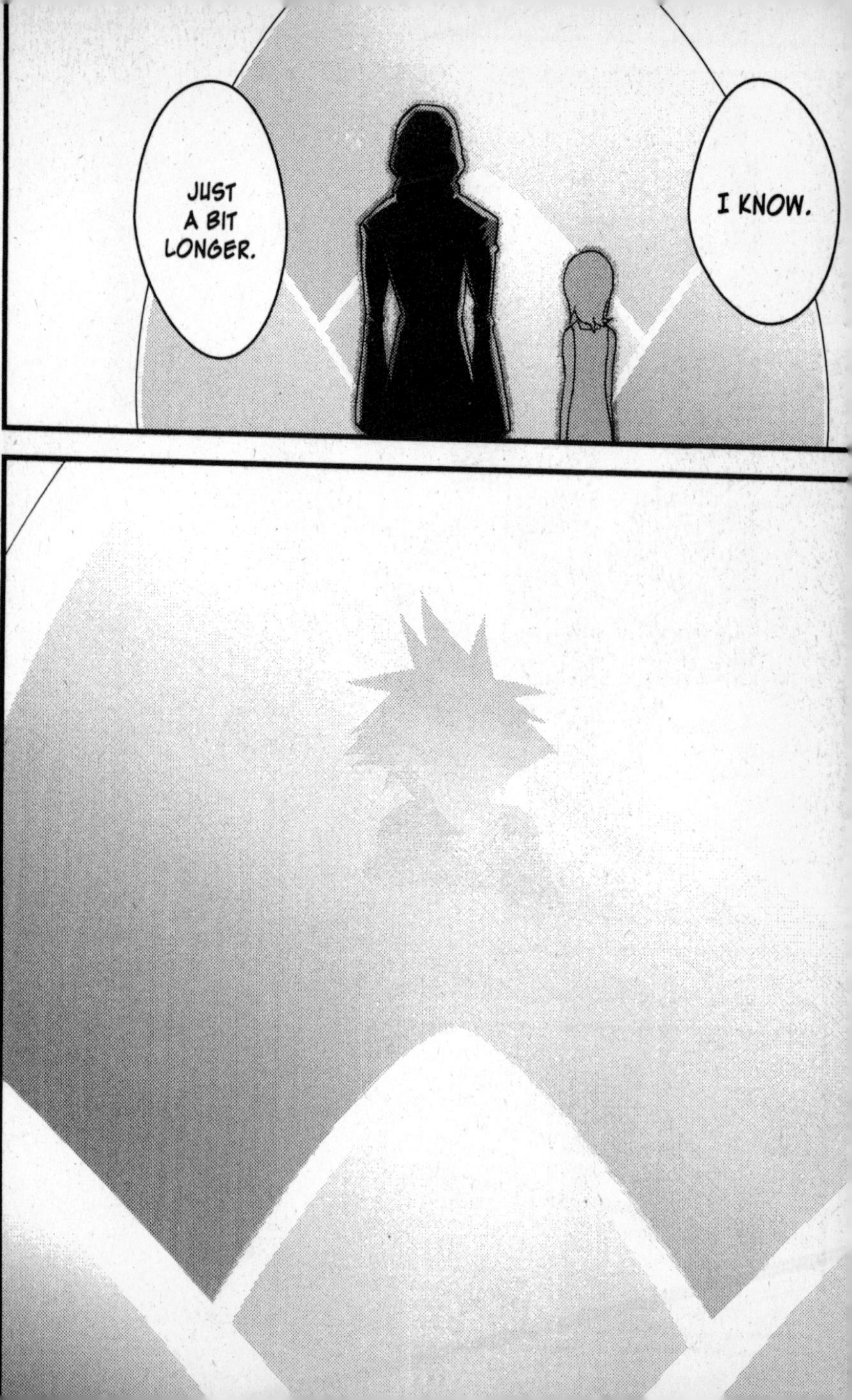
JUST A BIT LONGER.
I KNOW.

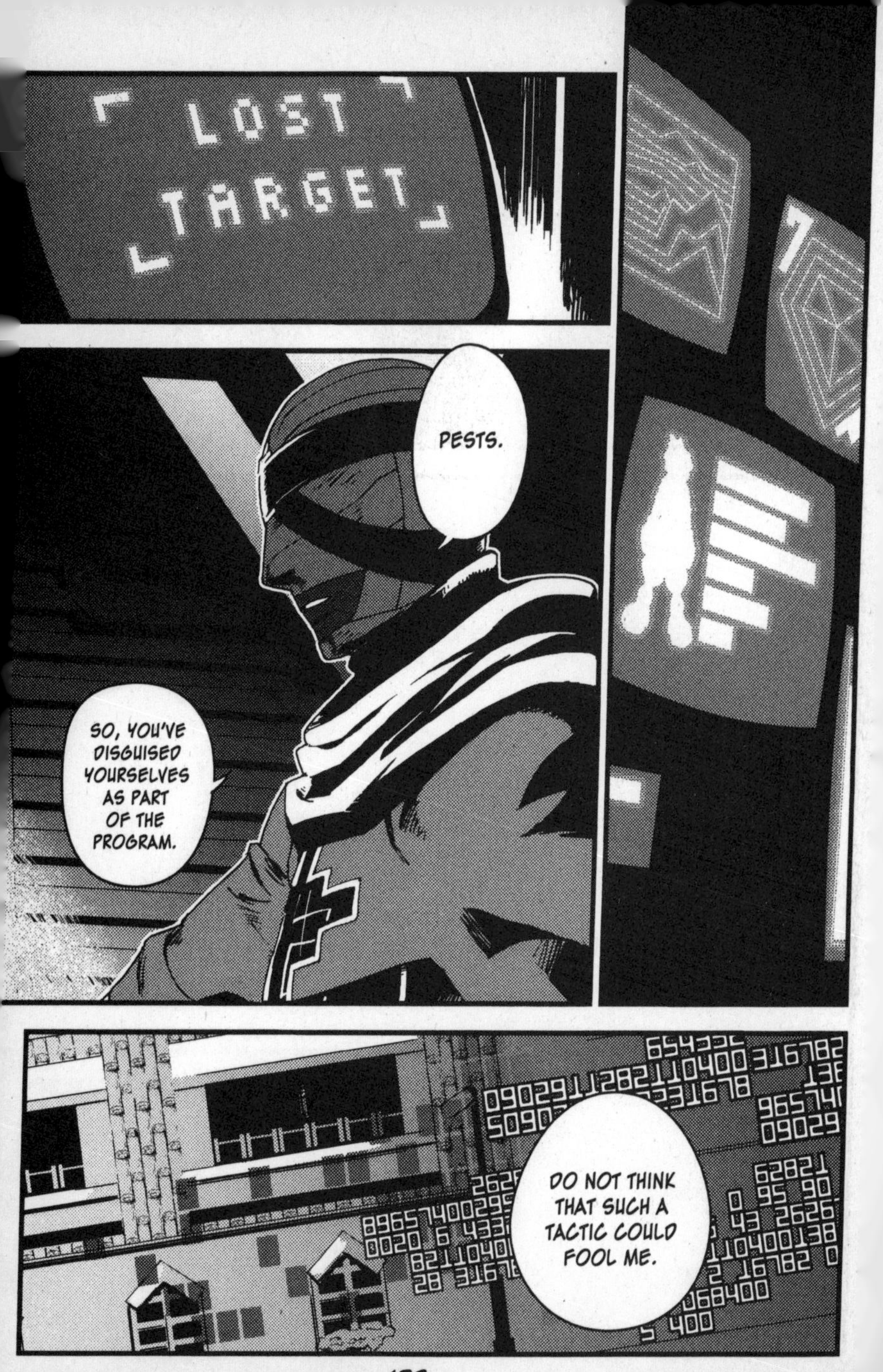
LOST TARGET
PESTS.
SO, YOU'VE DISGUISED YOURSELVES AS PART OF THE PROGRAM.
DO NOT THINK THAT SUCH A TACTIC COULD FOOL ME.

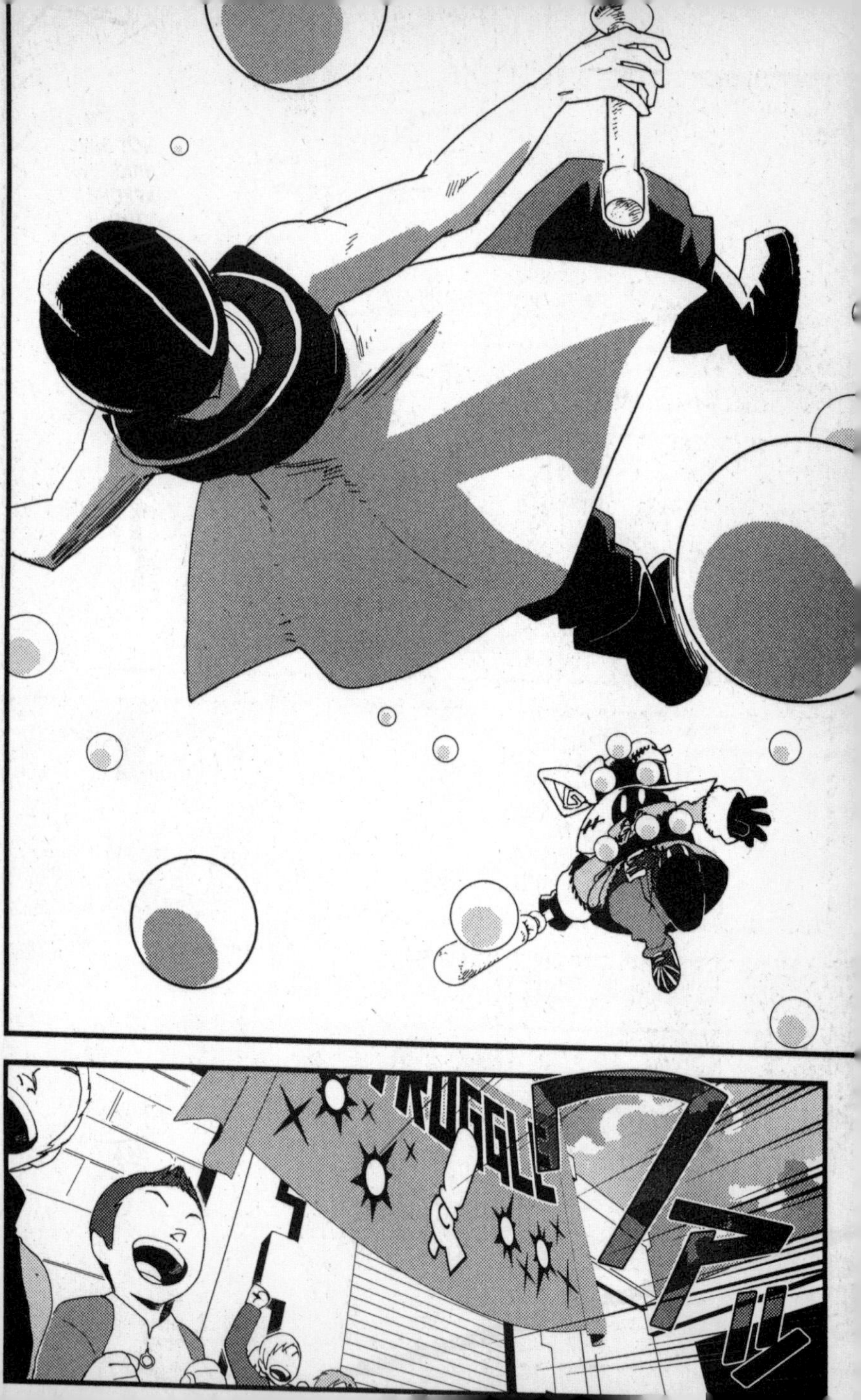
RUGGLE

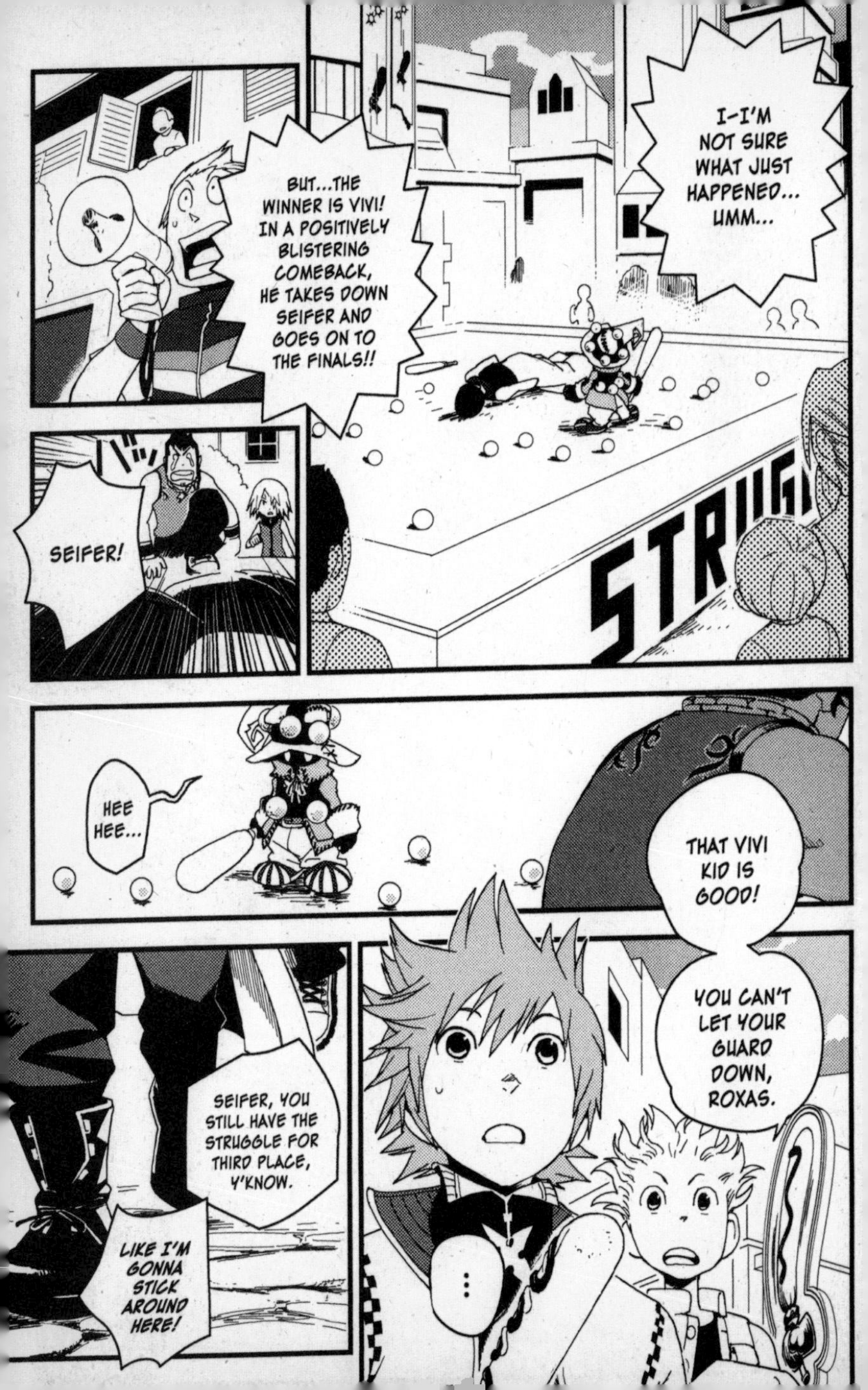
I-I'M NOT SURE WHAT JUST HAPPENED... UMM...
BUT...THE WINNER IS VIVI! IN A POSITIVELY BLISTERING COMEBACK, HE TAKES DOWN SEIFER AND GOES ON TO THE FINALS!!
SEIFER!
STRUG
HEE HEE...
THAT VIVI KID IS GOOD!
YOU CAN'T LET YOUR GUARD DOWN, ROXAS.
...
SEIFER, YOU STILL HAVE THE STRUGGLE FOR THIRD PLACE, Y'KNOW.
LIKE I'M GONNA STICK AROUND HERE!

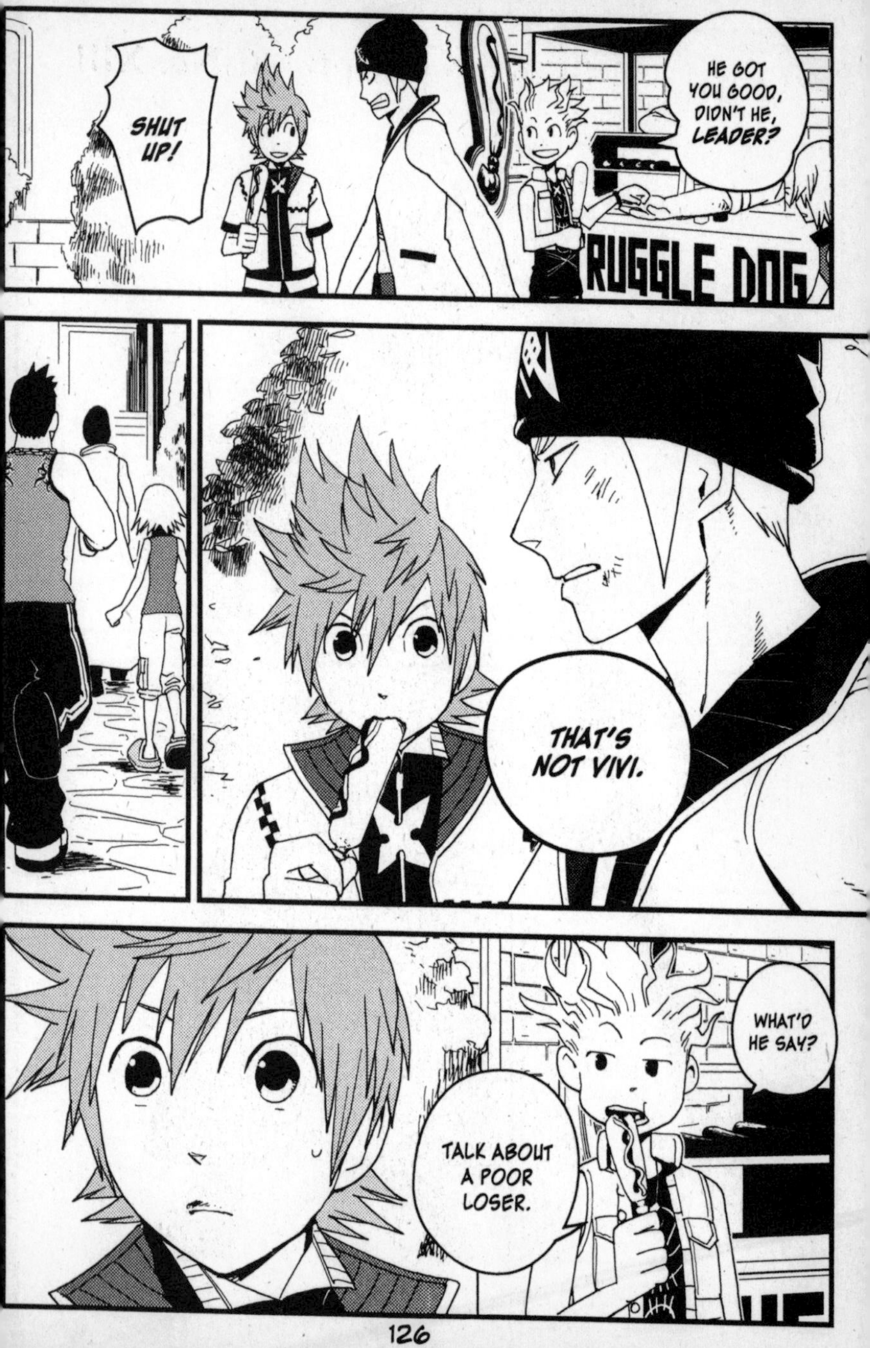
HE GOT YOU GOOD, DIDN'T HE, LEADER?
SHUT UP!
RUGGLE DOG
THAT'S NOT VIVI.
WHAT'D HE SAY?
TALK ABOUT A POOR LOSER.

# Chapter 5: No. XIII

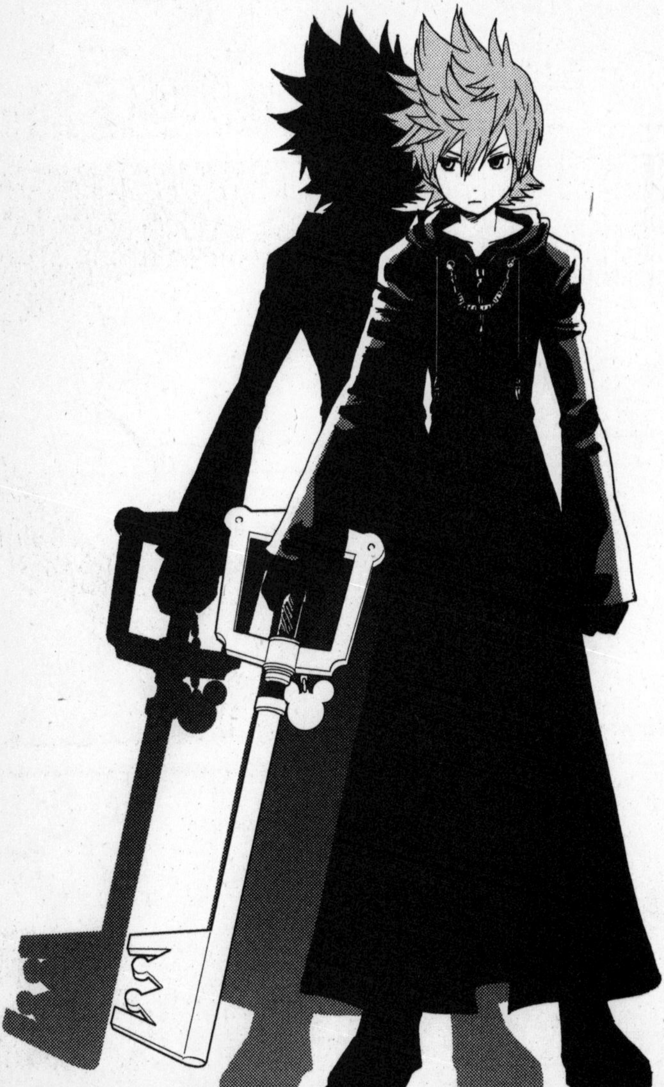

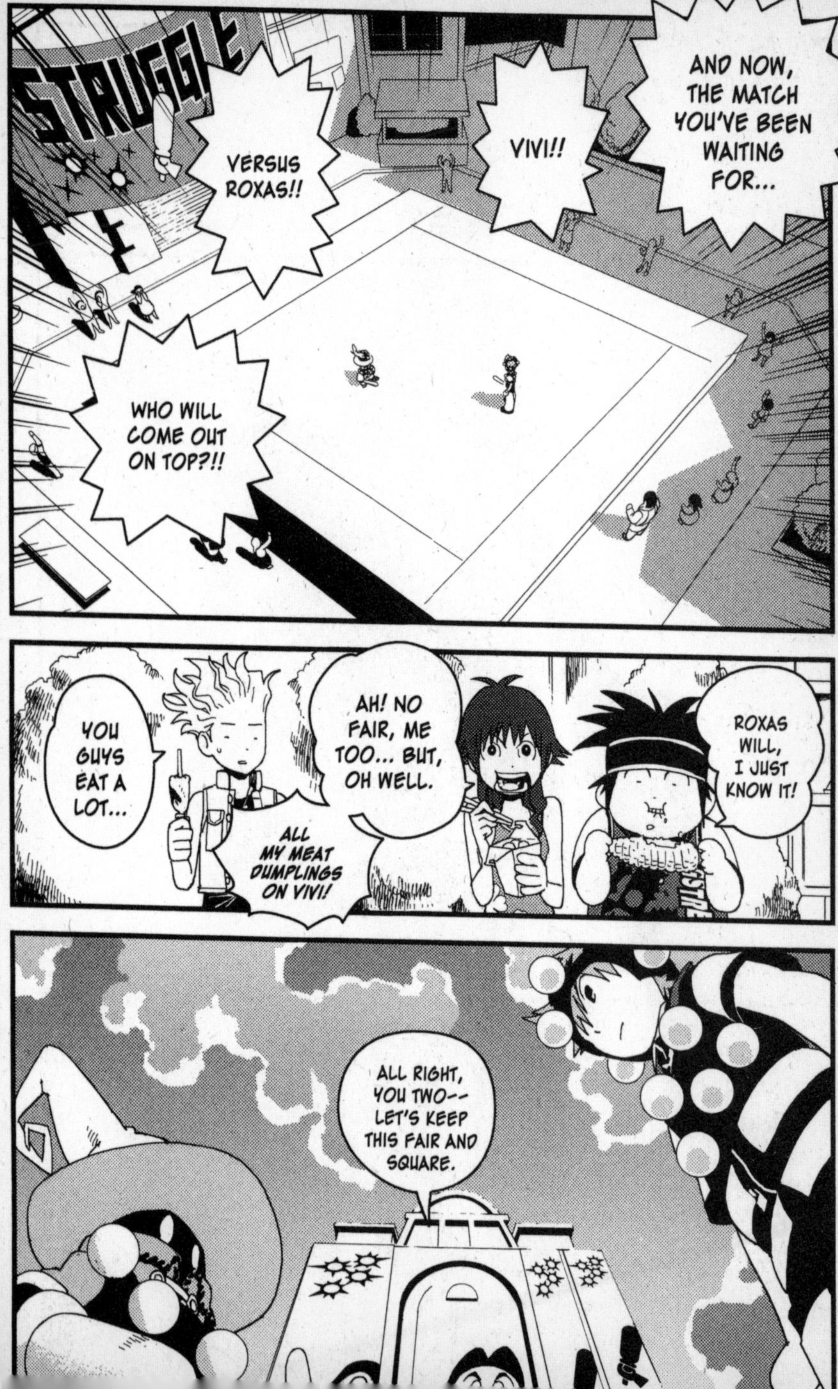
STRUGGLE
AND NOW, THE MATCH YOU'VE BEEN WAITING FOR...
VIVI!!
VERSUS ROXAS!!
WHO WILL COME OUT ON TOP?!!
ROXAS WILL, I JUST KNOW IT!
AH! NO FAIR, ME TOO... BUT, OH WELL.
ALL MY MEAT DUMPLINGS ON VIVI!
YOU GUYS EAT A LOT...
ALL RIGHT, YOU TWO-- LET'S KEEP THIS FAIR AND SQUARE.

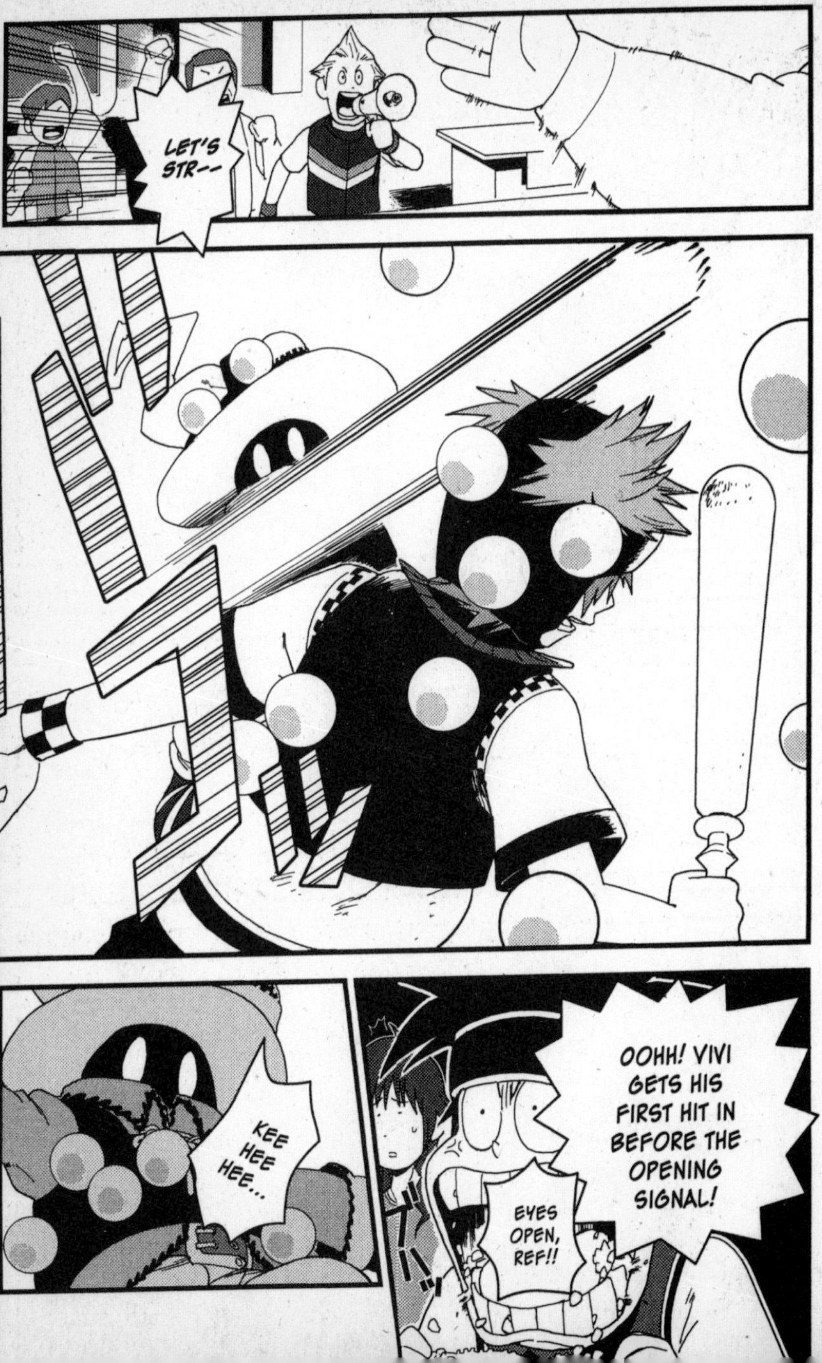
LET'S STR--
OOHH! VIVI GETS HIS FIRST HIT IN BEFORE THE OPENING SIGNAL!
EYES OPEN, REF!!
KEE HEE HEE...

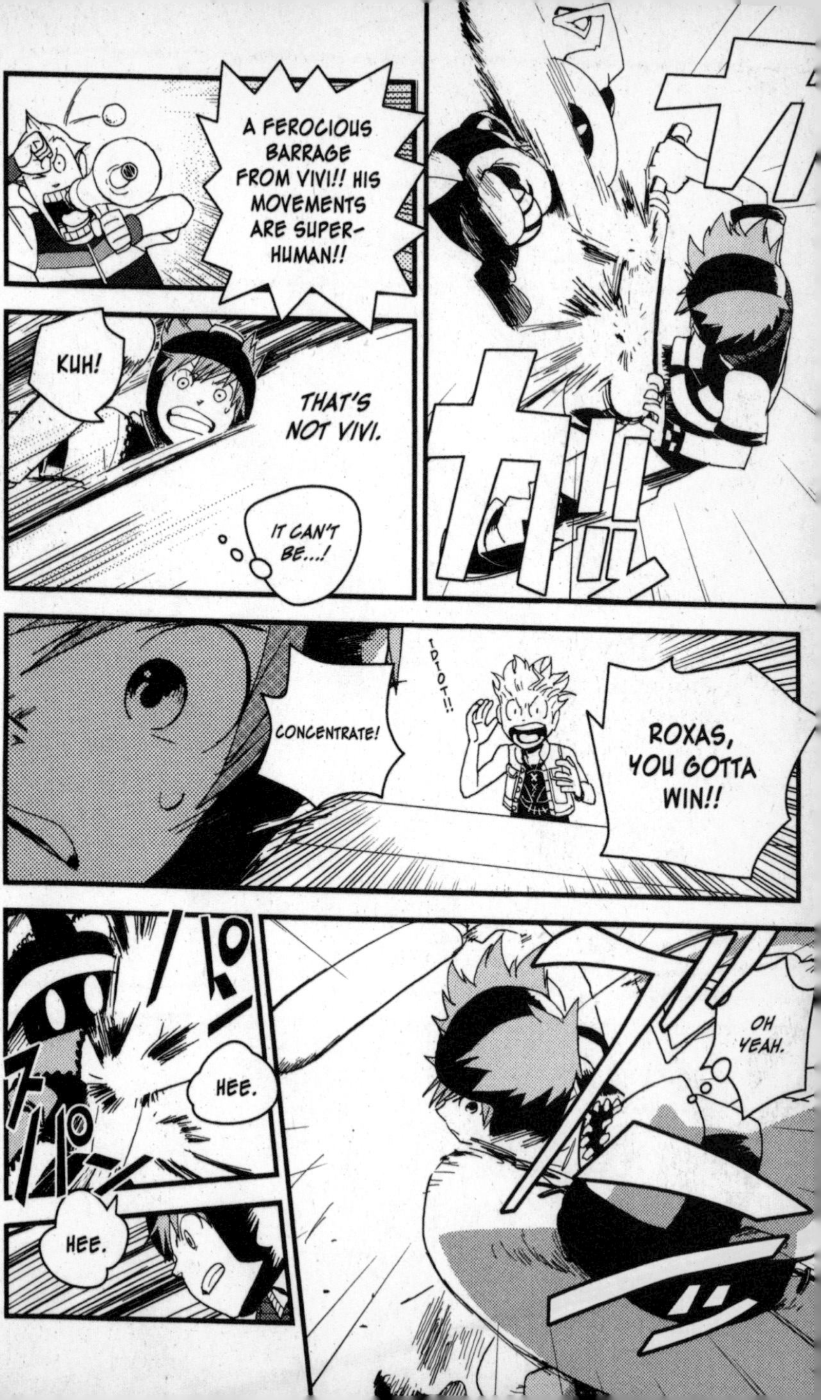
A FEROCIOUS BARRAGE FROM VIVI!! HIS MOVEMENTS ARE SUPER-HUMAN!!
KUH!
THAT'S NOT VIVI.
IT CAN'T BE...!
ROXAS, YOU GOTTA WIN!!
IDIOT!!
CONCENTRATE!
OH YEAH.
HEE.
HEE.

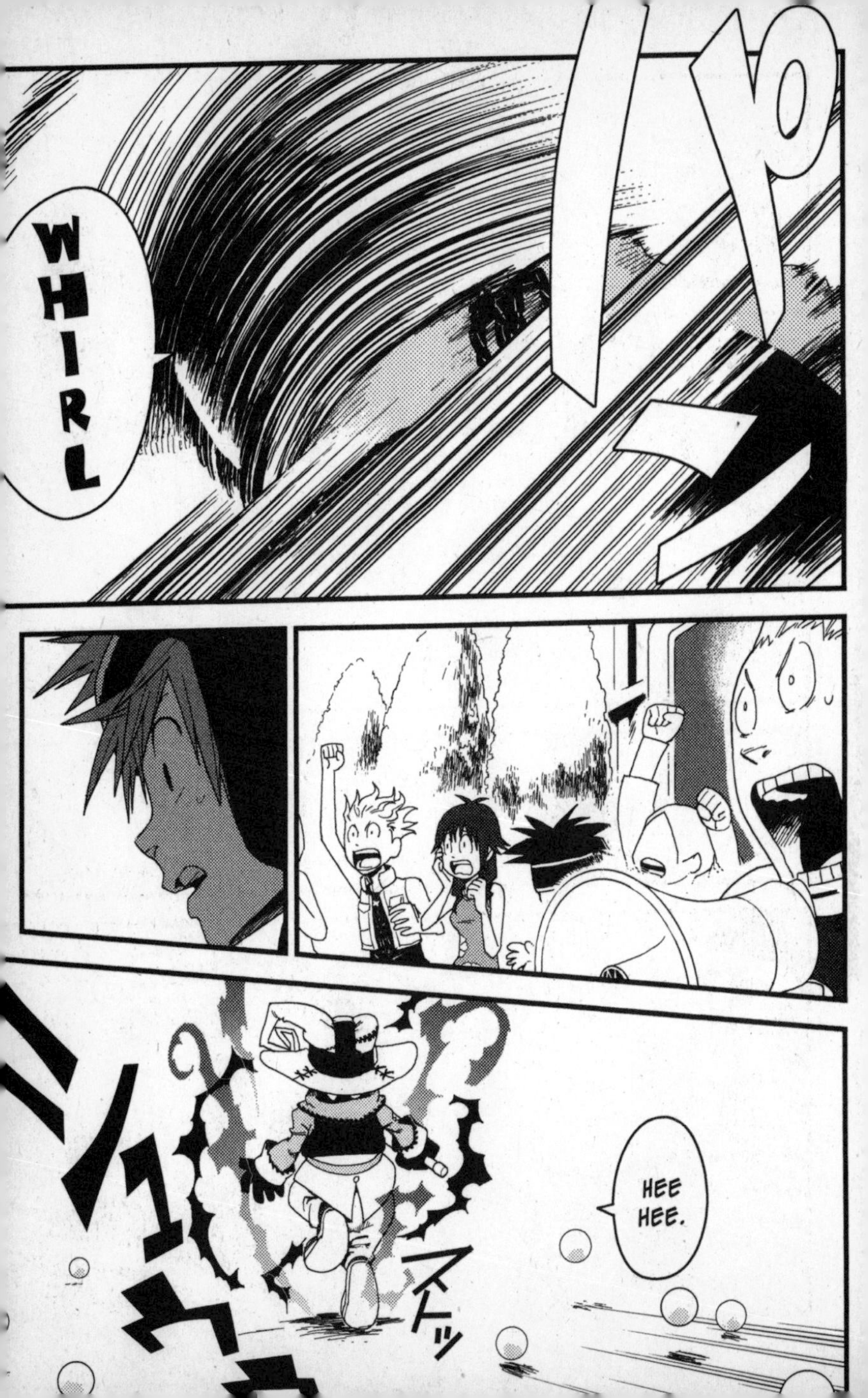
WHIRL
HEE HEE.

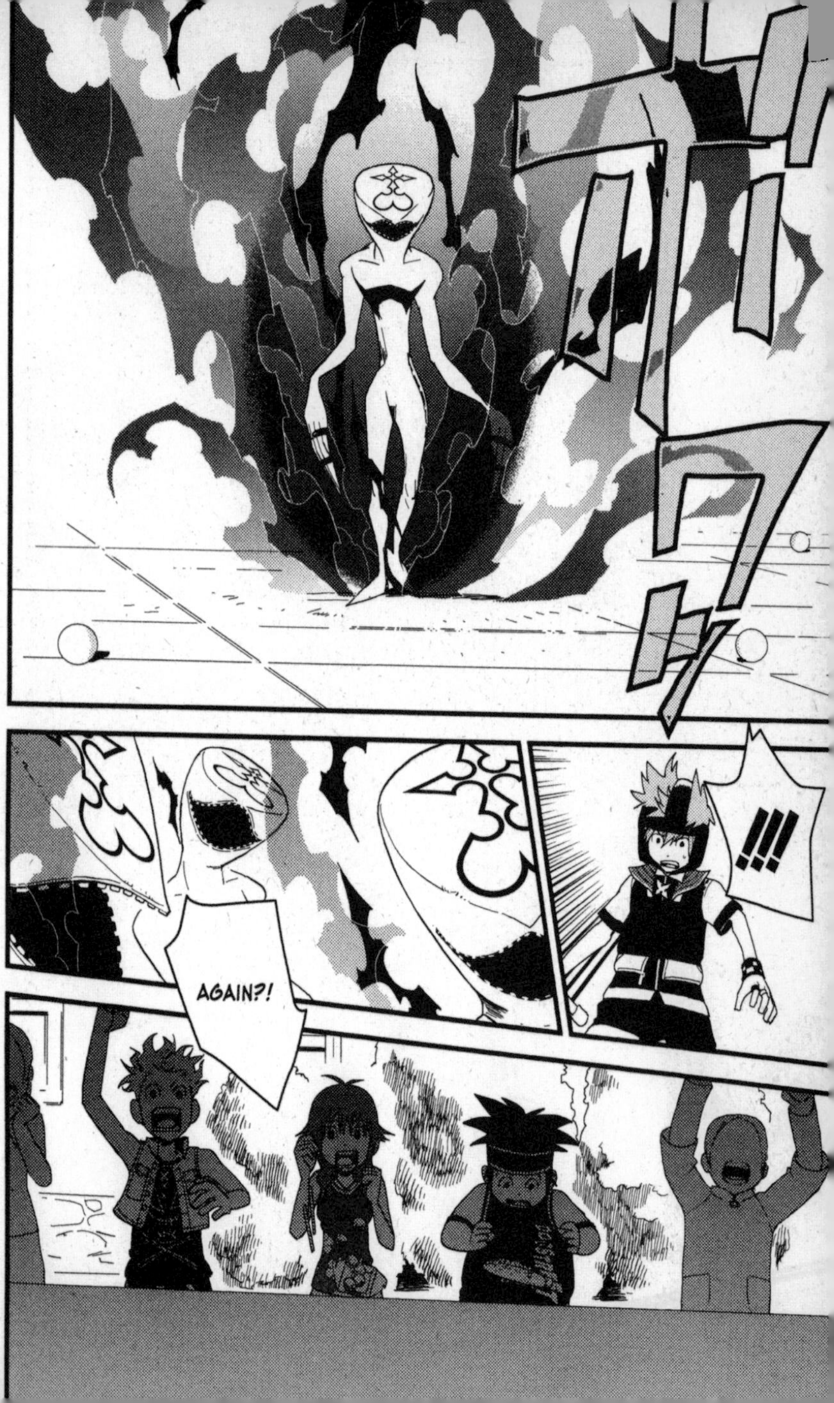
!!!
AGAIN?!

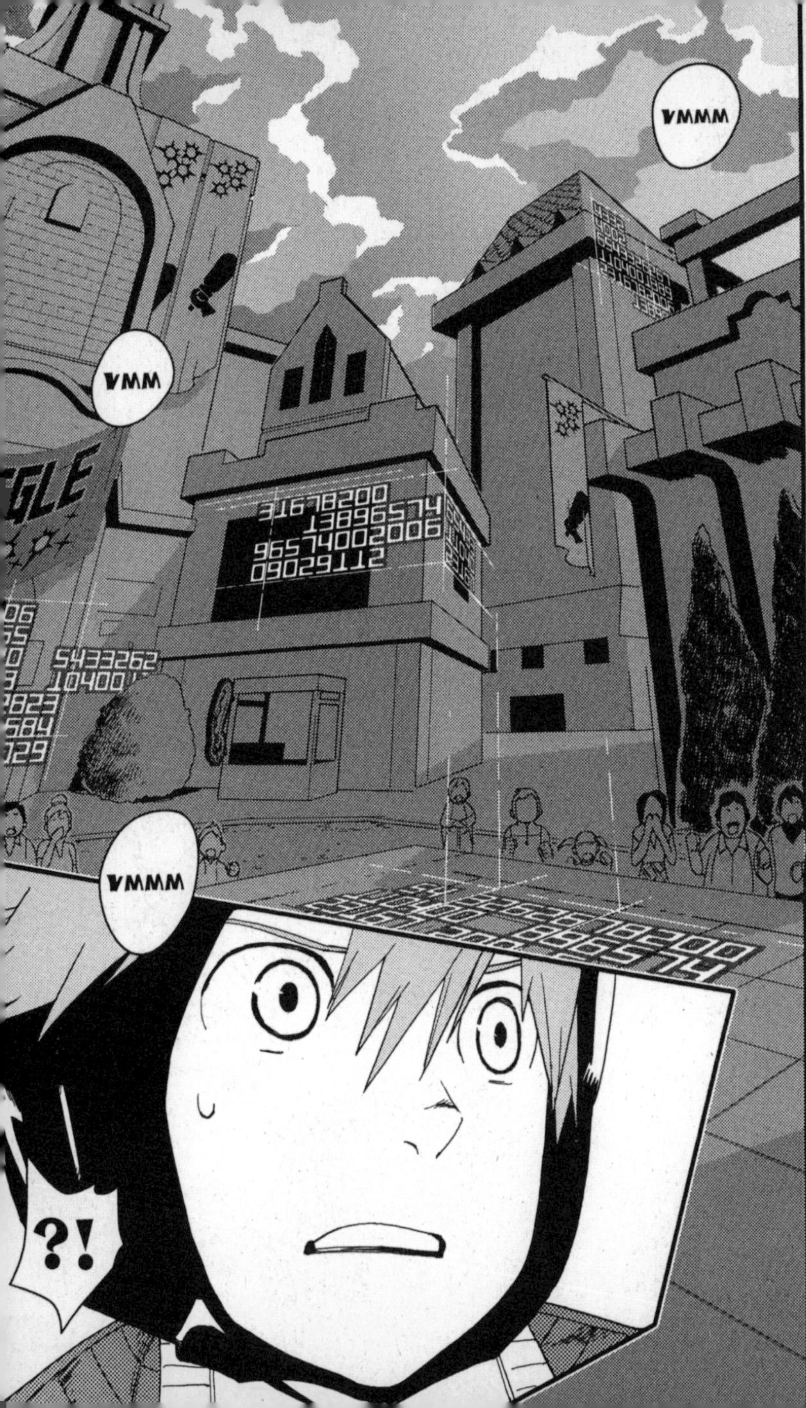
VMMM
VMM
VMMM
?!

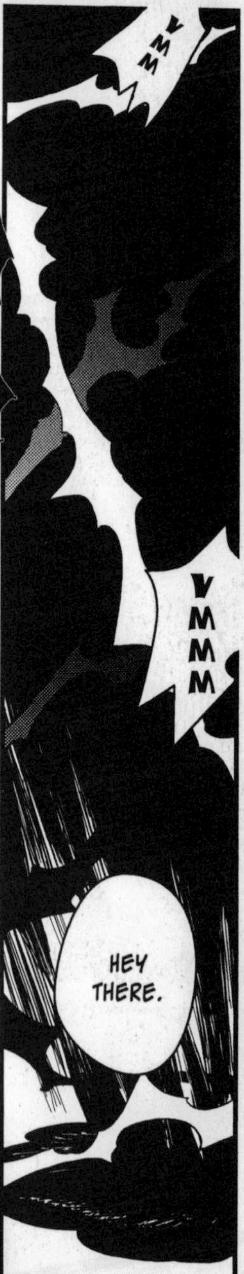
VMM
VMMM
HEY THERE.
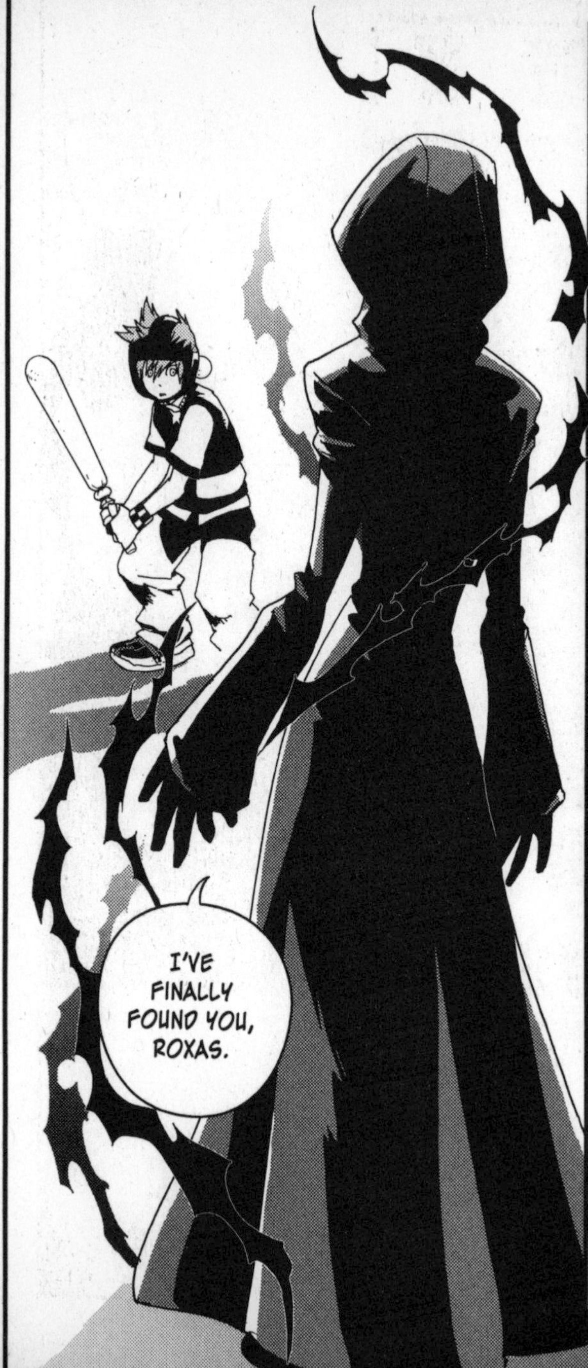
I'VE FINALLY FOUND YOU, ROXAS.

WHO ARE YOU?

MAN, I HAD A HECK OF A TIME GETTING HERE.

YOU REALLY DON'T REMEMBER?

THE GUY WHO TOOK OUR MONEY?

BUT WHAT'S WITH THAT GETUP? IT'S HILARIOUS.

IT'S ME.

YOU KNOW, AXEL.

HMPH.

SO, THE REPORTS WERE TRUE...

ボケー

135

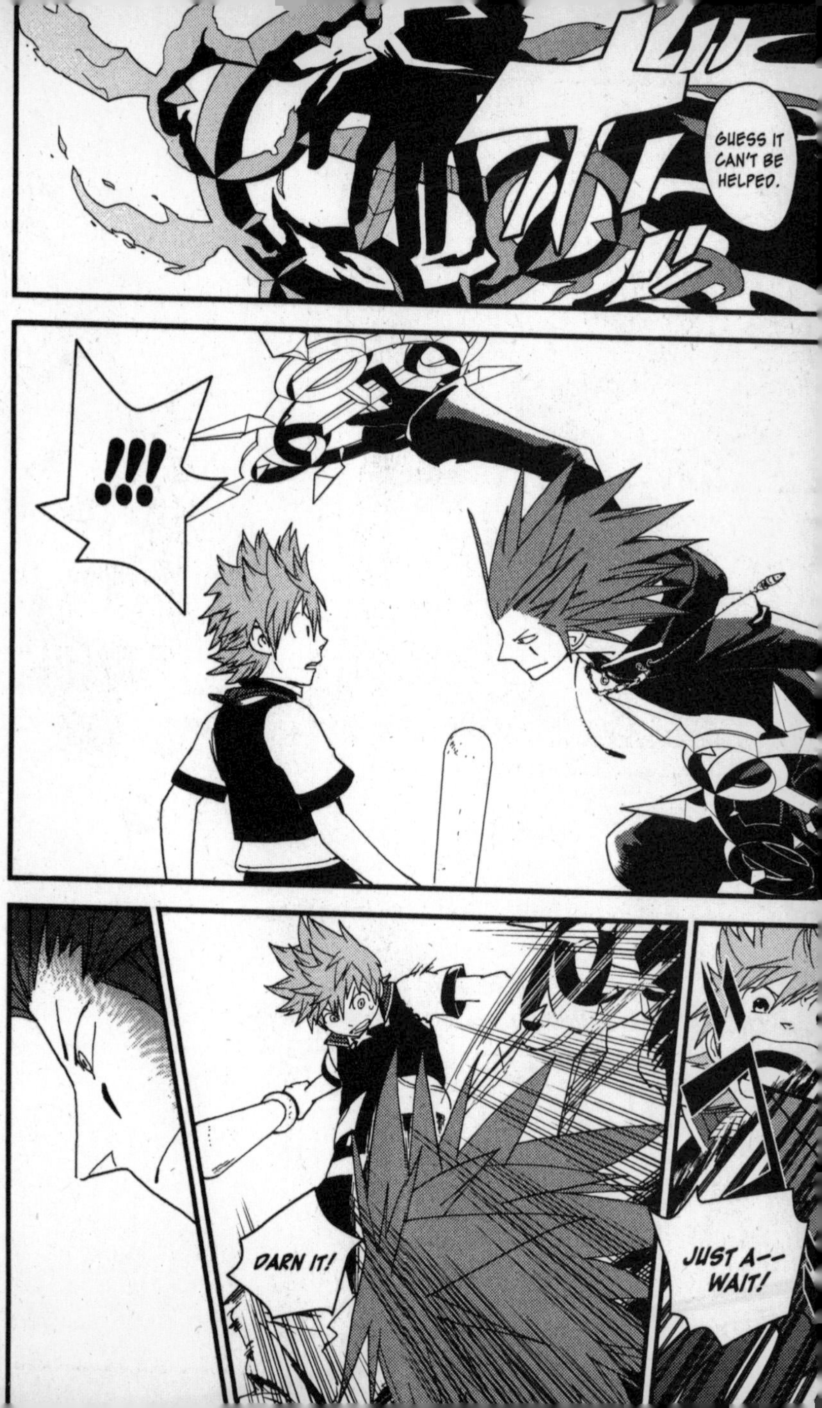
GUESS IT CAN'T BE HELPED.
!!!
JUST A-- WAIT!
DARN IT!

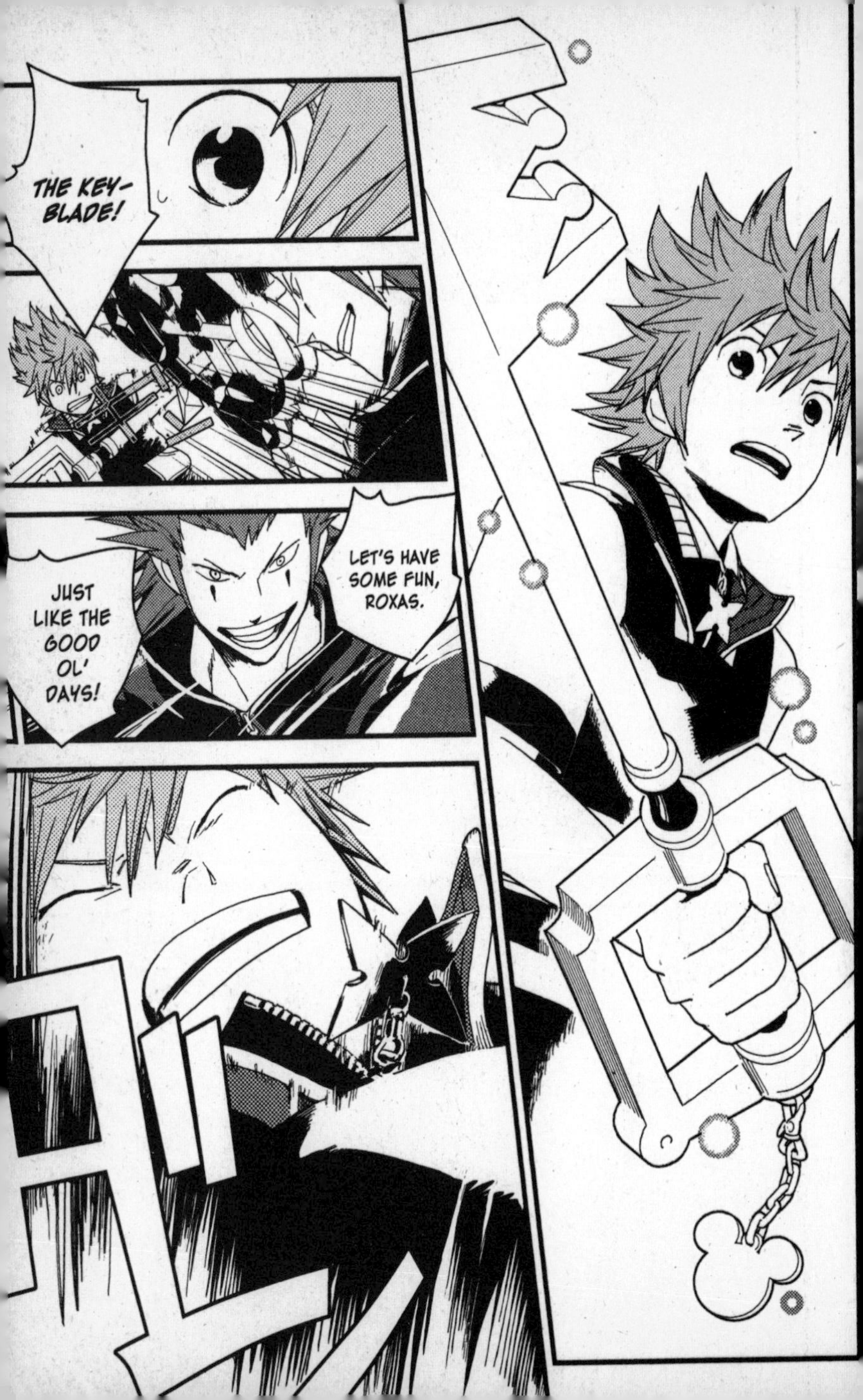
THE KEY-BLADE!
LET'S HAVE SOME FUN, ROXAS.
JUST LIKE THE GOOD OL' DAYS!

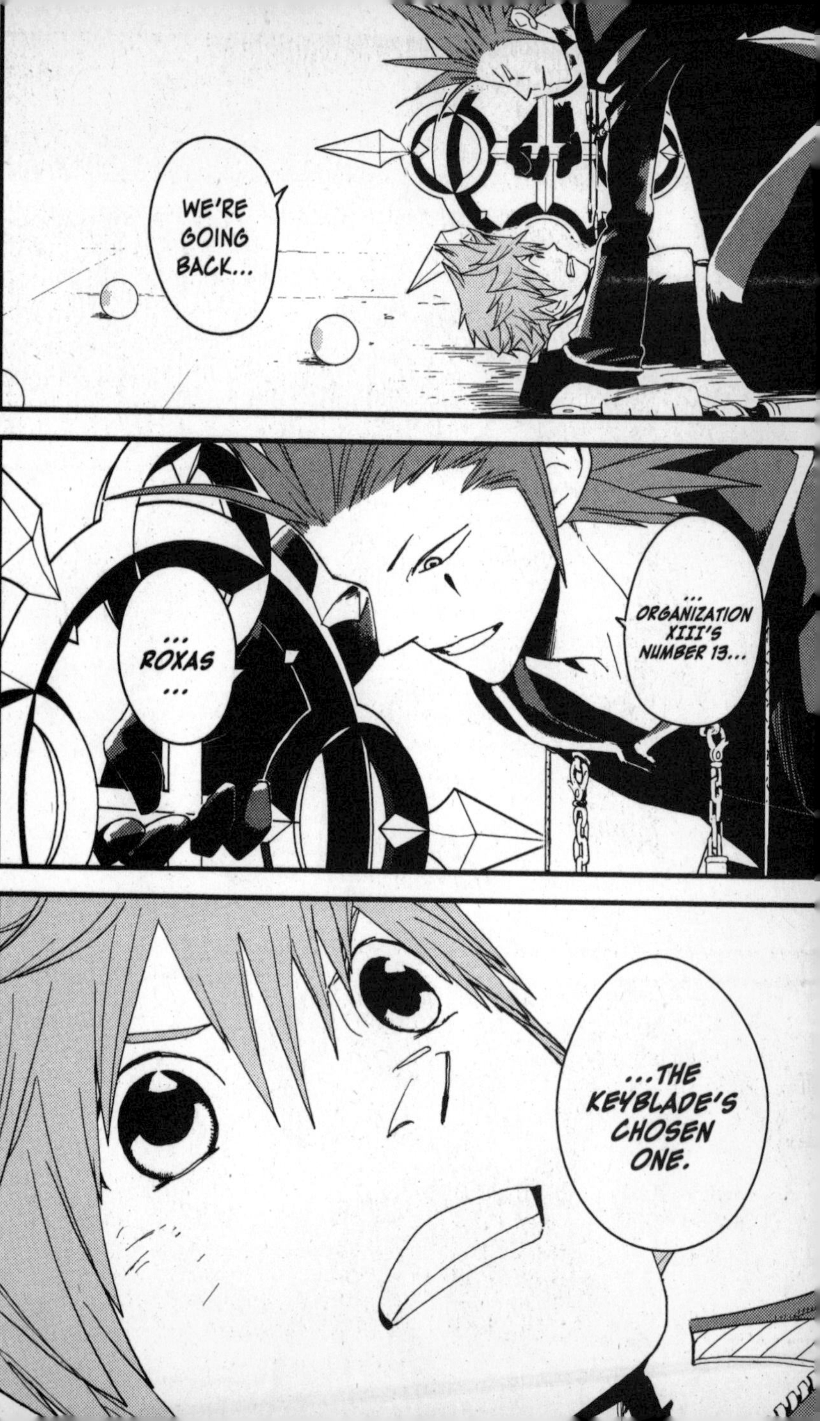
WE'RE GOING BACK...
...ORGANIZATION XIII'S NUMBER 13...
...ROXAS...
...THE KEYBLADE'S CHOSEN ONE.

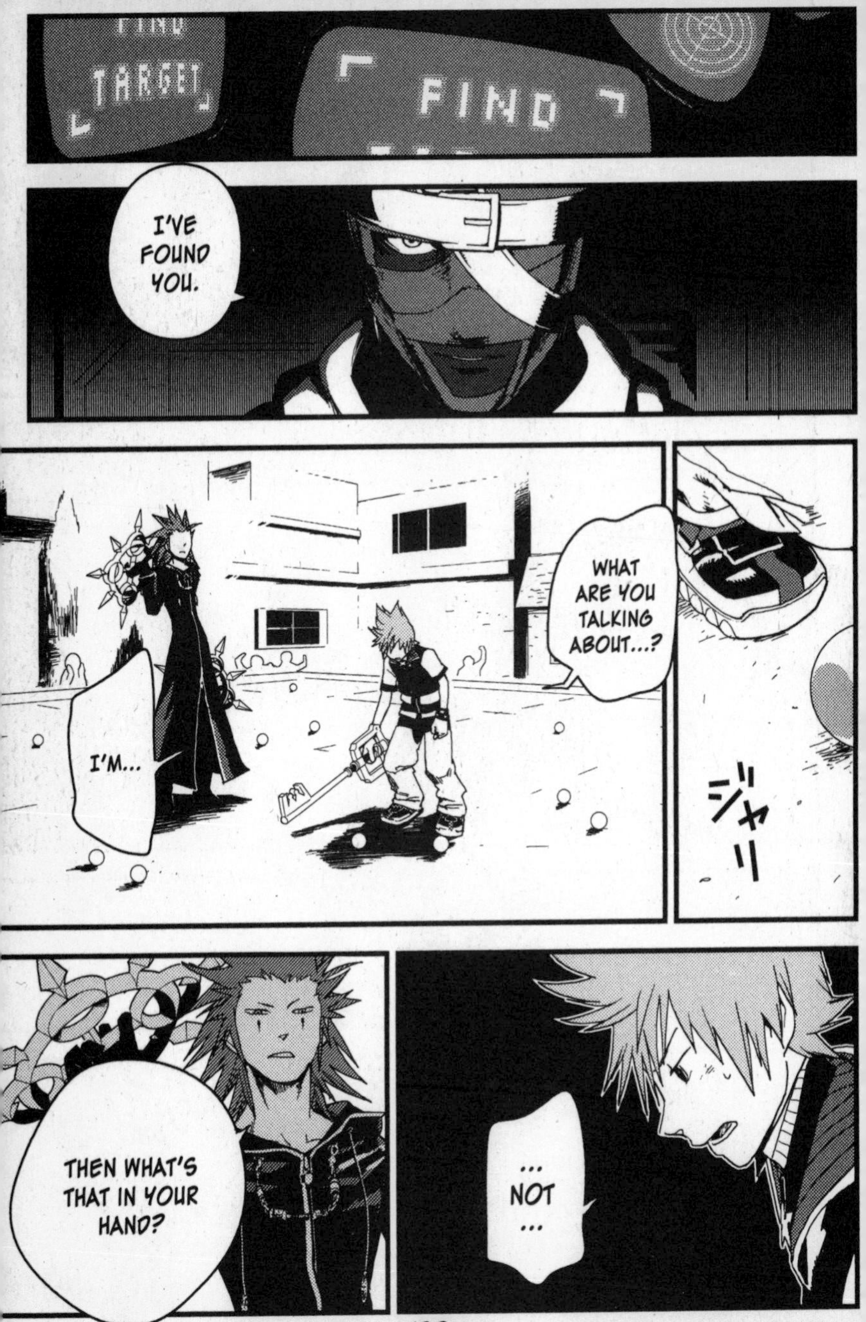
TARGET
FIND
I'VE FOUND YOU.
ジャリ
WHAT ARE YOU TALKING ABOUT...?
I'M...
... NOT ...
THEN WHAT'S THAT IN YOUR HAND?

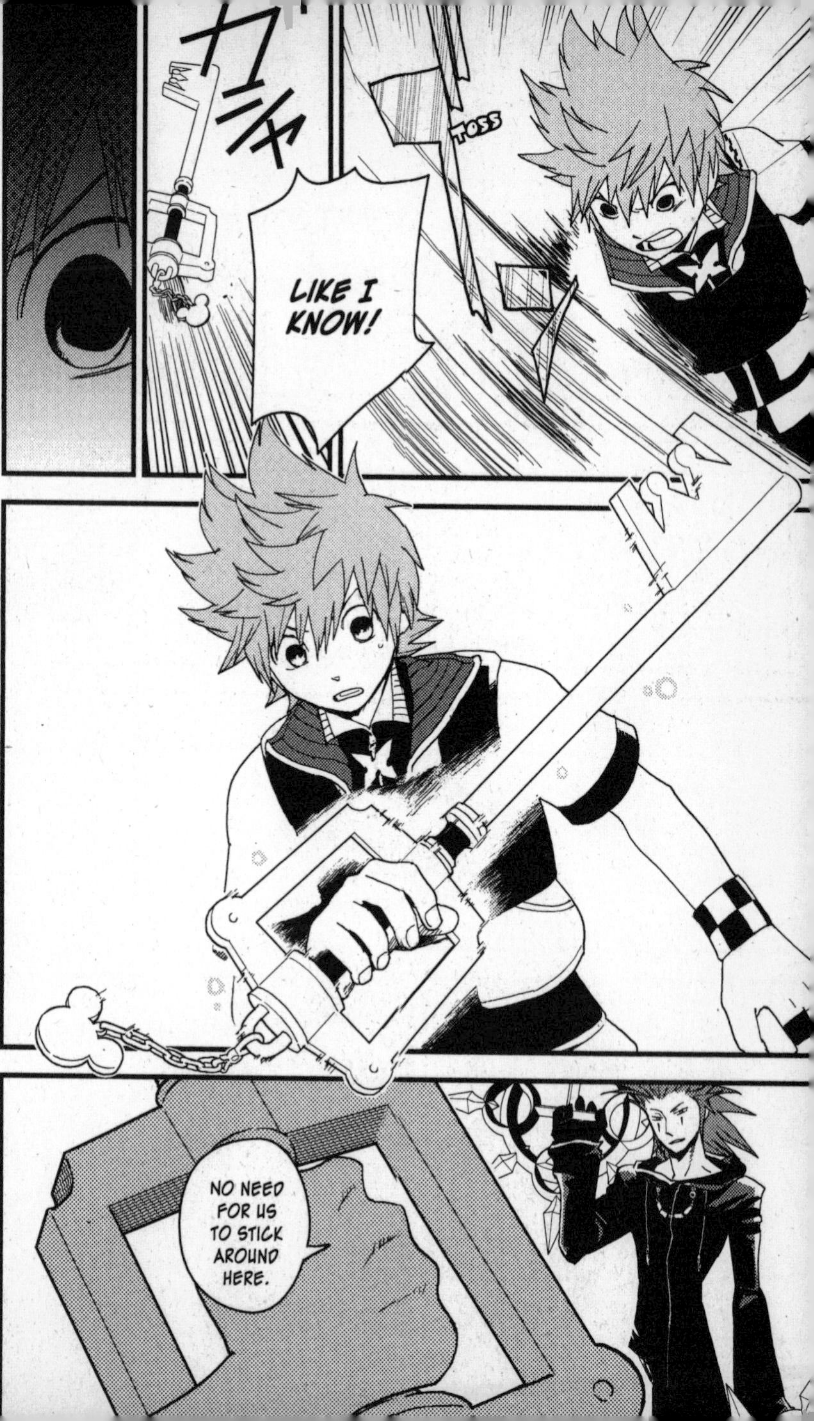
TOSS
LIKE I KNOW!
NO NEED FOR US TO STICK AROUND HERE.

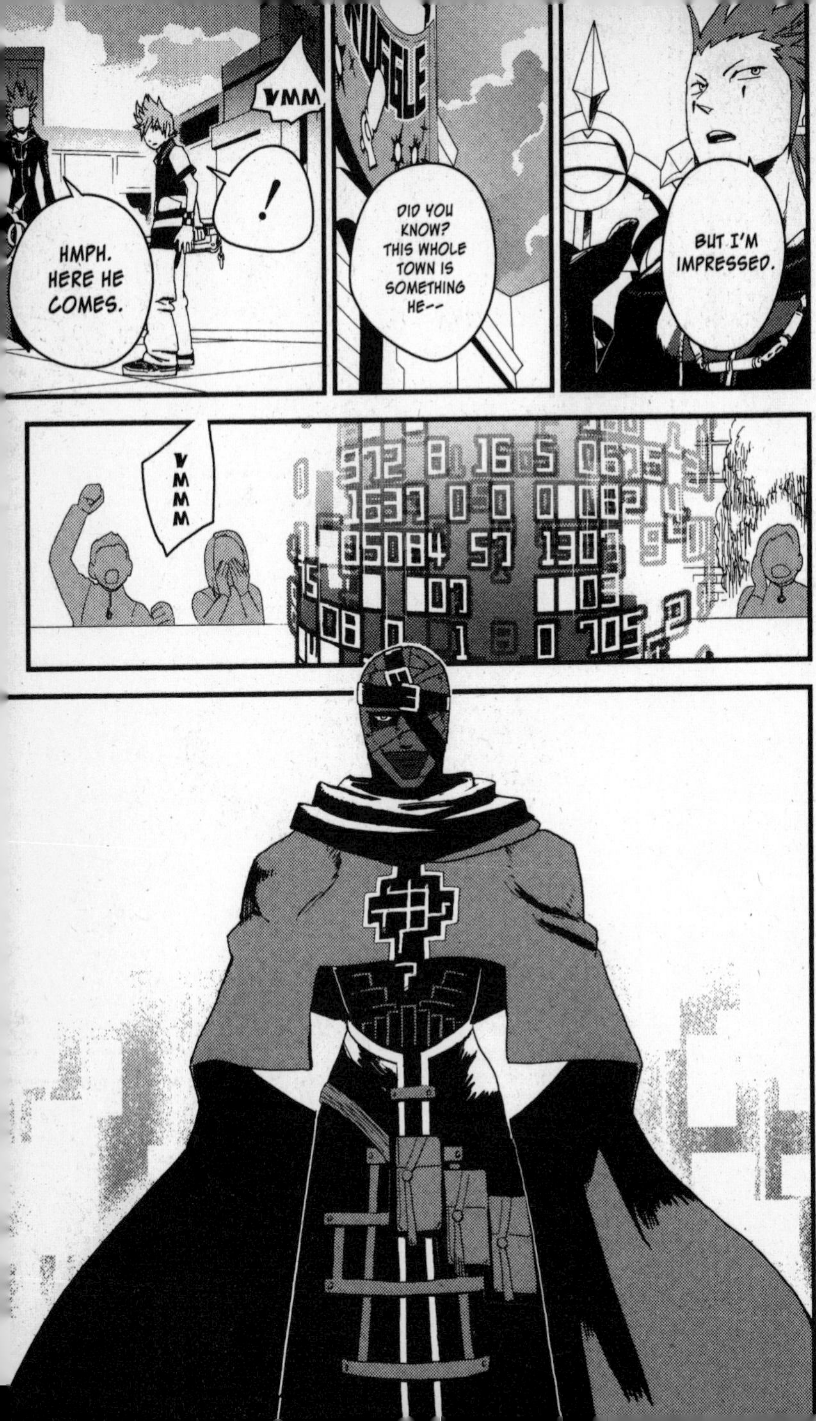
VMM
!
HMPH. HERE HE COMES.
DID YOU KNOW? THIS WHOLE TOWN IS SOMETHING HE--
BUT I'M IMPRESSED.
VMMM

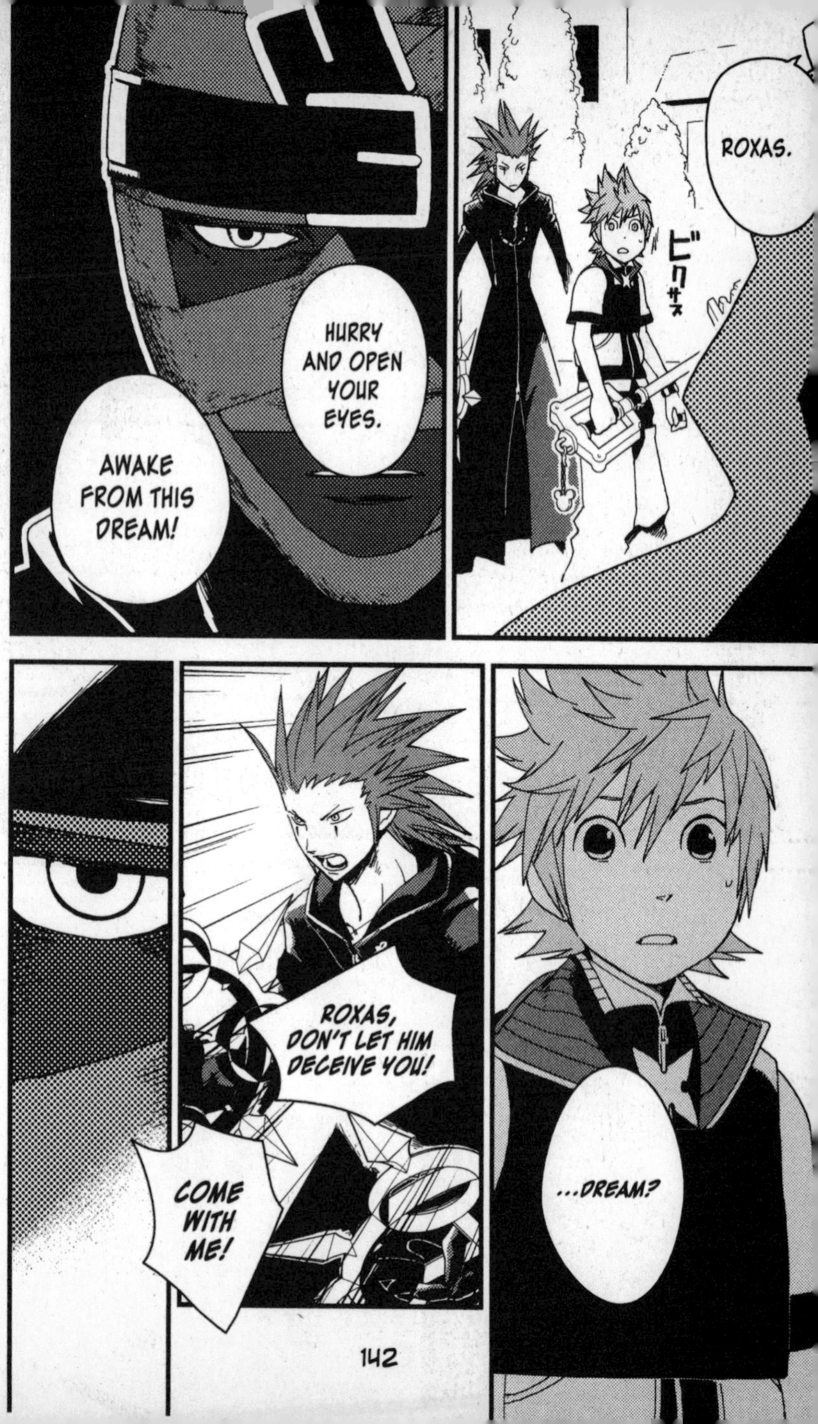
ROXAS.
HURRY AND OPEN YOUR EYES.
AWAKE FROM THIS DREAM!
...DREAM?
ROXAS, DON'T LET HIM DECEIVE YOU!
COME WITH ME!

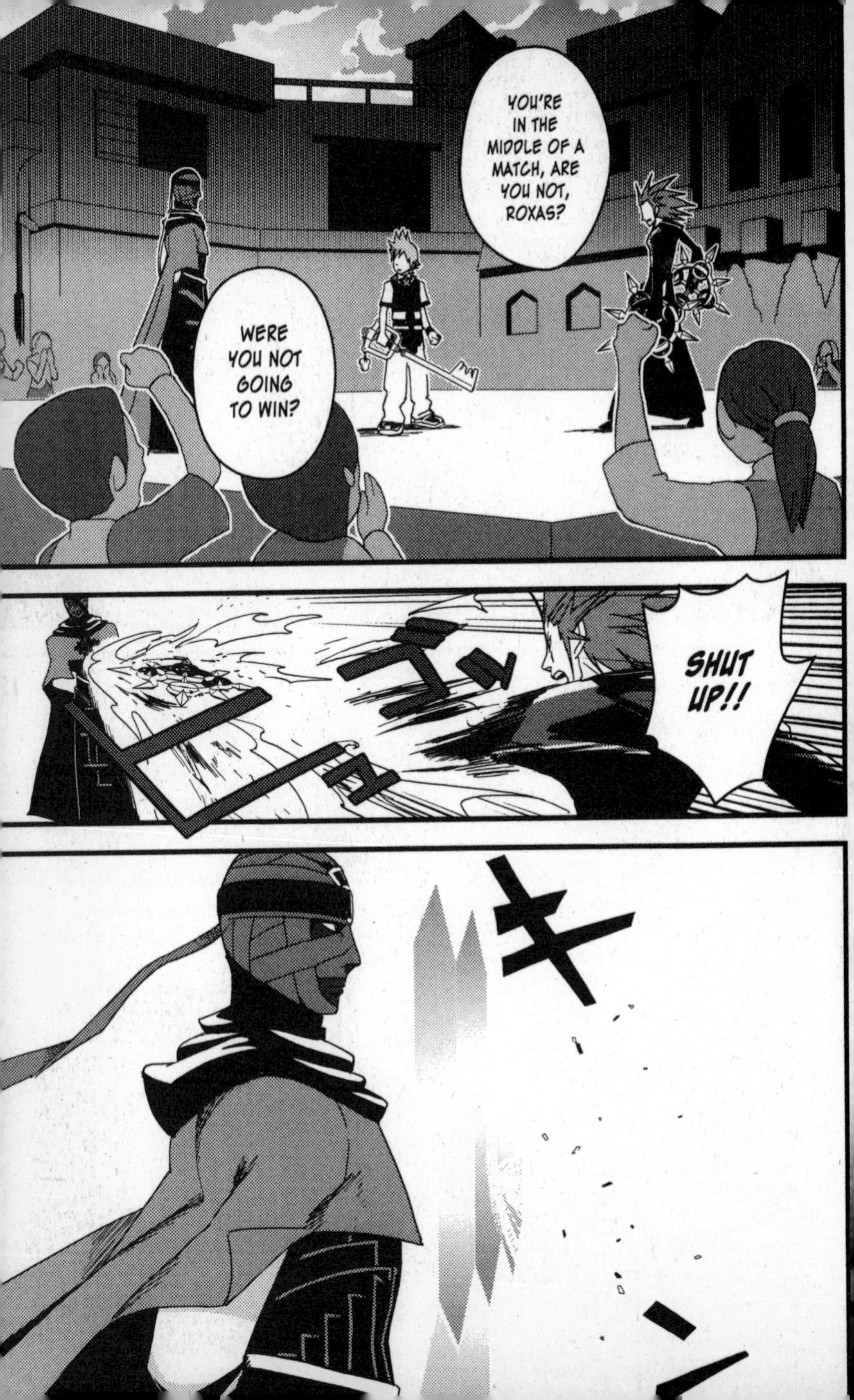
YOU'RE IN THE MIDDLE OF A MATCH, ARE YOU NOT, ROXAS?
WERE YOU NOT GOING TO WIN?
SHUT UP!!

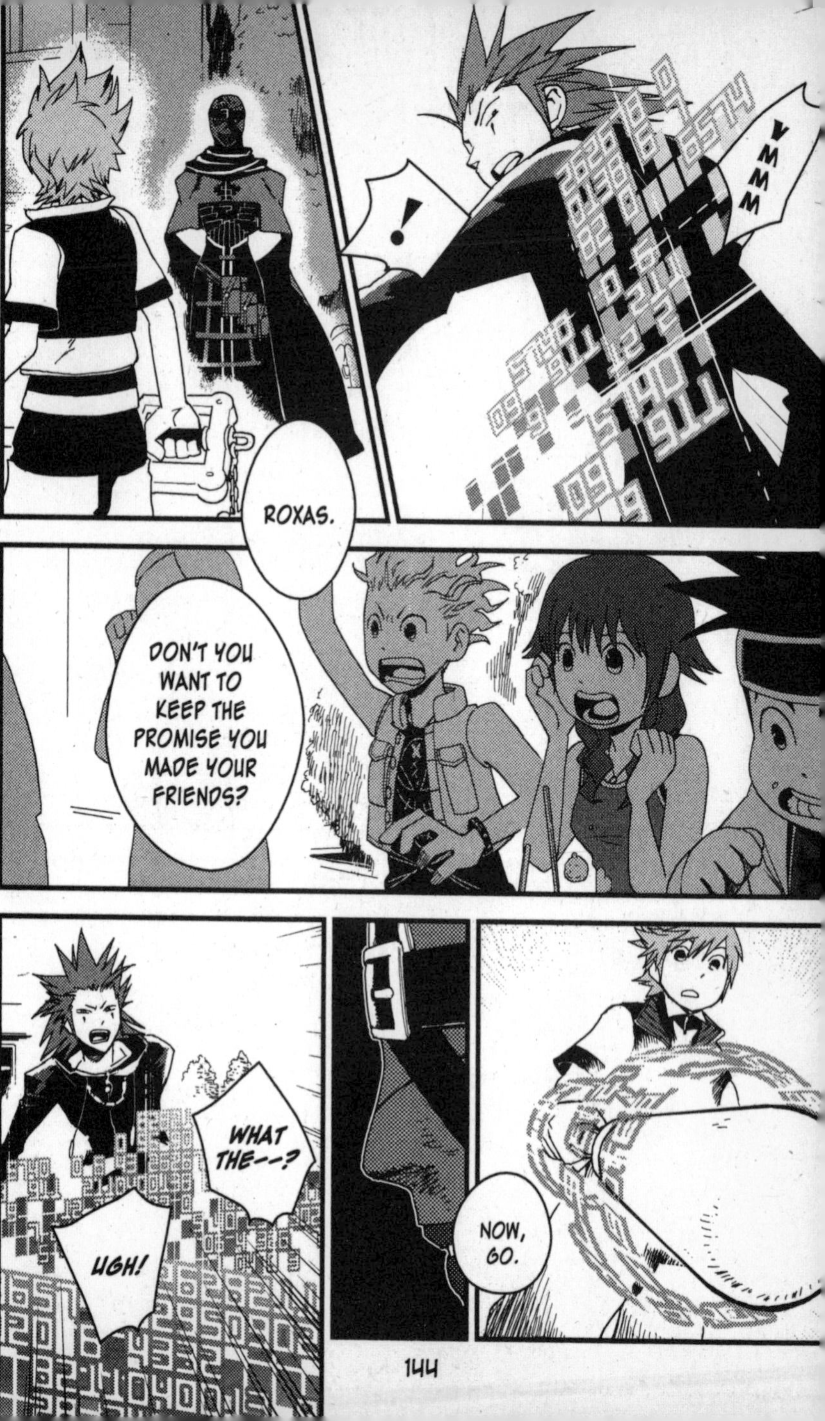
VMMM
!
ROXAS.
DON'T YOU WANT TO KEEP THE PROMISE YOU MADE YOUR FRIENDS?
NOW, GO.
WHAT THE--?
UGH!

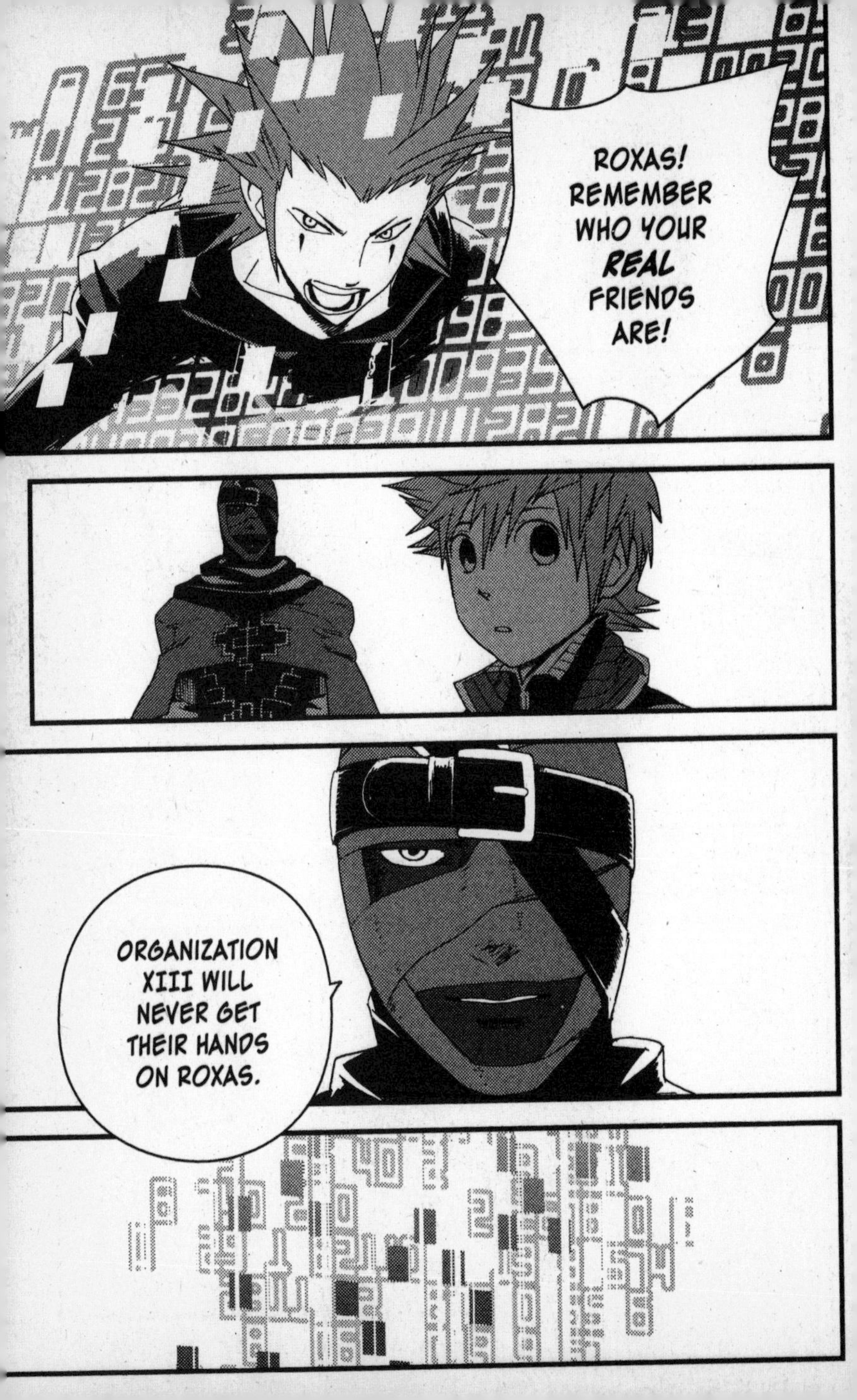
ROXAS! REMEMBER WHO YOUR *REAL* FRIENDS ARE!
ORGANIZATION XIII WILL NEVER GET THEIR HANDS ON ROXAS.

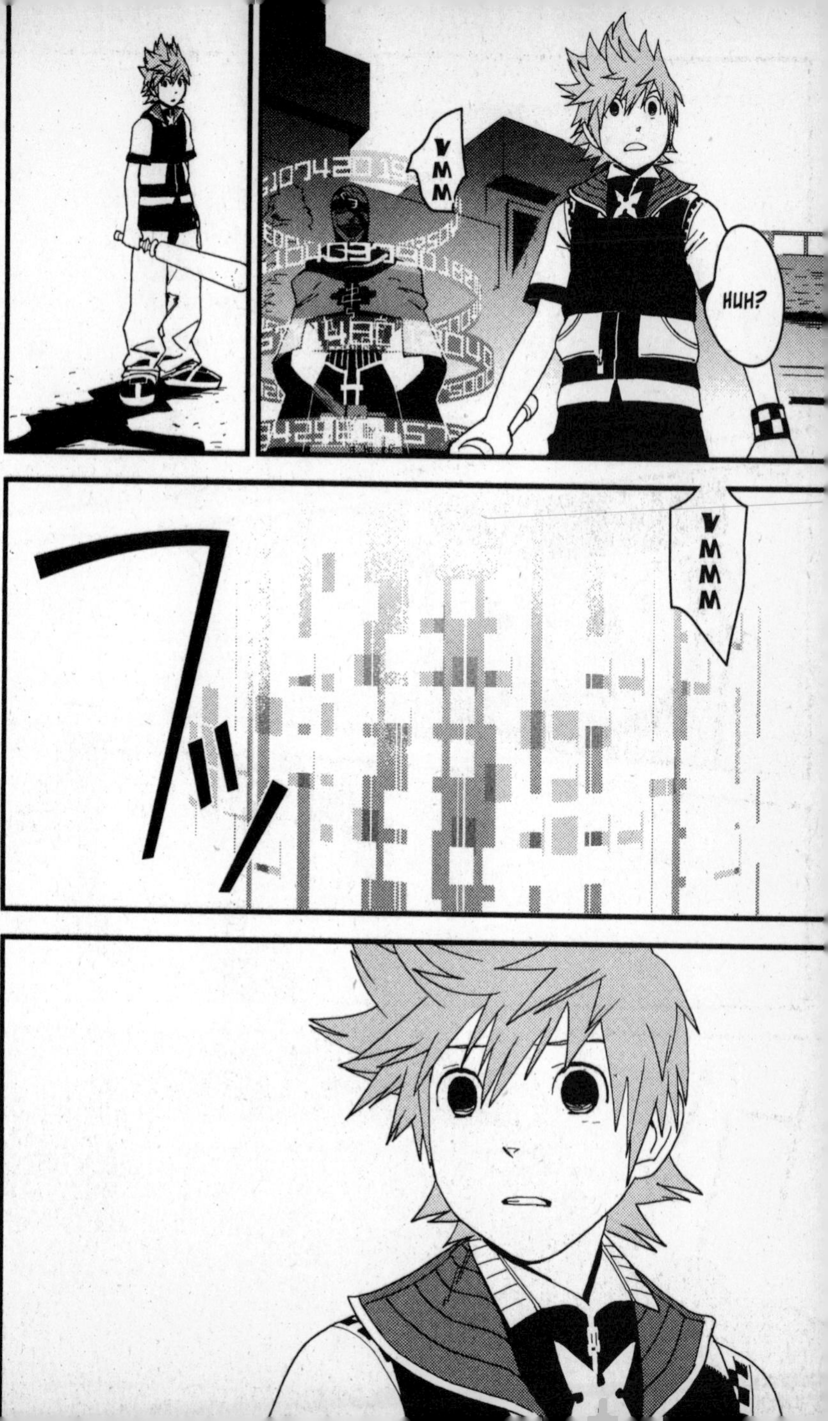
HUH?
VMM
VMMM

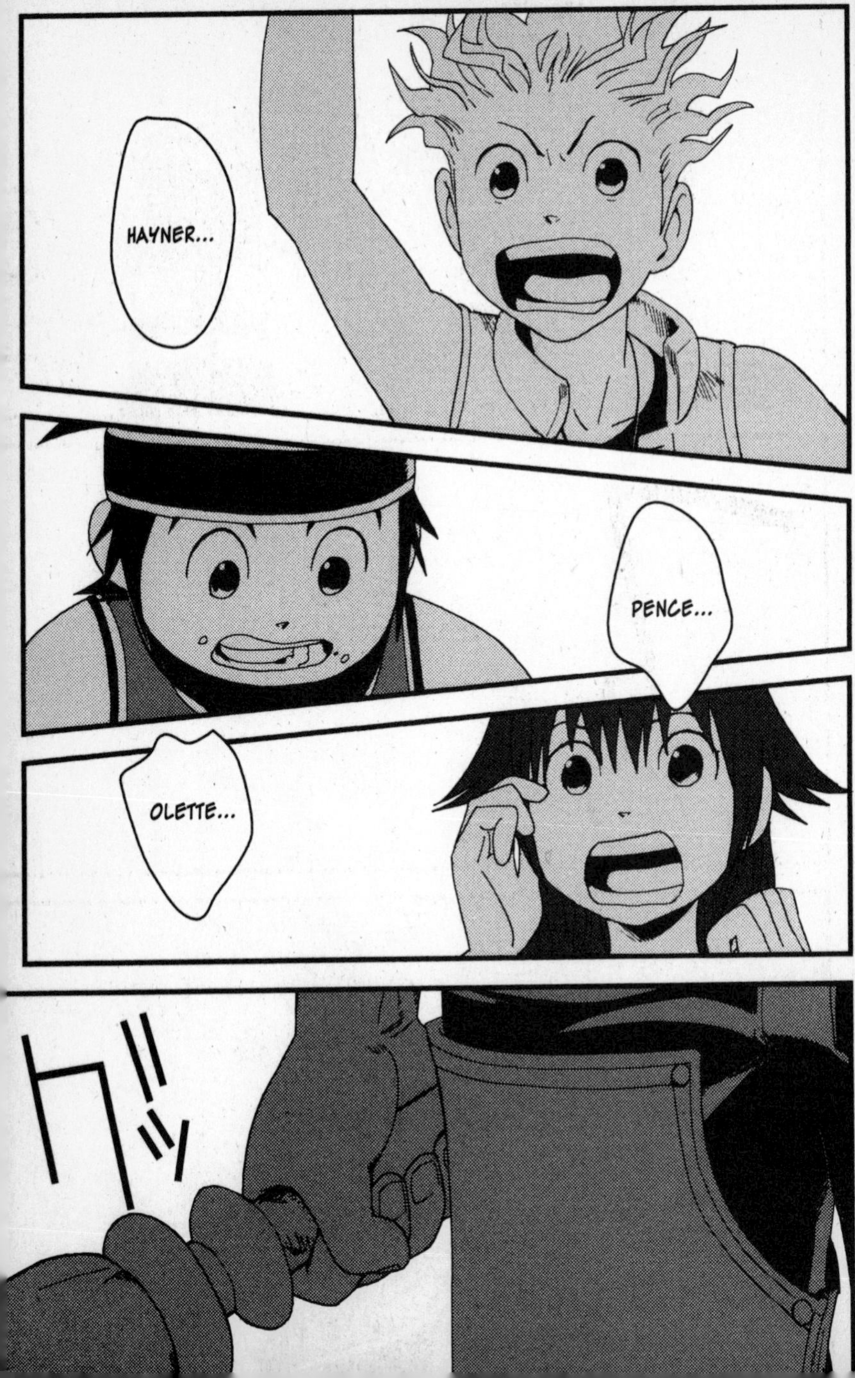
HAYNER...
PENCE...
OLETTE...
グッ

DO YOU REMEMBER YOUR TRUE NAME?

ROXAS.

I DON'T KNOW.

...ORGANIZATION XIII'S NUMBER 13, ROXAS...

WE'RE GOING BACK...

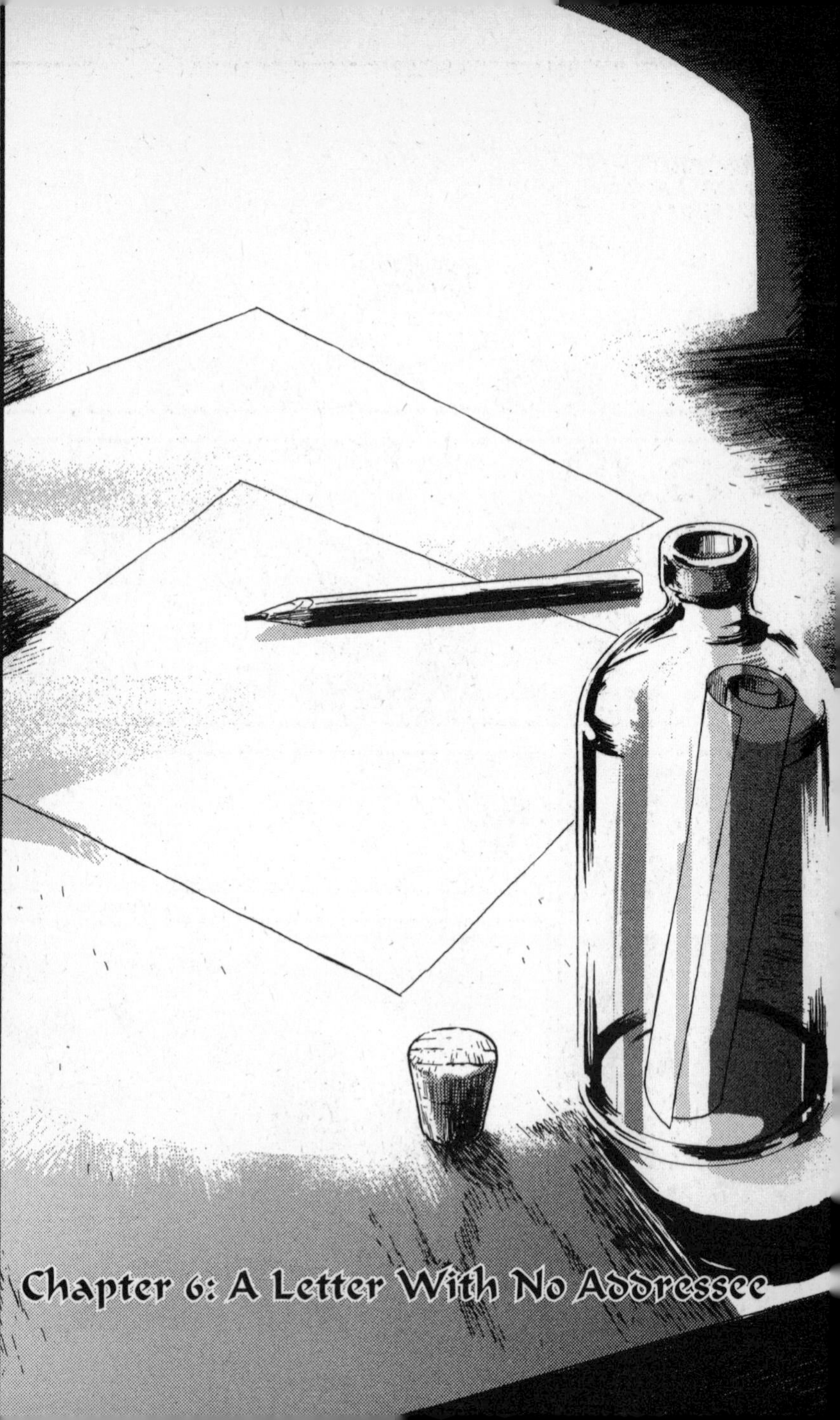
Chapter 6: A Letter With No Addressee

HEY, PULL YOURSELF TOGETHER!!

ROXAS!

SHAKE SHAKE

HUH...? EVERY-BODY...

?

DREAM-ING...

WERE YOU DREAMING OR SOMETHING?

LOOK, MAN, YOU DID IT! YOU WON!!

SOMETHING WRONG?

NOW YOU GOTTA WIN THE TITLE MATCH, TOO!

RIP THAT FAT BELT RIGHT OFF HIM!!

IT'S NOTHING.

...NO.

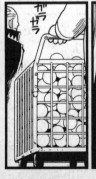

ARE YOU DRUNKEN ON THE SWEET WINE OF VICTORY, BOY?

CONTENDERS TO THE STAGE, PLEASE!

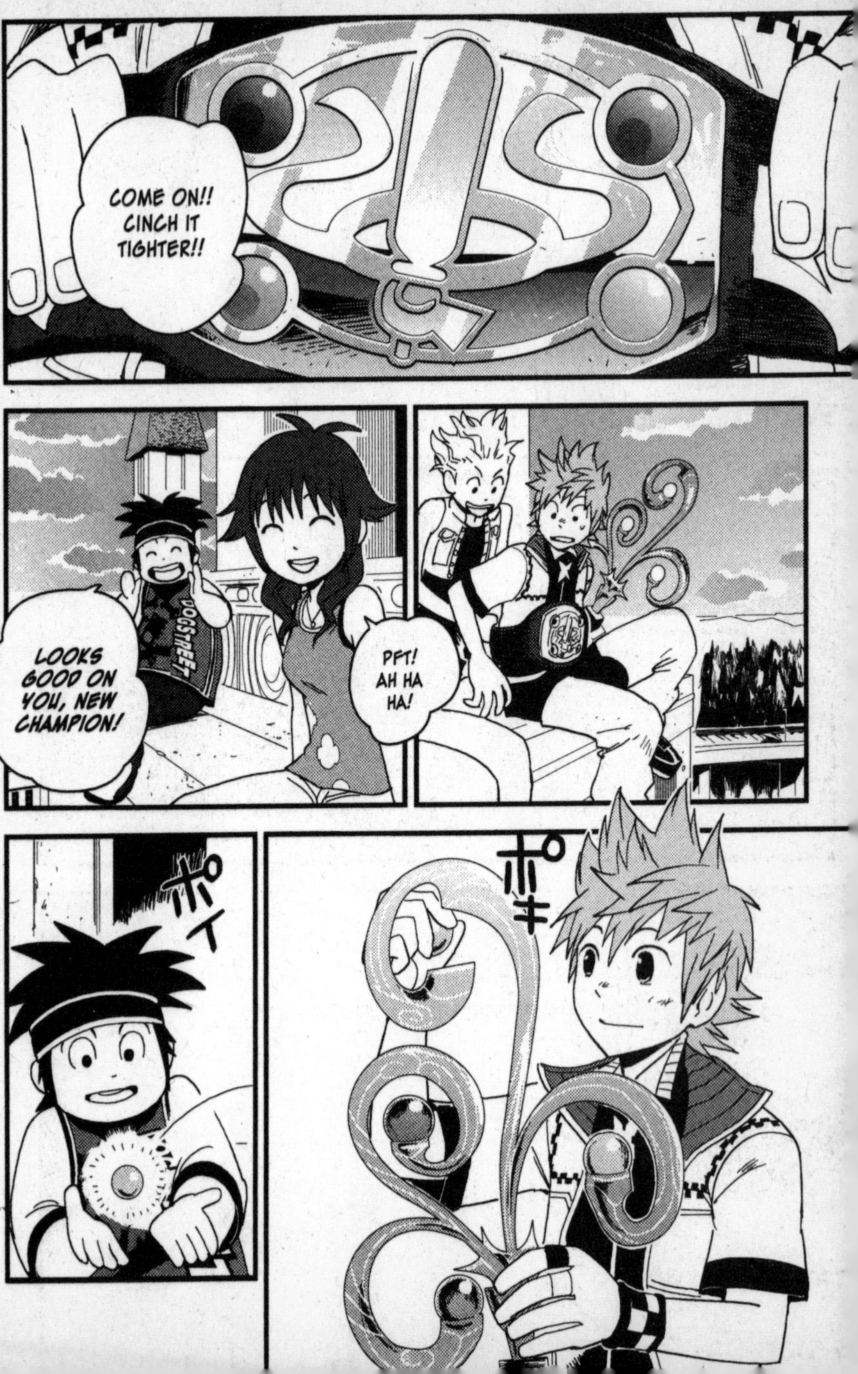
COME ON!! CINCH IT TIGHTER!!
PFT! AH HA HA!
LOOKS GOOD ON YOU, NEW CHAMPION!
ポキ
ポイ

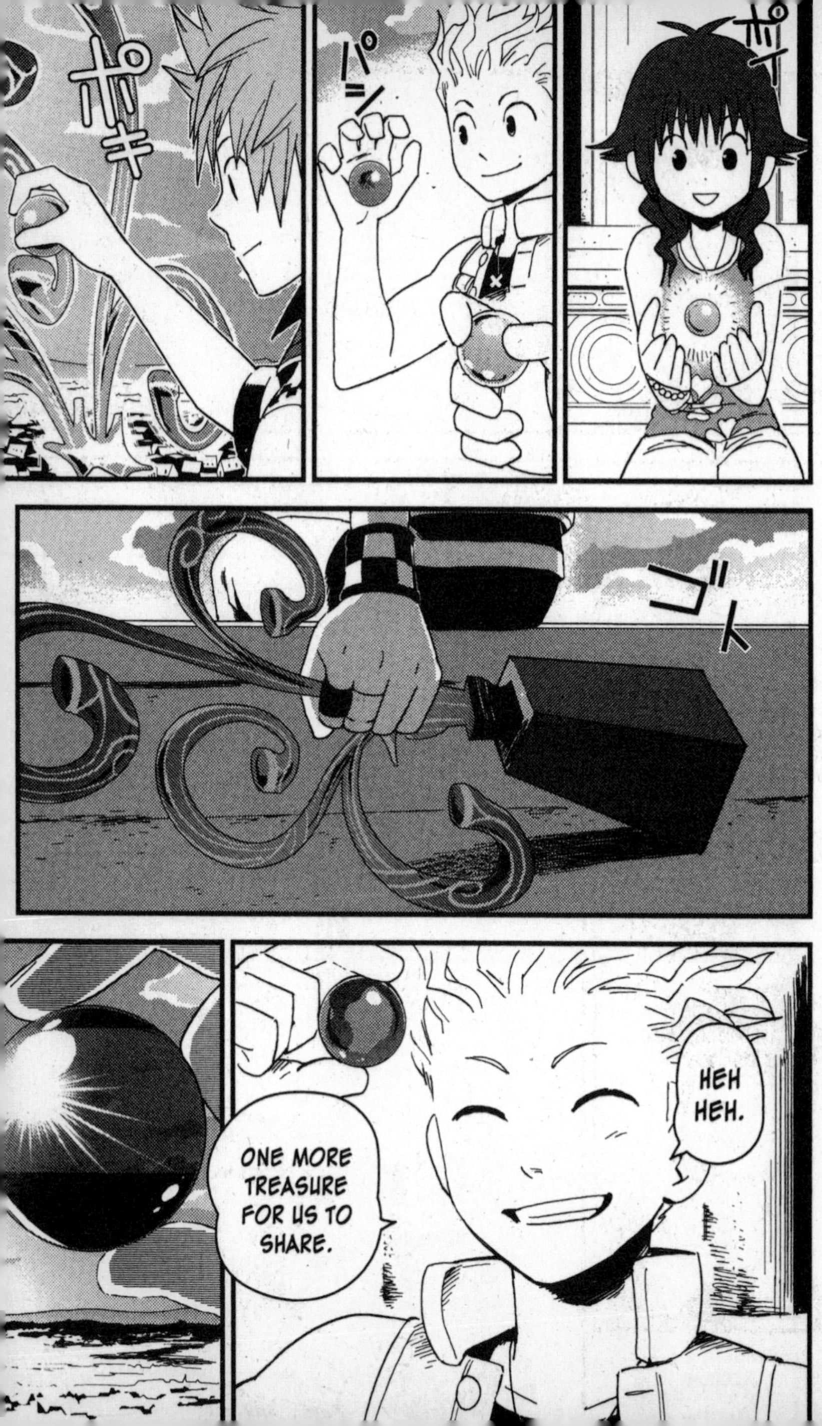
ポイ
パン
ポキ
ゴト
HEH HEH.
ONE MORE TREASURE FOR US TO SHARE.

SHUT UP!

YEAH, UNTIL ROXAS TOOK YOU OUT!

I TRIED HARD, TOO!

IT'S ALL THANKS TO YOU, ROXAS.

OOHH!

TADAH!

WITH ICE CREAM!

NOW, LET'S HAVE A TOAST...

?

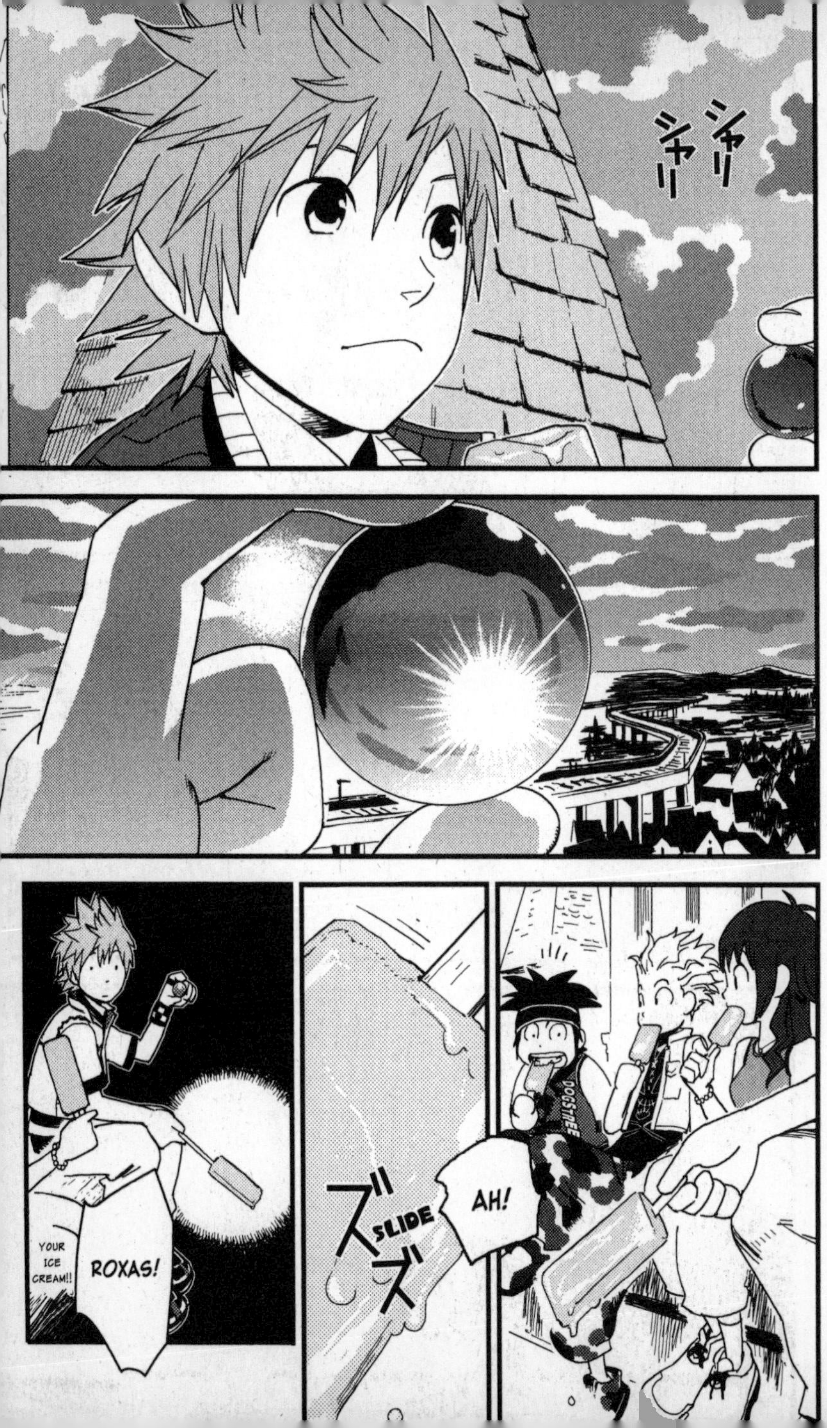
シャリ
シャリ
AH!
SLIDE
ズズ
ROXAS!
YOUR ICE CREAM!!

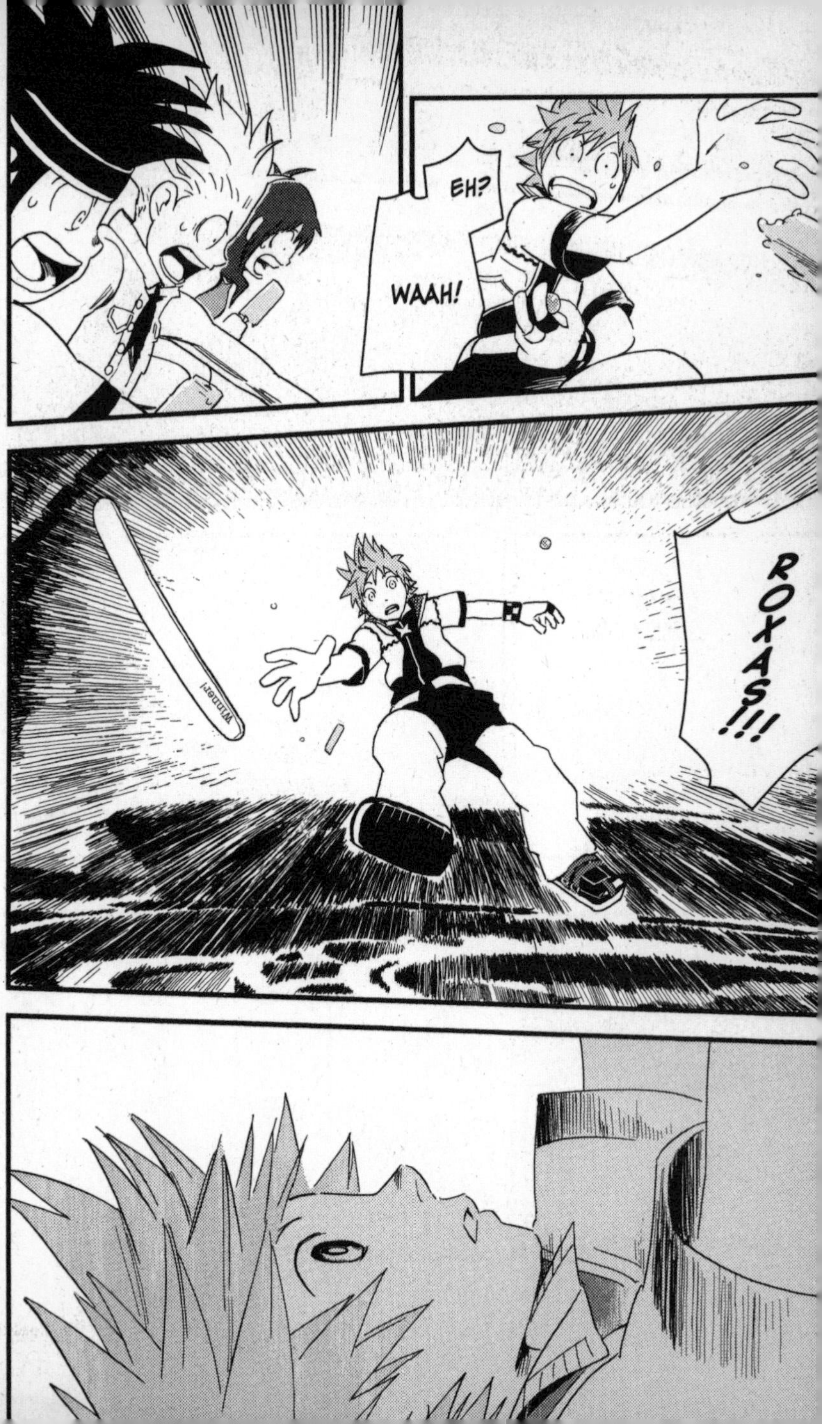
EH?
WAAH!
ROXAS!!!
Winner!

IT'S SO HIGH UP.

AM I GONNA DIE?

WHAT'S GOING ON?

THAT'S STRANGE.

I'M NOT HITTING THE GROUND...

...NAMINÉ?

KAIRI!

EH HEH HEH.

WAIT UP!

LET'S WALK HOME TOGETHER.

HEY.

IT'S SUCH A BEAUTIFUL DAY.

DO YOU FEEL LIKE GOING OUT TO THE ISLAND?

YOU CAN SEE THE ISLAND REALLY WELL.

NOT TODAY, SORRY.

...

YOU'RE STILL THINKING ABOUT THAT BOY...?

...IS THE PLACE WHERE *HE* USED TO BE.

TO ME, THAT ISLAND...

I TOLD MYSELF I'M NOT GOING TO THE ISLAND UNTIL I REMEMBER EVERYTHING ABOUT HIM.

KAIRI.

IT'S STRANGE, ISN'T IT?

THAT YOU CAN'T REMEMBER HIS FACE OR HIS NAME.

I DON'T REMEMBER HIM AT ALL.

BUT...ARE YOU SURE YOU DIDN'T MAKE HIM UP?

IT'S TERRIBLE, ISN'T IT?

...YEAH.

ALL OF A SUDDEN, HE WAS JUST GONE.

THOUGH I DO WONDER WHATEVER HAPPENED TO RIKU.

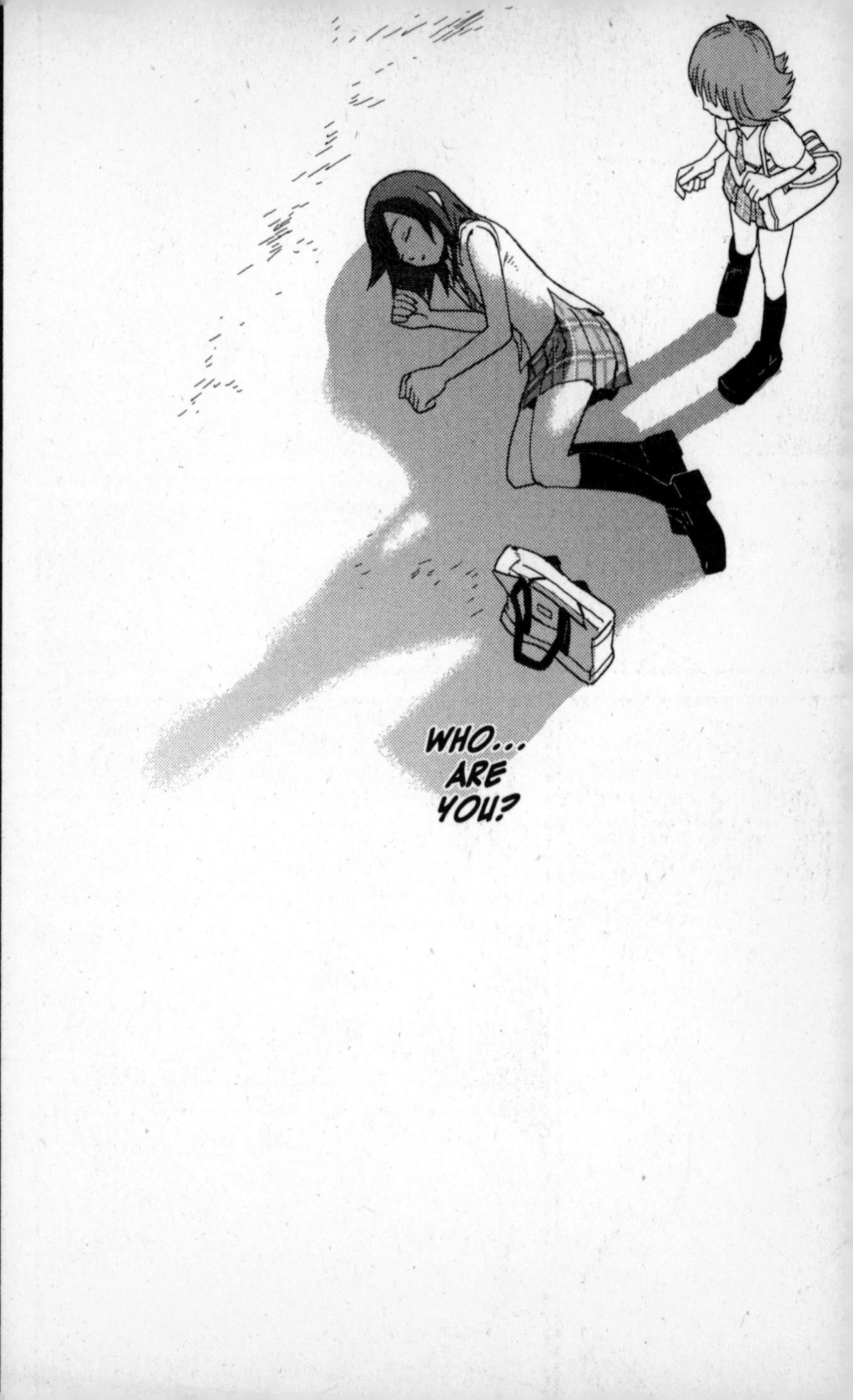
WHO... ARE YOU?

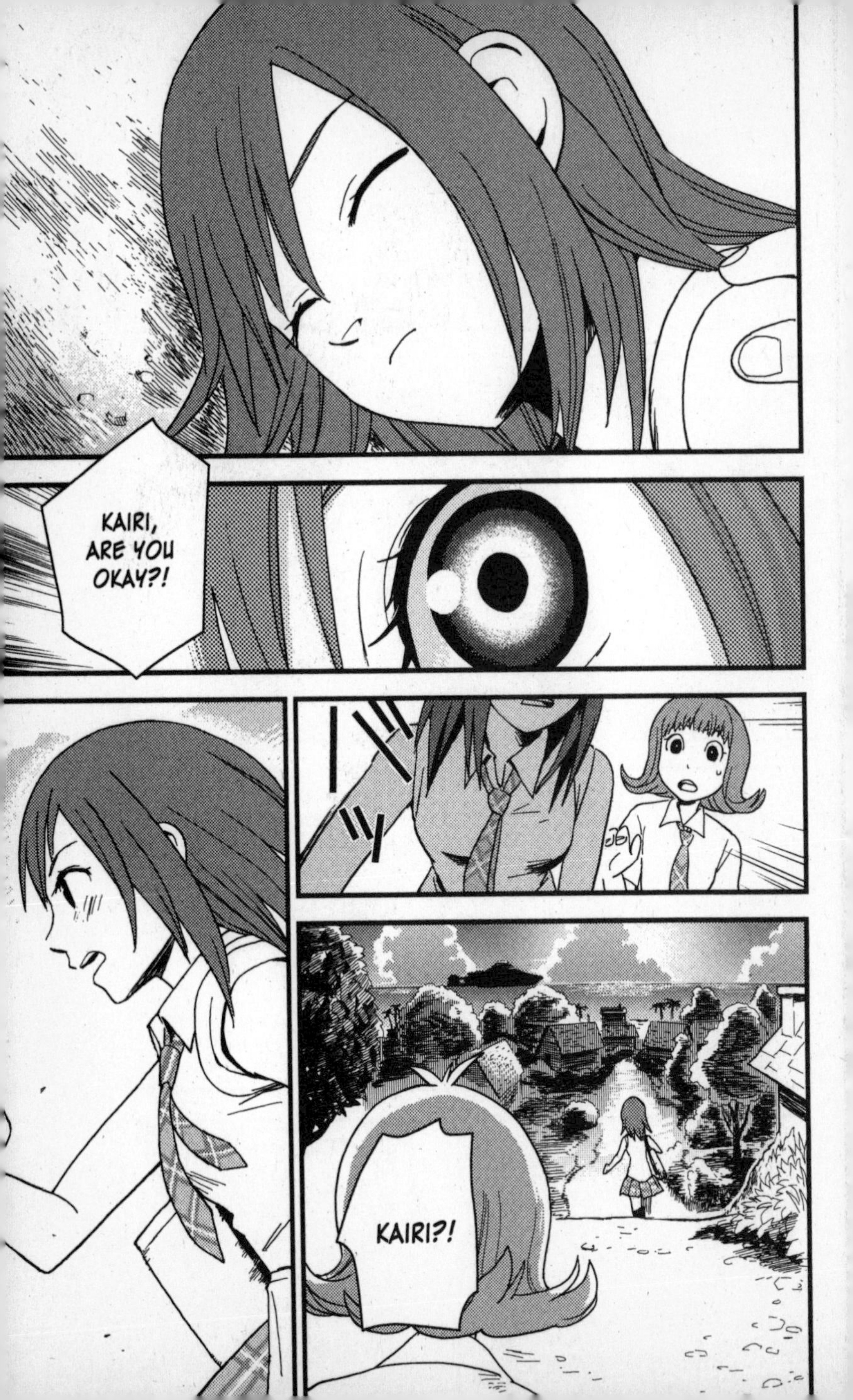
KAIRI, ARE YOU OKAY?!
KAIRI?!

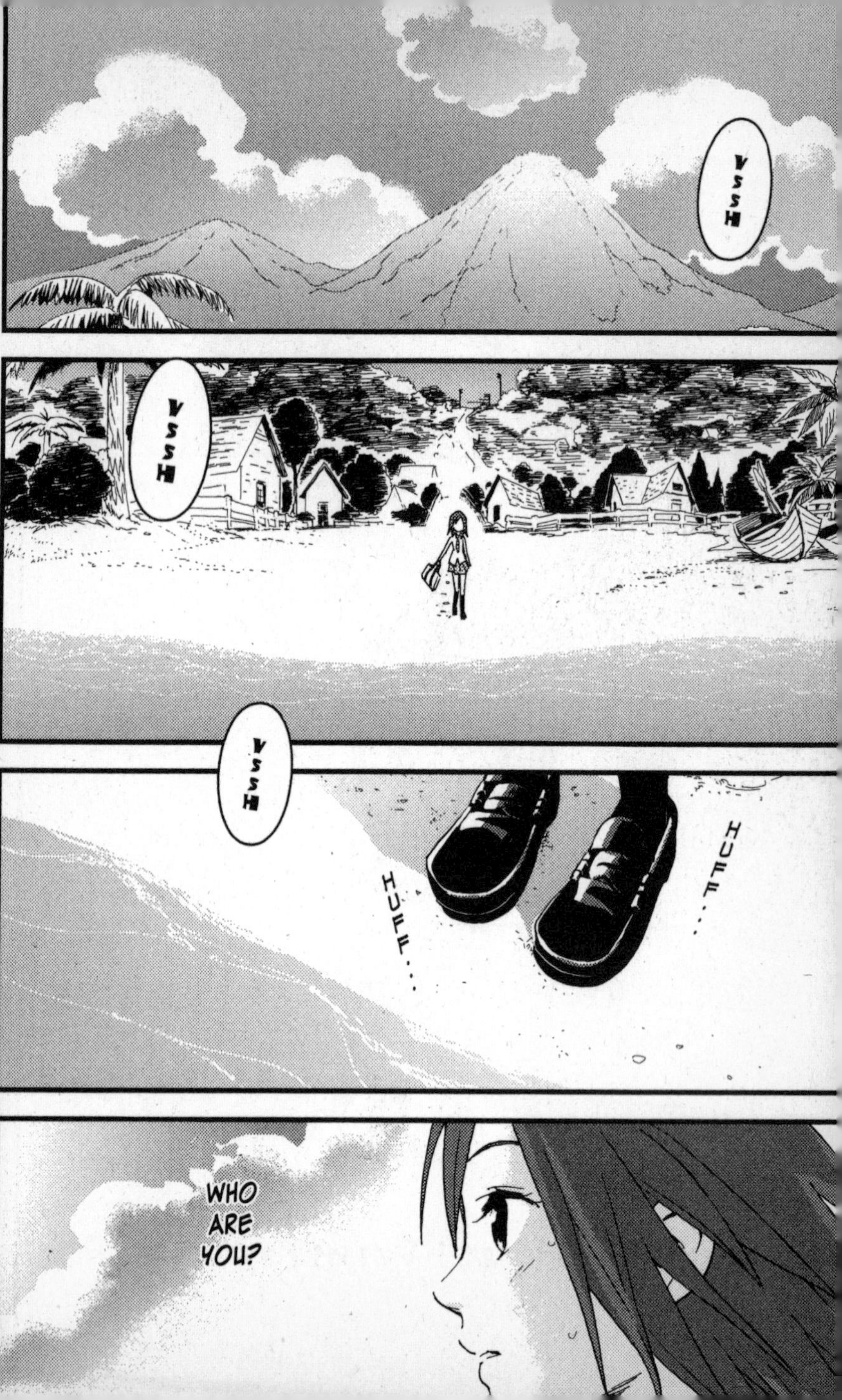
VSSH
VSSH
VSSH
HUFF...
HUFF...
WHO ARE YOU?

# Chapter 7: What I Want to Ask Is...

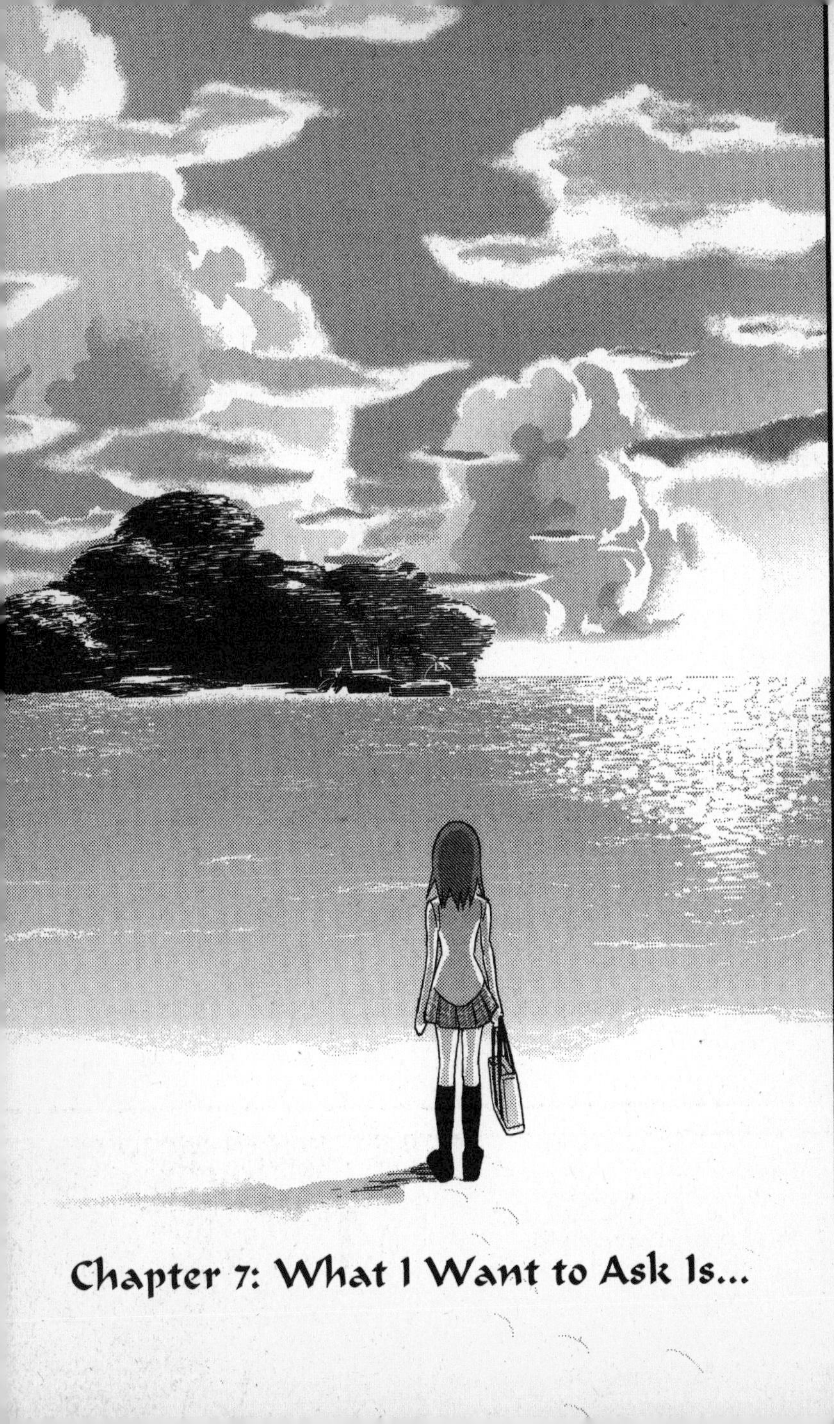

WHO...?

...WHO ARE *YOU*?

WHO... ARE *YOU*?

I'M KAIRI.

ROXAS...

I'M ROXAS.

KAIRI?

THAT'S STRANGE. IS THIS A DREAM...?

EH?

I'VE SEEN YOU SO MANY TIMES IN MY DREAMS...

YOU WERE BUILDING A RAFT ON AN ISLAND WITH A COUPLE OF BOYS.

EH...?

...IT MIGHT BE.

YOU'RE SPEAKING INTO MY MIND.

YOU KNOW THEM...?

YEAH...

AND THE OTHER ONE?!

AH... UM, RIKU...

PLEASE!

TELL ME THOSE BOYS' NAMES!

OKAY, I GUESS I CAN...

STARTS WITH AN "S"!

...GIVE YOU A HINT.

YOU DON'T REMEMBER MY NAME?

THANKS A LOT, KAIRI!

!

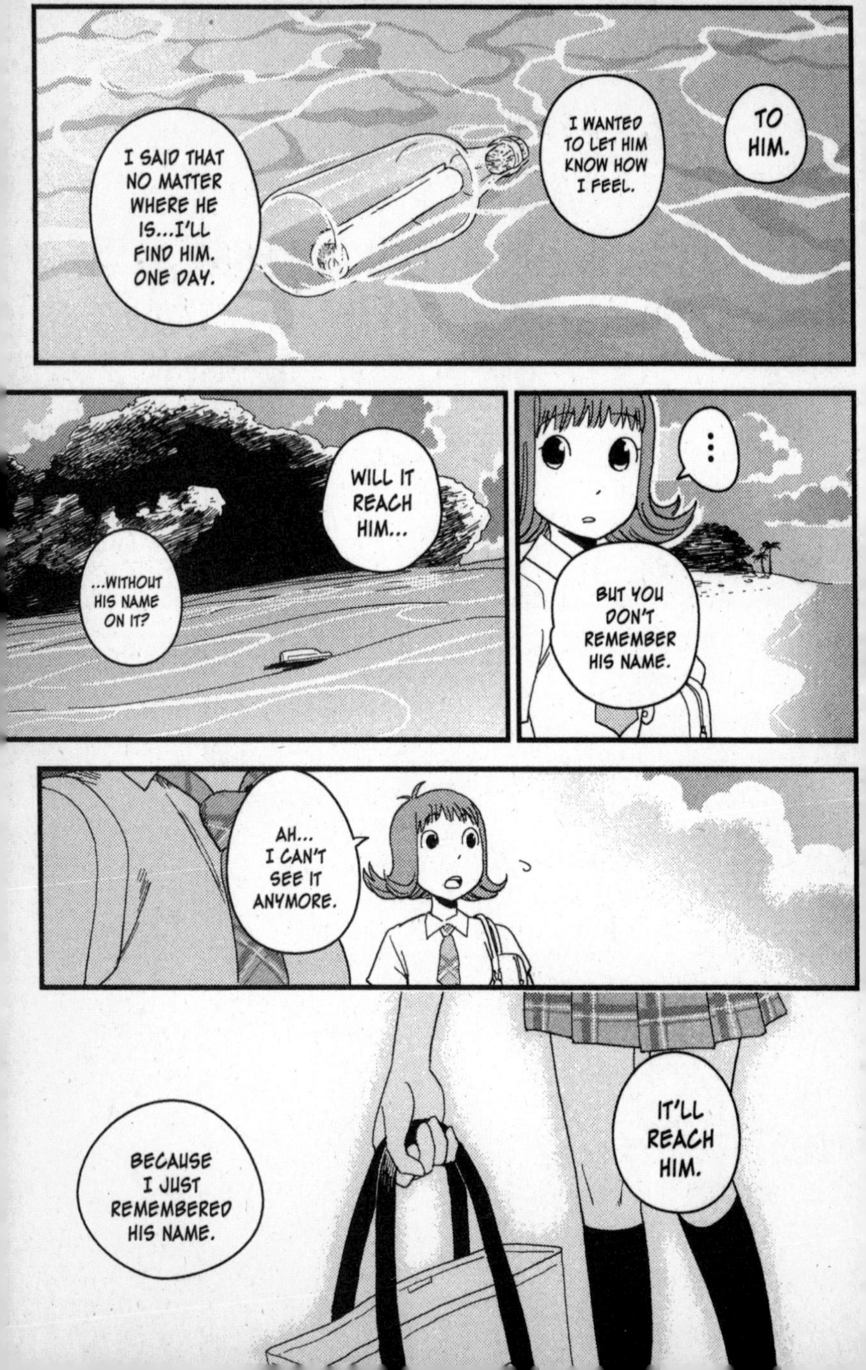
I SAID THAT NO MATTER WHERE HE IS...I'LL FIND HIM. ONE DAY.
I WANTED TO LET HIM KNOW HOW I FEEL.
TO HIM.
WILL IT REACH HIM...
...WITHOUT HIS NAME ON IT?
...
BUT YOU DON'T REMEMBER HIS NAME.
AH... I CAN'T SEE IT ANYMORE.
IT'LL REACH HIM.
BECAUSE I JUST REMEMBERED HIS NAME.

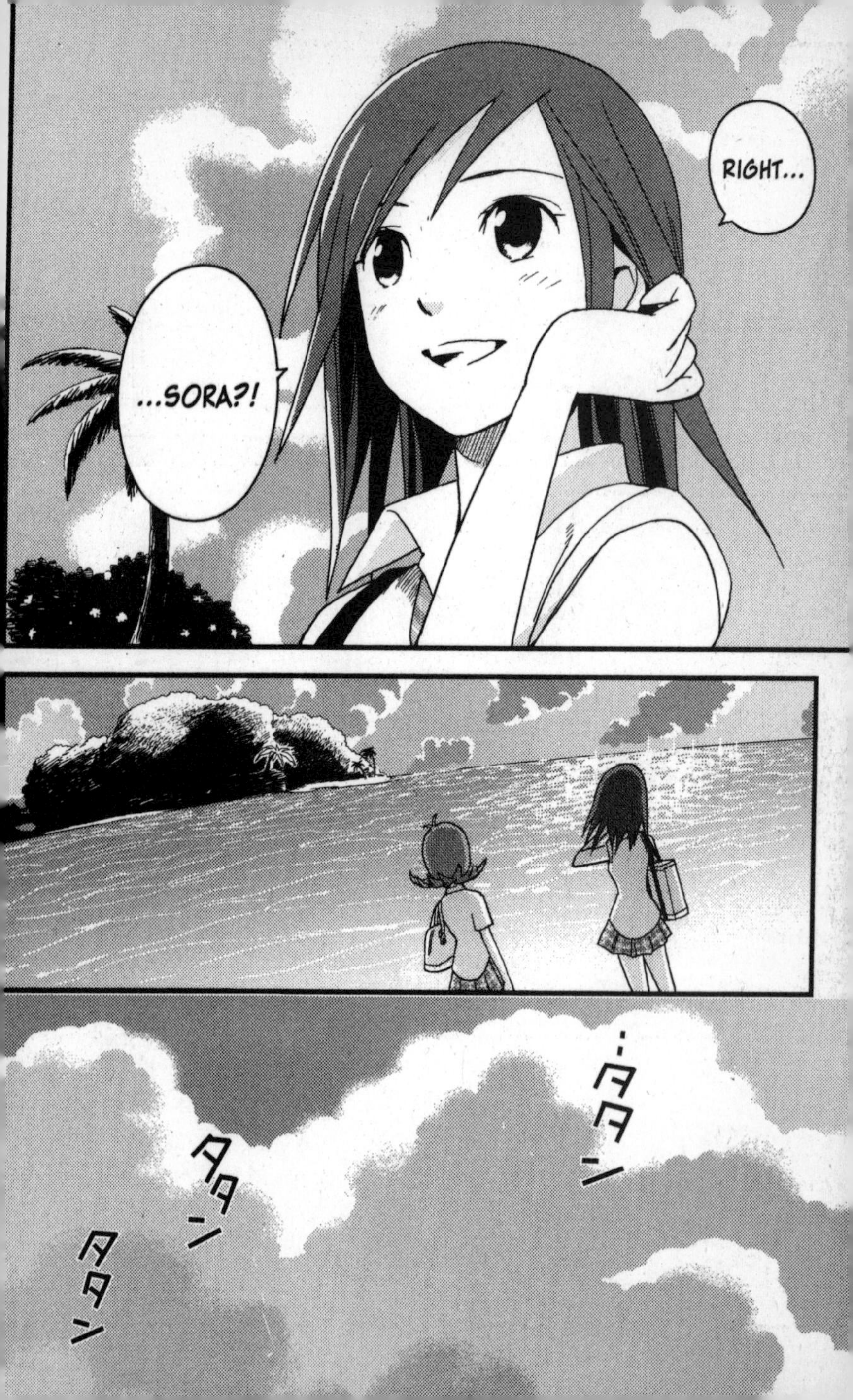
RIGHT...
...SORA?!
‥タタン
タタン
タタン

I FELL FROM THE STATION TOWER--

WHY AM I AT MY HOUSE...?

......

WAS THAT...

...A DREAM...?

PLEASE!

I'M KAIRI.

TELL ME THOSE BOYS' NAMES!

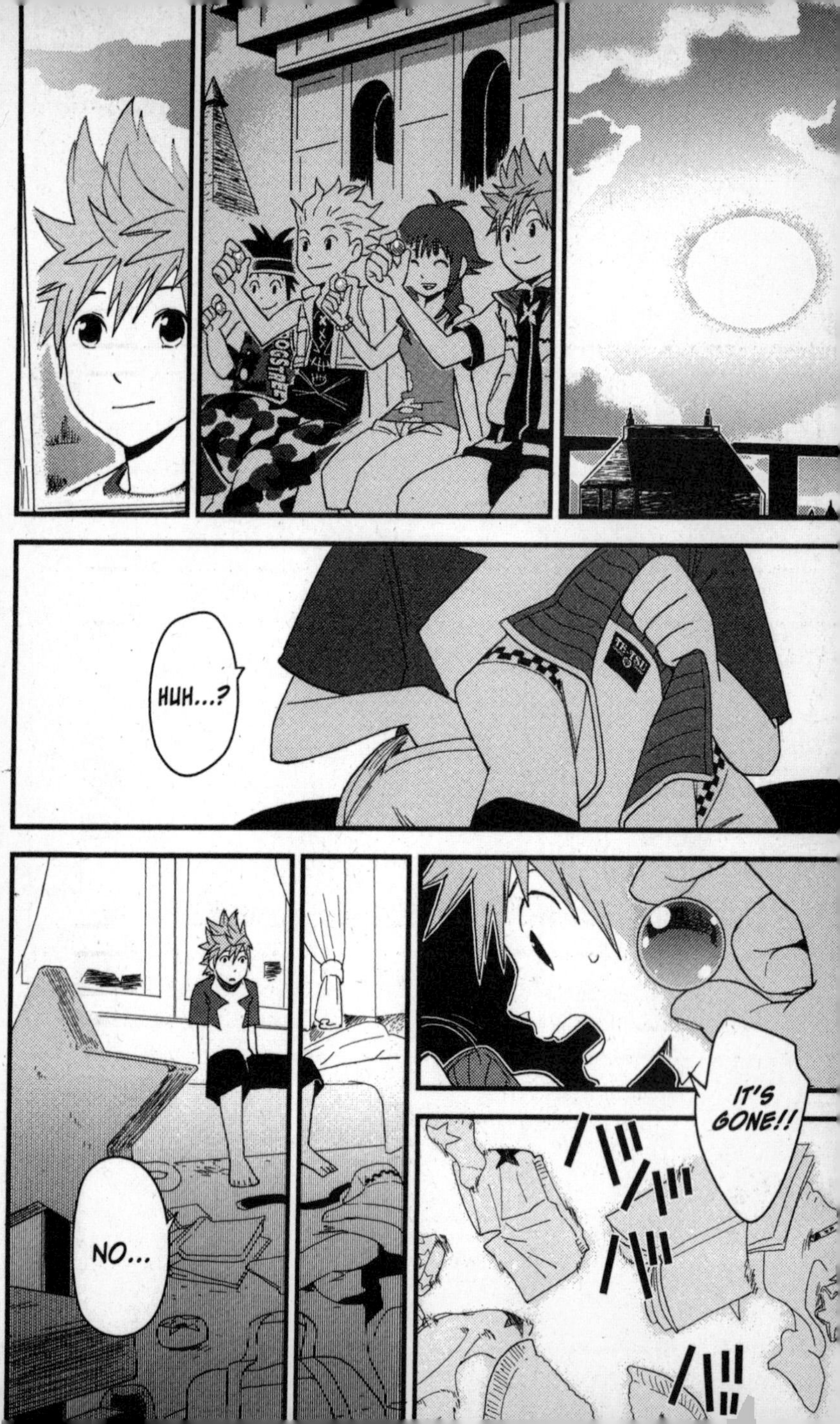
HUH...?
IT'S GONE!!
NO...

I DIDN'T FALL OFF THE STATION TOWER... WAS WINNING THE TOURNAMENT A DREAM TOO?

I'M DREAMING... BUT WHICH PARTS...WERE THE DREAM?

HEY, ROXAS, WHAT DO YOU THINK?! HAYNER SAYS OUR HOMEWORK DOESN'T MATTER!

AH... SORRY.

YOU'RE LATE, ROXAS!

UGH!

YOU WON THE TOURNAMENT YESTERDAY! YOU GOTTA BASK IN THE GLORY A LITTLE LONGER!

YOU'RE ON MY SIDE, RIGHT, ROXAS?!

AW, MAN!!

SEE?! SEE?! I KNEW IT!!

WE SHOULD DO OUR HOMEWORK.

I... THINK...

YEAH, SEE?

UH... UM, WELL...

LIKE WHAT?

THERE ARE PLENTY OF THINGS YOU COULD DO.

QUIT EXAGGER-ATING.

STUPID INDEPENDENT STUDY... SO, ANYBODY GOT ANY BRIGHT IDEAS FOR A TOPIC?

HMM, THEN...

NO WAY.

WHAT ABOUT *BLACK MAGIC* OR SOMETHING?

HOW ABOUT EXPLORING THE HAUNTED OLD MANSION?

LET'S GO CATCH SOME GHOSTS!!

ALLL RIGHT!!

BE CAREFUL, HAYNER.

PIECE OF CAKE!

HUP.

THUD

DAAAH!!

YEOW!!

BNNT

HUH...?

WHY AM I... RELIEVED ...?

UGH, WHAT NOW? ARE YOU OKAY?!

NO!

SOMETHING ZAPPED ME!!

WHAT ARE YOU BLOCKHEADS DOING?

WE CAME...

...TO EXPLORE THE HAUNTED OLD MANSION.

FOR OUR INDEPENDENT RESEARCH PAPERS.

SEIFER!

WE SHOULD ASK YOU THE SAME QUESTION!

WHO WOULD WANNA COPY YOU?

HUH?!

DON'T COPY US!

WHAT?!!

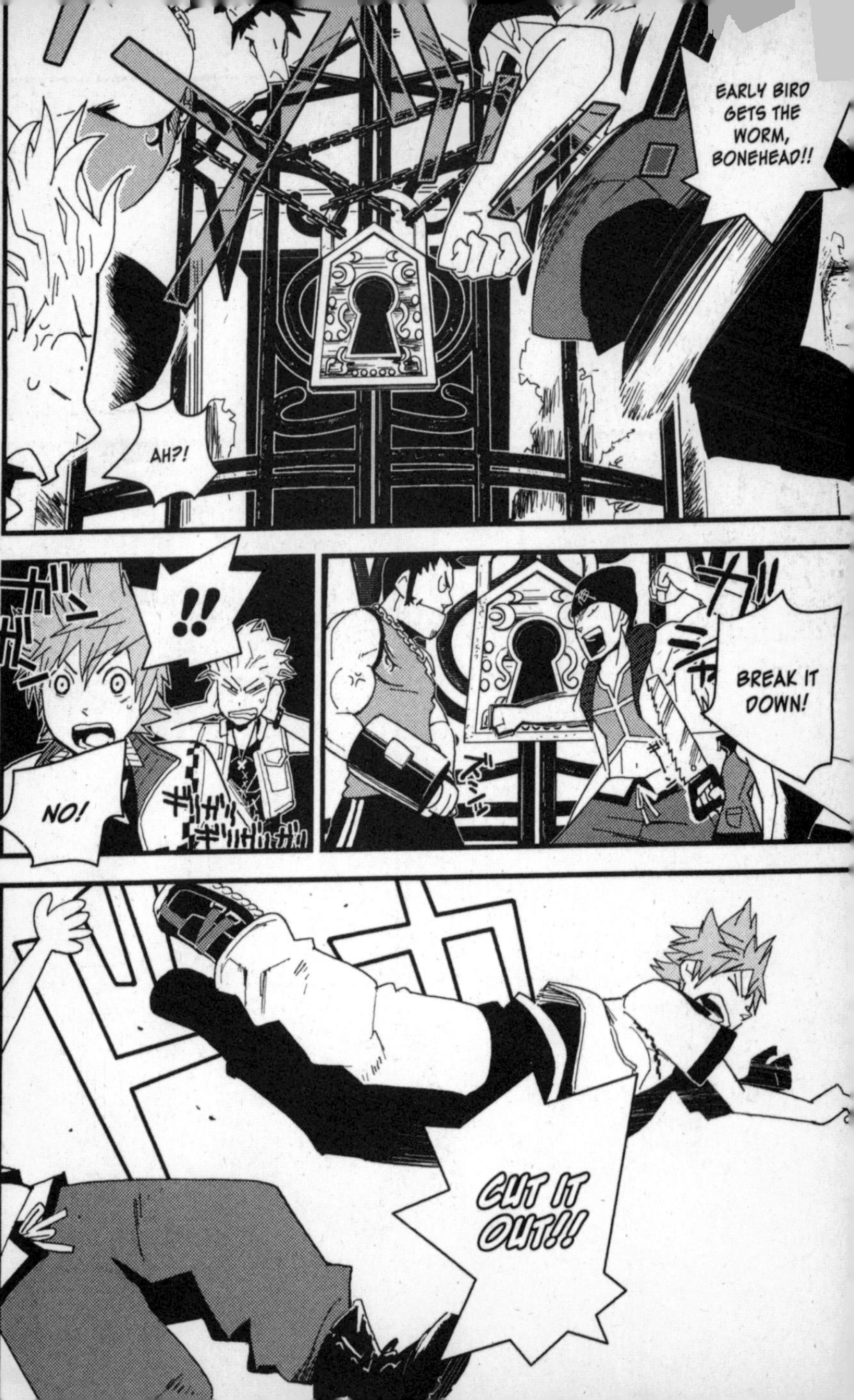
EARLY BIRD GETS THE WORM, BONEHEAD!!
AH?!
BREAK IT DOWN!
!!
NO!
CUT IT OUT!!

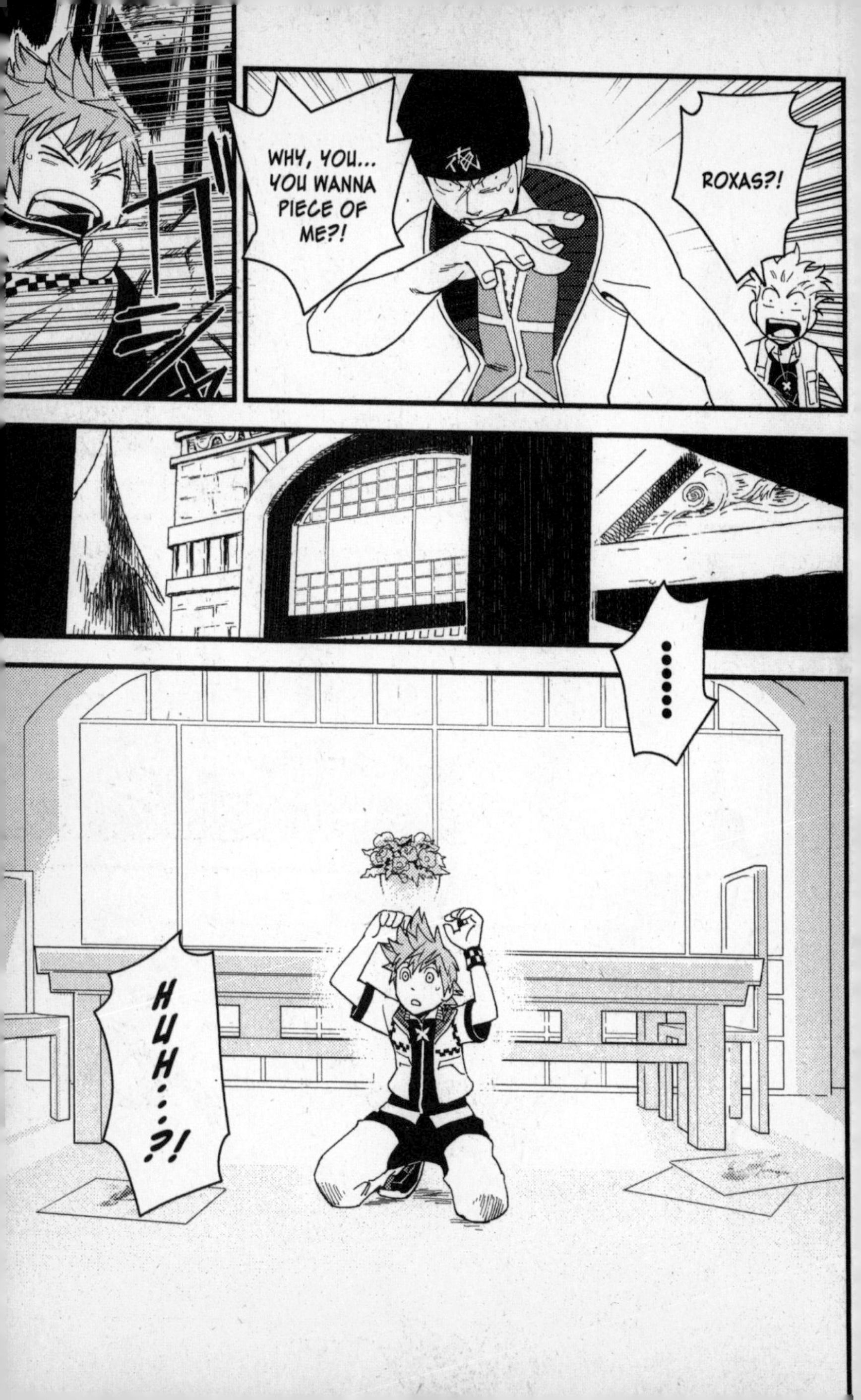
ROXAS?!
WHY, YOU... YOU WANNA PIECE OF ME?!
......
HUH...?!

AM I INSIDE?

...

IS THIS... ME?

...BECAUSE YOU *ARE* BEST FRIENDS.

THAT PICTURE IS OF YOU AND AXEL...

NAMINÉ...

I'M...

...A WITCH WITH POWER OVER SORA'S MEMORIES AND THOSE AROUND HIM.

WHO ON EARTH **ARE** YOU?

... WHO?

THAT'S WHAT DiZ CALLED ME.

LIKE YOU CAN USE MAGIC OR SOMETHING?

WHAT'S THAT MEAN?

HEH HEH...

:

A WITCH?

DiZ MONITORS THIS ENTIRE TOWN.

MAGIC, HUH...

I WISH I COULD USE IT FOR SOMETHING GOOD.

EH...?

...AH!

UM, OH YEAH...

PLEASE TELL ME.

TELL ME EVERYTHING YOU KNOW ABOUT ME.

IS HE RELATED TO ME IN SOME WAY?

WHO IS SORA?

ME?

...YOU WOULD KNOW THAT BETTER THAN ANYONE.

ACTUALLY...

...IS SLEEPING SO HE CAN REGAIN HIS MEMORIES.

RIGHT NOW, SORA...

BUT NOW... I'M PUTTING THEM ALL BACK EXACTLY THE WAY THEY WERE.

...I HAD TO TAKE APART THE MEMORIES CHAINED TOGETHER IN SORA'S HEART.

ABOUT A YEAR AGO...

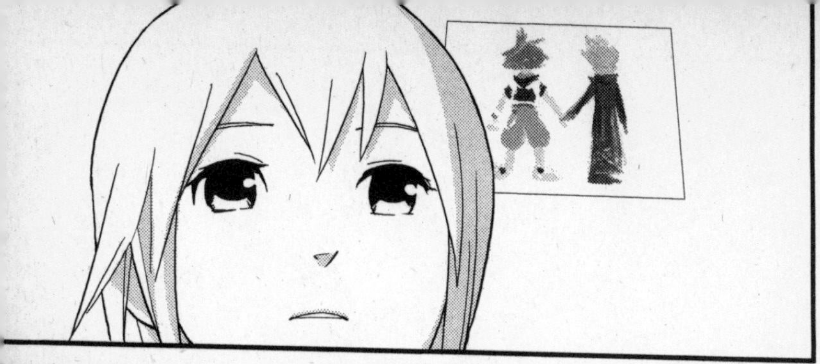

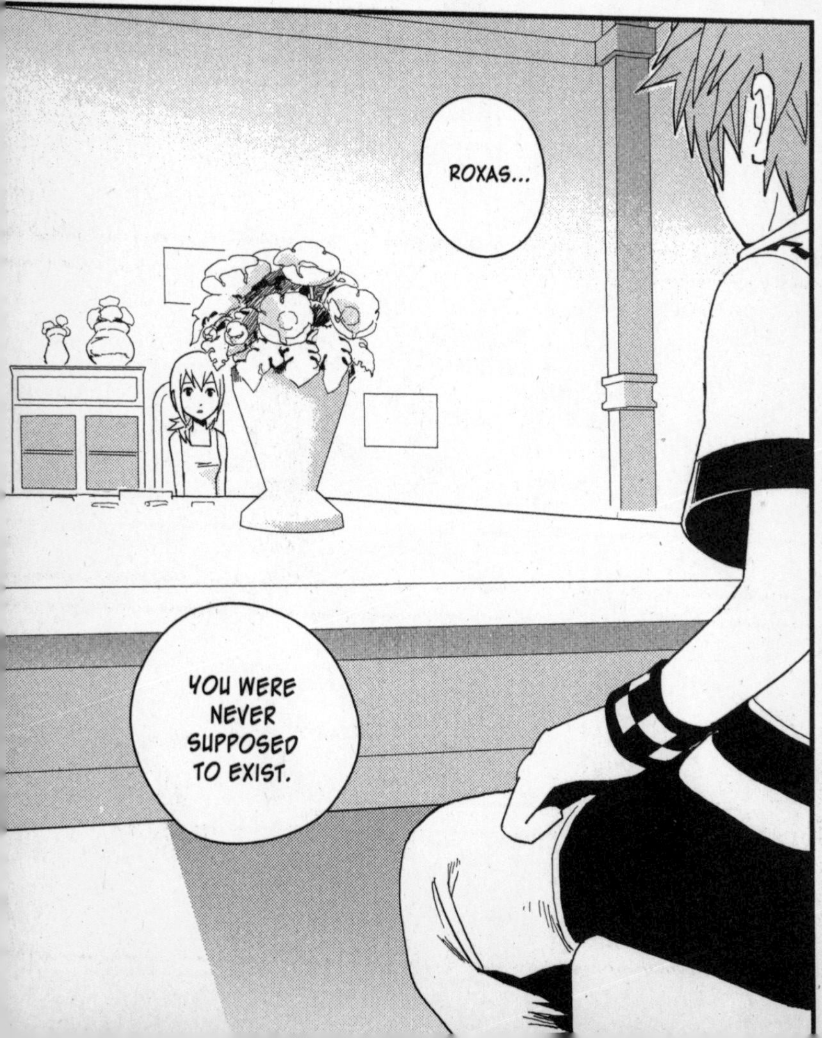
ROXAS...
YOU WERE NEVER SUPPOSED TO EXIST.

WAKE UP, ROXAS!

ROXAS!

BUT IT DOESN'T LOOK LIKE WE'LL BE ABLE TO GET INSIDE...

THOSE GUYS ARE ROUGH.

WE GOT RID OF SEIFER AND HIS GANG!

WE'LL JUST GO WITH WHAT WE HAVE.

YEAH...

EH, THERE'S NO SUCH THING AS GHOSTS ANYWAY.

AH! LOOK!

To be continued in volume 2

# KINGDOM HEARTS II

## What Dreams May Come...

Will Roxas finally learn the true nature of his connection to his dream-self, Sora? And what about Naminé? Will she be able to reveal the truth to Roxas before the ominous character DiZ "disposes" of her? And what about Axel? Just whose side is he on, anyway?

To find out the answers to these questions, and more, you'll have to return for the next fantastic volume of KINGDOM HEARTS II!

*TELL ME EVERYTHING YOU KNOW ABOUT ME.*

## R o x a s

An average, ordinary boy enjoying summer vacation with his friends--at least until certain events turn his whole life around and he gets wrapped up in strange happenings. Naminé says he holds half of Sora, but...

WE CAN DO IT, RIGHT? YOU AND ME.

As the leader of their gang, he is very good friends with Roxas. He's been trying to cheer Roxas up, since he's been feeling rather down lately...

**H a y n e r**

THIS MUST BE WHAT THEY MEAN BY SIMPLE PLEASURES.

**P e n c e**

He looks a little dull, but he's sharp as a tack. He's the information guy of the group, and he's well informed of rumors like the Seven Wonders of Twilight Town.

IT'S A REALLY NICE PHOTO OF OUR TREASURED TIMES TOGETHER.

**O l e t t e**

All the adults who know her unanimously say she's a levelheaded girl, but she's actually a natural at comic relief.

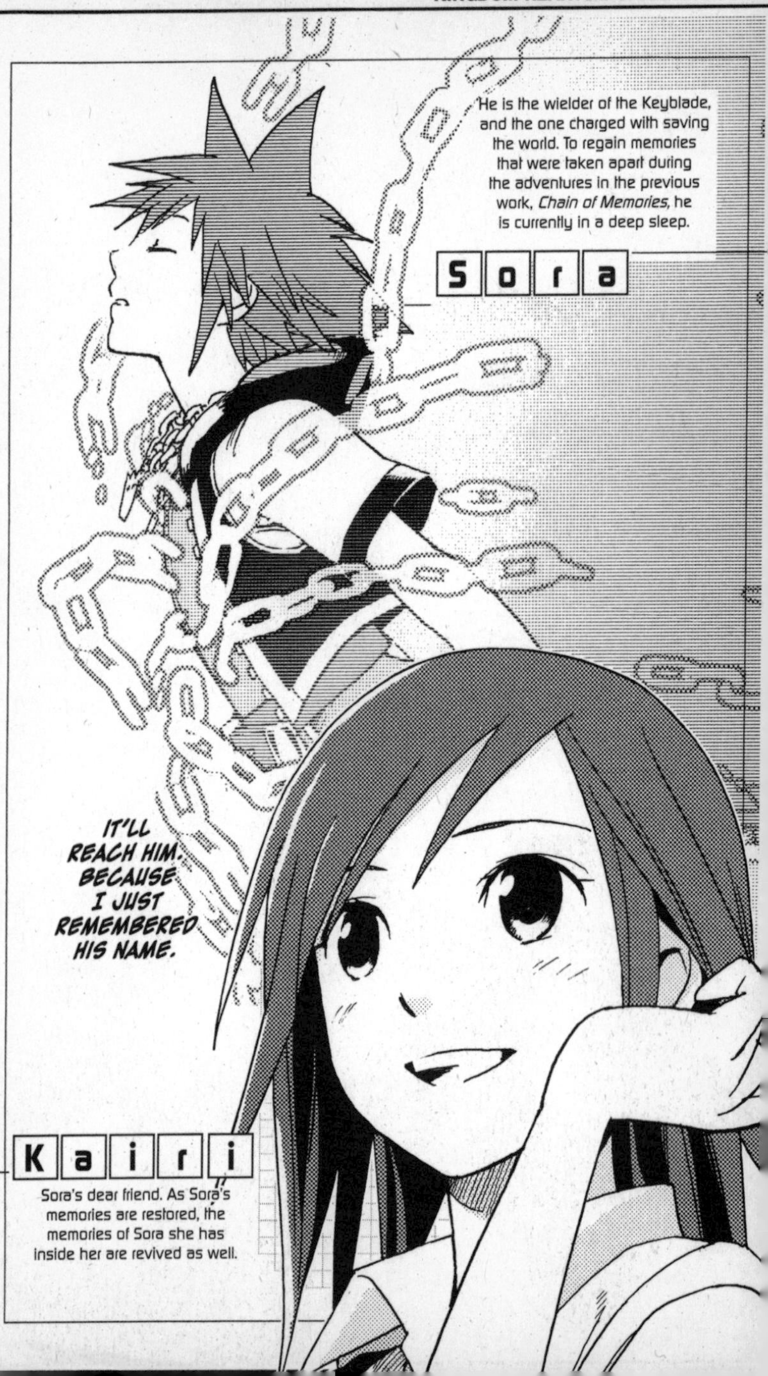
He is the wielder of the Keyblade, and the one charged with saving the world. To regain memories that were taken apart during the adventures in the previous work, *Chain of Memories,* he is currently in a deep sleep.
Sora
IT'LL REACH HIM. BECAUSE I JUST REMEMBERED HIS NAME.
Kairi
Sora's dear friend. As Sora's memories are restored, the memories of Sora she has inside her are revived as well.

YOU WERE NEVER
SUPPOSED TO EXIST.

# Naminé

She took apart Sora's memory,
but she's now doing everything
she can to help Sora regain it.
She approaches Roxas in an
effort to tell him something.

The redheaded man searching
for Roxas. In reality, he is
Organization XIII's Number 8 who,
though his enemy, gave advice
and help to Sora in *Kingdom
Hearts: Chain of Memories.*

# Axel

WE'RE
GOING
BACK,
ROXAS.

## DiZ

A man who gives orders to Naminé and the mysterious figure ???, and who continues to keep watch over Roxas. What is his true objective?

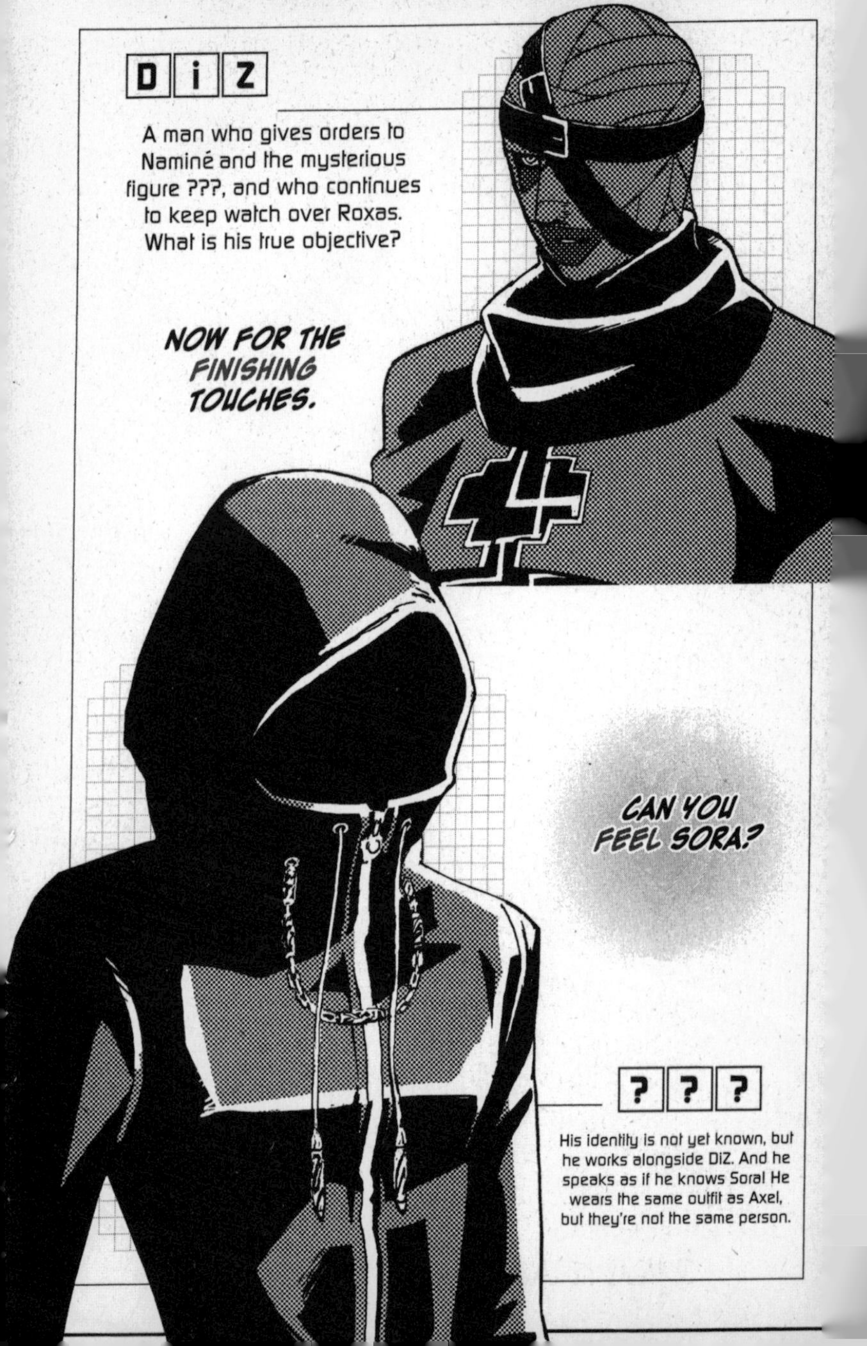
NOW FOR THE FINISHING TOUCHES.
CAN YOU FEEL SORA?

## ???

His identity is not yet known, but he works alongside DiZ. And he speaks as if he knows Sora! He wears the same outfit as Axel, but they're not the same person.

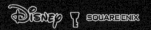

# STOP!

## This is the back of the book.
## You wouldn't want to spoil a great ending!

This book is printed "manga-style," in the authentic Japanese right-to-left format. Since none of the artwork has been flipped or altered, readers get to experience the story just as the creator intended. You've been asking for it, so TOKYOPOP® delivered: authentic, hot-off-the-press, and far more fun!

# DIRECTIONS

If this is your first time reading manga-style, here's a quick guide to help you understand how it works.

It's easy... just start in the top right panel and follow the numbers. Have fun, and look for more 100% authentic manga from TOKYOPOP®!